THE CONDOMINIUM BLUEBOOK®

CALIFORNIA

1995 Edition

Branden E. Bickel, Editor

B&B Publications

Seventh Edition

The Condominium Bluebook® is published by:

B&B Publications
4 Embarcadero Center, Suite 3440
San Francisco, CA 94111
(415) 433-1233

Library of Congress No. ISSN 1066-9310

PRINTED IN THE UNITED STATES OF AMERICA

The Basic Parliamentary Procedure segment of this book has been adapted, with permission, from a booklet entitled "The A-B-C's of Parliamentary Procedure" published by the Community Associations Institute in Alexandria, Virginia.

Please note: This publication is intended to provide you with the current statutes in force in California. However, such information may not be sufficient to address a particular legal problem. The user should retain a licensed attorney or financial advisor for assistance in resolving a specific problem.

PREFACE

WARNING!

California statutory law undergoes constant revision by enactment and amendment in the California legislature. Reliance on past editions of The Condominium Bluebook® may be misleading.

Generally, new legislation takes effect on January 1st of the year following enactment. A new edition of The Condominium Bluebook® is published at the beginning of each year incorporating changes from the most recent legislative session. The reader may wish to submit the subscription card provided at the front of this book to automatically receive next year's edition.

IMPORTANT NOTE!

Changes to existing and entirely new statutes for 1995 are highlighted in ***italic type.***

QUICK LOCATOR

TABLE OF CONTENTS

Section	*Content*	*Page*

Chapter 4 RESTRAINT ON ALIENATION; REGULATION OF SIGNS ADVERTISING SALE OF PROPERTY (Civil Code §§ 711-714.5)

Chapter 5 DISCLOSURE REQUIREMENTS UPON TRANSFER OF RESIDENTIAL PROPERTY (Civil Code §§ 1102-1102.15)

Chapter 9 — *NONPROFIT MUTUAL BENEFIT CORPORATIONS FORMATIONS & POWERS (Corporation Code §§ 7110-7160)*

Chapter 10 — *CORPORATE DUTIES AND RESPONSIBILITIES UNDER THE CALIFORNIA NONPROFIT CORPORATION LAW (Corporation Code §§ 7210-7215)*

Chapter 13 *MEMBERSHIP: ISSUANCE, TERMINATION & NOTICES TO (Corporation Code §§ 7312, 7341, 5016)*

Chapter 14 *MEETINGS AND VOTING (Corporation Code §§ 7510-7516)*

Chapter 15 *ADDITIONAL PROVISIONS RELATING TO ELECTION OF DIRECTORS (Corporation Code §§ 7520-7527)*

Chapter 18 *STANDING OF AN OWNERS' ASSOCIATION TO SUE; STATUTES OF LIMITATION (Code of Civil Procedure §§ 383, 337-339.5)*

INTRODUCTION

California has witnessed a phenomenal growth in the number of common interest developments (CIDs) over the past 25 years. According to one recent survey, there are now some 25,000 CIDs consisting of more than two million residential units. By comparison, there were fewer than 5,000 CID residential units in 1965. The social and economic implications of this growth pattern are tremendous. The Condominium Bluebook® is designed to be a basic reference source for those involved in the day-to-day operation of CIDs.

1. WHAT IS A COMMON INTEREST DEVELOPMENT?

A CID is a unique form of residential ownership. It combines a separate interest in the ownership of a residential "unit" or "lot" with a shared interest in the ownership of certain "common elements". All owners within a CID are automatically members of an owners' association that has the responsibility for maintaining the physical premises and operating the association in accordance with the provisions of the governing documents. The authority of an association is derived from enumerated powers that is, the authority of the association must be found in, or necessarily implied from, the governing documents in order for the association to legally act. If the power to act does not exist in the governing documents, the association has no authority to act, regardless of how reasonable or beneficial the proposed action might be. If the power to act does exist, that power is nonetheless limited by California law to what is reasonable under the circumstances.

There are four basic types of CIDs in California: condominiums, planned developments, stock cooperatives and community apartments. Some mobilhome parks and timeshare projects also qualify as CIDs when the residents share an ownership interest in a common element. In all CIDs, an owners' association is established for the purpose of operating and maintaining the CID in accordance with the governing documents. This system normally involves an operations program to maintain, preserve and protect the physical character of the subdivision and a financial program to levy and collect regular and special assessments from the owners to cover the cost of operations. The business of managing a CID is normally conducted through its board of directors within the framework of its declaration and by-laws. The role of the board, the tasks for which it is responsible, its obligation to act, and how these actions should be taken are normally described in the governing documents and the statutory law of California.

The vast majority of CIDs are condominiums (71%) and planned developments (26%). Ownership of a condominium unit is similar to ownership of a lot in a planned development in that the owner of both owns a separate residence and has the right to use the common facilities. The main difference lies in the nature of the separate interests and how title to the common elements is held. Typically, the separate interest or "unit" in a condominium project consists of the unfinished interior surfaces of the unit inward. Frequently it is said that a condominium "unit" is nothing more than "air space", although this is somewhat inaccurate since a "unit" usually includes the interior finished surfaces and all non-bearing walls. The exact boundaries of a unit are depicted schemat-ically on the condominium plan recorded in the office of the county recorder. A condominium unit owner also owns an undivided interest in the common elements as a tenant-in-common with the other owners.

A planned development is distinguished by the fact that the separate interest, or "lot" or "parcel", consists of everything within the lot lines that bound the owner's lot, including the earth beneath, the air above and all physical improvements within the lot lines. The owners' association in a planned development normally holds title to the common elements, which includes all property and improvements that lie outside the individual lots. In order to preserve uniformity of appearance and ensure proper maintenance, the association usually has the responsibility for maintaining the landscaping and the exterior of the structures even within the individual lots.

In a stock cooperative, the owner owns a share of stock or a membership interest in a corporate entity that owns all of the land and structures. In a community apartment, the owner holds a title interest in the development as a tenant-in-common. In both, the owner has similar exclusive rights to use a designated residential unit, but with no fee simple interest in a separate parcel of real estate.

2. HOW IS A CID MANAGED?

Today most CIDs are organized as non-profit mutual benefit corporations organized under the provisions of the Non-Profit Mutual Benefit Corporations Law found in California Corporations Code §§ 7110 through 10841. A few older CIDs or those comprised of a few units continue to operate as unincorporated associations. The operational differences are minimal in light of California Civil Code § 1363, which provides that regardless of whether a CID is governed by an incorporated or unincorporated association, the association may exercise the same powers granted to a non-profit mutual benefit corporation by the California Corporations Code. Nonetheless, most legal practitioners recommend incorporation of an association because of the legal protection that the corporate form affords to officers, directors and members from certain types of legal liabilities.

An association, whether incorporated or unincorporated, is typically run by a board of directors. The board usually consist of an odd number of directors elected by the members at the annual membership meeting. The governing documents normally specify the term of office, limitations on successive terms, the procedures for elections, whether the election of directors will be staggered to provide continuity in transition and similar matters.

The fundamental responsibility of a director is to represent the interests of the association and supervise its business affairs in a prudent manner. A non-profit association should be managed with the same degree of care as a for-profit corporation. Unfortunately, association officers and directors sometimes ignore prudent business practices on the mistaken belief that there is minimal exposure for mismanagement given the relative degree of informality with which business is conducted and the lack of an internal organizational structure found in for-profit corporations. However, the board has numerous constituents who may have standing to bring claims for mismanagement. Directors should demand that an association be operated in a manner similar to a for-profit business and require a well-defined management program, a risk evaluation program and rigorous financial controls.

The law imposes three basic duties on directors. First, they must act with the care that a reasonably prudent person in a similar position would use under similar circumstances. They must perform their duties in good faith and in a manner they reasonably believe to be in the best interest of the association. Prior to making a decision, they must inform themselves of all material information reasonably available to them. This duty requires not only reasonable action with respect to matters submitted for approval, but also requires reasonable inquiry into and monitoring of association affairs. Although directors are not insurers of the physical condition of the subdivision or proper operation of the organization, they are required to preserve and protect the physical assets and operate the association in a responsible and businesslike manner.

Second, directors are required to refrain from acting for personal gain. Directors are prohibited from using their position of power to further their private interests.

For example, a director must not take a secret profit from association transactions, use position to gain a personal advantage or put personal friendship ahead of loyalty to the association.

Third, directors owe a duty to obey and enforce the governing documents and provisions of law. Since they may be held liable if they authorize actions which are beyond the powers conferred by law, it is essential that directors become familiar with the federal, state and local statutes, rules and regulations governing the operation of CIDs as well as the governing documents. A director may be held personally liable for damage caused by his or her illegal or unauthorized acts.

A director is presumed to have acted properly if he or she satisfies three basic duties. This is called the business judgment rule. To obtain the benefit of this important protection, a director must act in good faith and with a reasonable basis for believing that his or her conduct is in the lawful and legitimate furtherance of the association's purposes. He or she must exercise honest business judgment after due inquiry and consideration of what is believed to be the relevant factors. The business judgment rule protects a director even for a decision that proves to be wrong. However, inaction, either by inattention or refusal to act, will not protect a director from failure to act unless the inaction follows a conscious decision after proper deliberation documented in the minutes. The protection can also be lost if a director is not sufficiently disinterested, fails to exercise due care, lacks good faith, or acts on the basis of motives other than the best interests of the association.

Although a director may not avoid ultimate responsibility for his or her actions, a director may rely in good faith on advice or input from committees, officers, employees or outside consultants. The board may also delegate authority to act on its behalf to an individual or a committee, but it cannot delegate its ultimate responsibility to supervise the delegated activity. Action under delegated authority is legally the action of the board itself. The board should periodically evaluate the scope of delegated authority and ensure that those to whom the authority has been delegated are competent and willing to perform the necessary tasks and are performing those tasks in a diligent manner.

Finally, an association should develop a program for orientation and education of directors and committee members to ensure that decision making process functions properly and on an informed basis. The board and the individual directors stand in a fiduciary relationship with the members and owe the members a high duty of care. Education is the first step in satisfying that duty.

3. WHAT ARE THE RIGHTS AND DUTIES OF AN OWNER?

A CID homeowner is entitled to all of the same rights and responsibilities attendant ownership of a private parcel of real estate, but subject to the restrictions set forth in the governing documents and as otherwise provided by California law. These restrictions create both rights and duties. While the restrictions vary from project to project, there is a degree of similarity among them in all CIDs and those will be addressed here.

Every owner has the right to quiet enjoyment and possession of his or her own residence and the right to use and enjoy the common facilities for their intended purpose. This means that neither the association nor any other owner may unlawfully interfere with an owner's access or peaceful enjoyment of his or her residence. Both the association and an owner have a legal right to restrain unlawful interference with an owner's quiet possession, to abate a nuisance and to enforce the restrictions of the governing documents. In addition, an owner has a legal right to require the association to protect and preserve his or her right of quiet enjoyment and possession since the association has an independent duty to enforce the governing documents.

A violation of the right to quiet enjoyment and possession must be more than a mere inconvenience or imposition. It must substantially affect an owner's beneficial enjoyment of the premises. What constitutes a "substantial" interference is a question of fact that must be determined by reference to the facts and circumstances of a specific incident.

Each owner also has a right to be informed about association business and participate in the process of governance. An owner is entitled to access to association records by following the procedures set forth in the California Corporations Code. An owner has a legal right to attend meetings of the membership and the board of directors, except when the board adjourns to executive session to consider litigation, matters that relate to the formation of contracts or personnel matters. Adjournment to executive session is done by a motion reflected in the minutes. An owner has a right to review and copy the minutes of all board meetings (other than executive session minutes) within 30 days after the date of the meeting.

California law also requires that each owner be provided current financial information about the association on an annual basis. The association must provide each owner with a *pro forma* operating budget for the upcoming fiscal year not less than 45 days nor more than 60 days prior to the beginning of the fiscal year. Under certain circumstances, the board may elect to distribute a summary of the *pro forma* operating budget, but the *pro forma* operating budget must nevertheless be available for inspection by any member in the association business office.

An owner may make alterations or improvements within the boundaries of his or her separate interest, unless specifically prohibited by the governing documents. Generally speaking, preservation of uniformity of appearance is one of the most important elements in a CID regime. Therefore, modifications must be carried out in accordance with the policies and procedures set forth in the governing documents and all applicable federal, state and local regulations. Improvements or alterations may not impair the structural integrity, mechanical systems or the support of any portion of the CID. Handicapped, blind, deaf and physically disabled owners have the additional right to make modifica-tions at their own expense to facilitate access. Such modifications must be reasonably necessary to accommodate the disability and not present an unreasonable risk of harm to others. Common area modifications to accommodate the handicapped must be removed at the owner's expense when a handicapped person no longer occupies a unit.

An owner is entitled to all of the rights and privileges of association membership by virtue of his or her status as an owner. Under certain circumstances, the right to use common area facilities may be limited by the board when an owner is in violation of the governing documents. However, an owner is normally entitled to notice and an opportunity to be heard on whether a violation exists before the right to use common area facilities can be restricted. An owner may not sell, transfer or assign his or her rights of membership to any other person. Membership and ownership cannot be legally severed.

Along with the rights of ownership come responsibilities. An owner must obey the governing documents. An owner is also responsible for the actions of his or her guests, family members and pets, and must ensure that they do not create a nuisance or unreasonably interfere with the rights of others. An owner is responsible for maintenance and upkeep of the interior of his or her residence and usually any appurtenant exclusive use common area. The governing documents will specify who is responsible for exterior maintenance of individually owned parcels in a planned development. An owner is also responsible for damage caused through his or her own fault.

An owner has the duty to make timely payment of assessments. Failure to fulfill this obligation can impose a financial burden on the association and other owners. An association operates on a fixed budget. Prompt payment of assessments is essential to its successful operation. It is the association's duty to require prompt payment by all members.

Finally, both the owner and the association have a right and a duty to take steps to enforce the governing documents in the event of a violation. Failure to do so may result in a waiver of the right to enforce and the inability to preserve the original regime contemplated by the governing documents. If it is necessary to institute legal proceedings to enforce the governing documents, the prevailing party is entitled to recover all litigation expenses, including reasonable attorney's fees. It is important to note that the losing party in an enforcement action may be required to pay not only their own legal expense and also those of the other party as well.

4. HOW CAN THIS BOOK HELP IN MANAGING A CID?

The Condominium Bluebook® is a compilation of useful statutes, procedural guidelines and forms which can be used by individuals involved in the operation of CIDs. The statutory segment is a selection of statutes from various California codes that pertain to the operation of a CID. The reader may wish to review the table of contents in order to gain a general familiarity with the statutory material set forth in the book.

CHAPTER 1

HOW TO USE THE CONDOMINIUM BLUEBOOK®

1. What's in the Bluebook?

The Condominium Bluebook® is a comprehensive compilation of useful information about common interest developments or "CIDs". It includes a summary of the essential laws (called statutes) that relate to the management and operation of a CID, and to the rights and obligations of an association and its members. It is a reference guide for all owners, officers, directors, property managers and others involved in the community association industry. The book covers association taxation, asbestos abatement, vehicle towing, disclosure of public records, injury prevention programs, recent judicial and legislative developments, standard parliamentary procedure, helpful checklists, and commonly used forms. All major subjects are alphabetically indexed at the end of the book.

Most of the statutes contained in the Bluebook are drawn from the following sources:

> California Corporations Code (abbreviated as "Corp. C."): These provisions govern the operation of most types of owner associations. They address voting rights, meetings, record keeping, and responsibilities of directors and officers. The Corporations Code applies only to owner associations which are incorporated, although unincorporated associations

are granted the same "powers" as an incorporated association. The first few pages of the CC&Rs usually state whether the association is incorporated or unincorporated.

California Code of Civil Procedure (abbreviated as "CCP"): These provisions govern procedural aspects of a lawsuit or arbitration which an owner and/or the owner association might be involved. Sections 337 to 339.5 are common statutes of limitation that describe when legal rights expire. Sections 1281 to 1288 set forth legal procedures that can be used as guidelines for private arbitration or, to a lesser degree, mediation.

California Evidence Code (abbreviated as "Evid. C."): Section 1152.5 restricts the resulting use of statements and documents made or used during a legal arbitration.

2. *How do the laws in the Bluebook relate to the CID governing documents?*

It is important to read the Bluebook in conjunction with the governing documents. The statutes contained in the Bluebook provide a framework within which most CIDs must operate. Some statutory provisions may be duplicated or paraphrased in the governing documents, particularly statutes that deal with the duties and responsibilities of the officers and directors, and the rights of individual owners vis-a-vis the association. Not all CIDs fall within the purview of the statutes collected in the Bluebook. For example, a CID without common area, or established for commercial or industrial purposes, is governed by only a few of the statutes.

3. *What if the governing documents do not address an issue?*

CIDs are relatively new forms of residential ownership and the body of statutory and case law governing their operation after initial formation is somewhat limited. Gaps may exist in both the statutory law and governing documents. Judicial decisions frequently deal with areas of ambiguity, uncertainty or ommission in the statutory scheme. Check the chapter on recent judicial highlights to find out if a problem in the association has been addressed in a recent court decision. Consult an attorney for professional advice when the answer is still not clear.

4. *What if the governing documents are in conflict with the statutes in the Bluebook?*

Statutes do not necessarily supersede contrary provisions in the governing documents. Statutes fall into two categories: 1) Those which take priority over the governing documents and apply no matter what the documents say; and 2) Those which only apply when the governing documents do not contradict them. To determine what type of provision is involved, look for introductory phrases like "unless otherwise provided in the declaration" or "subject to the provisions of the governing documents" in the text of the law which mean that inconsistent CC&R provisions will control over the statutory language. If no such introductory clause exists, then the statute will generally take priority over an inconsistent CC&R provision.

Occasionally, a statute will specifically state that it is intended to override an inconsistent CC&R provision. These statutes are usually introduced by such phrases as "notwithstanding anything in the governing documents to the contrary" or "notwithstanding the provisions of the declaration" or "unless the governing documents impose more stringent standards."

5. *What if the governing documents are ambiguous or unclear?*

When it is difficult, or impossible, to determine the meaning of a provision in the governing documents, examine the relevant statutes for clarification. If nothing can be found, the general test of reasonableness will normally be employed by a court. Look to custom and practice (how the law is applied by other associations) for guidance as to what may be considered reasonable. Consult an attorney if a significant legal issue is at stake.

6. *What if the governing documents seem unfair or unreasonable?*

Check the Bluebook to determine whether a statute has been enacted which takes priority over the unfair provision. Recent statutory changes are noted in the text of the statutes by *italics*. If this does not help, don't despair; the courts have been careful to protect the rights of associations, their members, their officers and directors, and the individual owners against unfair or unreasonable provisions in the governing documents. Check the Bluebook for recent court decisions and legislative changes that may address the issue. Consult a real estate attorney if it is still unclear.

7. *How can the Bluebook help an association make a proper decision?*

To implement the decision making process you should follow a step-by-step set of analytical guidelines to reach a resolution. The Bluebook has a checklist for the usual decision making process used by associations and members and can be used as a guide. In general, decision making should involve a 6-step process that is summarized as follows: 1) Does the association or board have the authority to act under the governing documents or statutory law? 2) If so, what is the proper method or procedure for deciding? 3) Must the membership approve the action? 4) Is the action reasonable and consistent with the overall purpose of the CID? 5) Is the action in the best interests of all the owners? 6) Finally, is there any overriding legal, or other reason why the action should not be taken?

When in doubt, consult an attorney before proceeding. If the action could have a significant impact on one or more owners, it may be wise to get a written opinion of counsel in advance confirming the validity of the action. This may protect the board in the event of a later challenge by allowing it to assert advice of counsel as a defense. Caution - the failure of an association to follow its own internal procedures will make any action vulnerable to challenge.

Also, check the Bluebook for recent court decisions involving public policy that impacts the reasonableness of association actions. If an association or an owner finds themselves in a dispute that leads to mediation, arbitration or court, the Bluebook along with professional advice will help the disputing parties to understand the procedural process.

8. How can the Bluebook help an owner who feels the association is not doing its job?

The Bluebook contains virtually all the statutory minimum standards of conduct for associations, directors, officers and managers. In addition, there is a common law rule prohibiting negligent conduct. Negligence is a concept created by the judicial system. Its intent is to require everyone to exercise reasonable care under the circumstances not to injure other people or damage their property. The failure to do so is considered negligence and exposes the offending person to a claim for damages by the victim.

To use the Bluebook, begin by reviewing the governing documents and statutes for provisions that pertain to the type of responsibility which you feel the association is not fulfilling. Then determine whether there is any inconsistency between the two. If so, determine whether the statutes or governing documents control the situation and analyze the conduct of the association against the relevant law. Once you are comfortable that you understand the applicable standards of conduct, attempt to discuss the matter with the president, a director, committee chair or property manager, as may be appropriate. If you don't get the result you want, consider attending a board meeting or calling an owner meeting to discuss the problem with the other owners. If you do not seem to be able to generate much interest, the problem may not be as important as you think. If you are unable to make any headway and still feel the problem is important to resolve, consult an attorney.

The Bluebook contains statutes that involve your right to attend a board meeting, your right to convene an owner meeting, your responsibility to notice meetings and your right to inspect association records. The Bluebook also provides all the rules, checklists and forms you will need to obtain a list of owners, give proper notice of a meeting and run the meeting under the rules of parliamentary procedure.

9. *How can the Bluebook help an owner who is unhappy with another owner's behavior?*

The unhappy owner should begin by consulting the governing documents and statutes in the Bluebook to determine whether the other owner is violating the documents or statutes, or both. If so, one option is to request that the association commence enforcement proceedings. This probably should be done in writing and specify, to the extent possible, the exact provisions of the governing documents or statutory law that are being violated. Alternatively, an owner could proceed directly with an enforcement himself. The one qualification is that of Civ. C. § 1354(a) which provides that the CC&Rs may be enforced by an owner or the association, unless the CC&Rs expressly limits that right for either party. Most CC&Rs do not have such a restriction on enforcement.

If the unhappy owner or the association decide to pursue enforcement, they must next consider whether they are dealing with a violation of the CC&Rs and, if so, whether the relief involves a claim for monetary damages of $5,000 or less, exclusive of association assessments. If so, the party initiating enforcement must first endeavor to submit the dispute to a form of alternative dispute resolution such as mediation or arbitration. The form of alternative dispute resolution is initiated by serving a "Request for Resolution" on the other party and will be non-binding unless the parties agree to make it binding. The Bluebook contains forms and checklists for alternative dispute resolution. Failure to pursue this preliminary procedure before filing a lawsuit, could result in a dismissal of the action as premature or refusal to award the enforcing party his attorney fees even if he prevails.

10. How can the Bluebook help an owner decide whether he can remodel his home?

The first step is to carefully review the governing documents. Normally, an owner may make improvements, or alterations, within the boundaries of his or her unit, or lot, that do not impair the structural integrity, mechanical systems or lessen the support of any building. Moreover, modifications to facilitate access for the handicapped and/or disabled, (or to eliminate hazards for these persons) must be allowed unless there is a very compelling reason for denial of the owner's right to modify. A good rule to go by is that the owner has the right to modify the area he or she is responsible for maintaining and only the association has the right to modify the area it is responsible for maintaining. But, the right to modify is subject to the provisions of the governing documents which may restrict the right to modify to an even greater degree.

Any modification that pervades a common area (including exclusive use common areas), or affects the structural integrity or mechanical systems of a building, must be approved by the association or its representative. Many large CIDs have an architectural review committee to review all such applications. Procedures for submitting an application are spelled out in the governing documents. Unless the governing documents clearly allow an owner to modify the common area or exclusive use common area, the association will probably want to obtain an opinion of counsel as to its authority to grant permission for an owner to modify the common area. The common area is owned by all owners jointly and cannot generally be allocated for use by any one person without approval of the other owners. Some governing documents flatly prohibit modification of the common area or require 100% approval of all owners.

Consult the governing documents and the Bluebook for the definitions of "unit" or "lot", "common area" and "exclusive use common area" to understand the dividing line between the owner's property and the common area. If the alteration requires approval, follow the procedures for obtaining approval. The Bluebook has the proper procedures and forms if you need to get the application onto a meeting agenda.

11. How can the Bluebook help an officer, director or manager asked to take action against an owner?

The first thing to do is to determine the exact nature of the violation and whether the conduct violates the governing documents or the law. It is always a good idea to check both the governing documents and the statutes to see if there is any inconsistency and, if so, which takes priority over the other. The next thing to do is to examine the evidence of the infraction and verify its occurrence. It should be standard practice to corroborate a violation through one or two independent sources before commencing enforcement proceedings, unless multiple infractions have occurred and further verification would serve no useful purpose.

The next step is to issue a warning. If this does not work, the final step is to commence an appropriate enforcement proceeding. The Bluebook contains a sample notice of violation and request for resolution. If a meeting or disciplinary hearing is required, the Bluebook provides procedures, rules and forms for mediation and arbitration.

12. How can I find the sections of the Bluebook relating to various questions?

The Bluebook is organized into chapters that deal with specific subjects. Each chapter is subdivided into sections. The heading in each section generally describes the content of the material. The chapter, section and subsection headings, as well as the title of each statute, are listed in the Table of Contents at the beginning of the book providing a sequential reference guide. The Bluebook has a Quick Locator at the front of the book before the Table of Contents that lists 21 major subjects and the page number where those subjects begin. Finally, a comprehensive alphabetical listing of subjects can be found in the Index.

13. Where are certain relevant statutes in the Bluebook?

The following list organizes issues commonly raised by category with references to relevant sections of the Bluebook:

A. Owner Issues

(1) Owner Rights and Procedures:

(a) Peace and quiet in the home: All owners have a legal right to quiet enjoyment of their home, and can enforce that right against others who interfere with it. This a basic legal principal rather than a statutory right.

(b) Making alterations: Civ. C. §§ 1360, 1361, 1362.

(c) Service from directors, officers and managers: Civ. C. § 1364 (maintenance); Civ. C. §§ 1365, 1365.5 (financial information); Civ. C. §§ 1365.7 (duties of all directors); Corp. C. §§ 7230-7238 (standards of conduct for corporate directors and officers); Civ. C. §§ 1363.1, 1363.2 (management companies).

(d) Obtaining financial information about the Association: Civ. C. §§ 1363, 1365 (association records and financial documents); Corp. C. §§ 8310-8338 (rights to inspect records of incorporated associations).

(e) Meetings and voting: Civ. C. § 1363 (general rules for all associations); Corp. C. § 7312 (fractional interests), Corp. C. § 7341 (termination of members); Corp. C. §§ 7510-7516 and 7610-7616 (general rules for owner meetings in incorporated associations); Corp. C. §§ 7210-7225 (general rules for director meetings in incorporated associations); Corp. C. §§ 7520-7527 (rules for electing directors and officers in incorporated associations).

(f) Enforcing owner rights: Civ. C. § 1354 (general rules); CCP §§ 337-339.5 (statutes of limitation); CCP §§ 1280-1288.8 (mediation or arbitration); see also checklists and forms in the Bluebook.

(2) Owner Responsibilities:

(a) Paying assessments and consequences of nonpayment: Civ. C. § 1366 (limits on association power to levy assessments); Civ. C. §§ 1366.1, 1367 (non-payment and collection).

(b) Maintenance: Civ. C. §§ 1360, 1361, 1362.

(c) Resale: Civ. C. §§ 1368, 1102-1102.15, 1134 (disclosures to prospective purchasers); Civ. C. § 51 (discrimination); Civ. C. §§ 712, 713 ("for sale" signs); see also checklists on the Bluebook pertaining to the sale of property.

B. Director, Officer, and Manager Issues

(1) Association rights and responsibilities:

(a) Limits of association power: Corp. C. § 7140 (incorporated associations).

(b) Maintenance: Civ. C. §§ 1360, 1361, 1362 (units); Civ. C. § 1364 (common areas); see also checklists in the Bluebook pertaining to major component inspection, rule enforcement, notices of violation, and alternative dispute resolution.

(c) Assessments: Civ. C. § 1365.5 (review of financial information, segregation of reserves, spending limits); Civ. C. § 1366 (limits on power to levy assessments); Civ. C. §§ 1366.1, 1367 (non-payment and collection); see also checklists and forms pertaining to delinquency policy, notices of violation, alternative dispute resolution, notice delinquent assessments and notice of assessment lien.

(d) Record Keeping: Civ. C. §§ 1363, 1365 (records and financial documents); Corp. C. §§ 8310-8338 (responsibility of incorporated associations to provide records to members); see also checklists pertaining to financial responsibility and annual reporting requirements.

(e) Vehicle Removal: VC §§ 22658-22658.2.

(f) Taxation of association funds: IRC § 528; RTC §§ 23701, 23701t.

(g) Amending the governing documents: Civ. C. §§ 1355-1357; see also checklist pertaining to amending the governing documents.

(h) Resolving disputes: Civ. C. § 1354 (general rules); CCP §§ 337-339.5 (statutes of limitation); CCP §§ 1280-1288.8 (mediation or arbitration); see also checklists and forms pertaining to rule enforcement, notices of violation, and alternative dispute resolution.

(2) Directors and officers responsibilities and liabilities:

(a) General responsibilities: Civ. C. § 1365.7 (all associations); see also checklists pertaining to annual reporting requirements, financial responsibility, and major component inspection.

(b) Minimum standard of conduct: Corp. C. §§ 7230-7238 (incorporated associations).

C. Calling and Running Meetings

(1) General rules for owner meetings: Civ. C. §§ 1363 (all associations); see also checklists and forms pertaining to owner meeting agenda, notices of owner meetings and proxies.

(2) Additional rules for owner meetings: Corp. C. §§ 7510-7516 and 7610-7616 (incorporated associations).

(3) Electing officers and directors: Corp. C. §§ 7520-7527 (incorporated associations).

(4) Director meetings: Corp. C. §§ 7210-7225 (incorporated associations); see also checklists and forms pertaining to board meeting agenda, notices of board meetings, meetings without notice and proxies.

(5) Meeting procedures: see Chapter 21 of the Bluebook for basic parliamentary procedure.

CHAPTER 2

JUDICIAL AND LEGISLATIVE HIGHLIGHTS OF 1994

INTRODUCTION

Published court decisions are an important part of the American legal system. They originate in the appellate courts and set forth both the result and reasoning underlying the disposition of a particular case. In order to understand the overall legal structure of a particular jurisdiction - here California - these decisions must be read in conjunction with the statutory law and the legal documents that govern a private community.

It is also important to understand the internal structure of the judicial system in order to appreciate the significance of a particular decision. There are two independent judicial systems that operate concurrently - the state court system and the federal court system. Each has three tiers. At the lowest level are the trial courts, known in the federal system as the Federal District Courts and in the California system as the Municipal and Superior Courts. Each system has intermediate appellate courts which decide appeals from the trial courts. At the top of each system sits one supreme court that has the ultimate and final authority over all judicial matters within its jurisdiction. Virtually all published decisions come from the appellate and the supreme courts. Published decisions carry precedential weight and may be relied on by trial courts in deciding future cases involving similar facts. Reported decisions also give society guidance on how it should conduct its affairs in areas of conflict.

Federal courts are generally concerned with enforcement of federal laws, including federal constitutional rights, and disputes between citizens of different states. State courts generally handle matters of local concern, such as the individual and property rights of state citizens. Most decisions involving community associations come out of the state court system.

JUDICIAL HIGHLIGHTS OF 1994

1. United States Supreme Court

City of Ladue v. Gilleo, 114 S. Ct. 2038 (1994).

A homeowner in the city of Ladue, Missouri placed a sign in a second story window of her home bearing a message against the war in the Persian Gulf. The city council enacted an ordinance prohibiting all signs except those that (1) fell within one of 10 exemptions, and (2) complied with special size limitations. Effectively, the ordinance prohibited homeowners from displaying any signs on their property except residence identification signs, signs advertising the sale or rental of real property, and signs warning of safety hazards.

The ordinance contained a statement of purposes, part of which recited that the proliferation of signs in the city would create ugliness, visual blight and clutter. The homeowner challenged the ordinance claiming that it violated her right of free speech guaranteed by the First Amendment of the United States Constitution. The United States Supreme Court unanimously agreed with the homeowner that the ordinance violated her First Amendment free speech rights, because (1) although the ordinance was supported by the city's valid interest in minimizing clutter, this interest was not compelling enough to restrict the constitutionally protected right of free speech, (2) the city had almost completely foreclosed an important means for a homeowner to communicate political expression, (3) adequate substitutes for political expression did not exist for the homeowner, and (4) the government's need to regulate temperate speech from within the home was less important than the public's right to control the aesthetic appearance of property.

CAVEAT: This is not a common interest development case, but consider the implications of attempting to regulate political free speech by a CC&R restriction or rule.

2. California Supreme Court

Nahrstadt v. Lakeside Village Condominium Association (1994) 8 Cal.4th 361.

Ms. Nahrstadt moved into the Lakeside Village Condominium complex with her 3 cats in direct violation of a CC&R restriction prohibiting any animals except domestic fish and birds. Lakeside Village is a high-density 530-unit condominium project in Culver City. The association threatened disciplinary action if the cats were not removed and Ms. Nahrstadt sued to prevent the association from enforcing the restriction. The trial court dismissed her complaint. The Court of Appeal reinstated her claim ruling that enforceability depended on reasonableness, and reasonableness depended on the facts of each case.

The California Supreme Court reversed the Court of Appeal stating that the restriction was reasonable on its face and that enforceability does not require a fact specific analysis in every case. It also noted that trial courts do not have "unbridled license to question the wisdom of the restriction's benefit." The Supreme Court held that "courts must enforce [CC&R] restrictions unless the challenger can show that the restriction is unreasonable because it is arbitrary, violates a fundamental public policy, or imposes burdens on the use of the affected property that substantially outweigh the restriction's benefit." In this case, the Supreme Court found no fundamental public policy would be served by invalidating the pet restriction.

SIGNIFICANCE: This case substantially expands the enforceability of CC&R provisions by limiting the basis for a legal challenge to a few specific grounds and creating a presumption of reasonableness.

3. California Court of Appeal

Booska v. Patel (1994) 24 Cal.App.4th 1786.

An adjoining landowner sued his neighbor for negligently severing the roots of a tree that extended into the defendant's yard, causing the tree to become unsafe and requiring subsequent removal. Established California law allows a property owner to cut tree limbs that extend onto his property without the neighbor's permission. Early California cases extended the same right to sever trespassing root systems. This is the first California case to hold to the contrary. The court held that a person who cuts the roots of a neighbor's tree can be held liable for the resulting damage when a tree is sensitive to root damage and the root system causes minimal interference to the neighbor's property. The court also noted that "neither party has considered what would be the neighborly thing to do to resolve this problem".

AFTERTHOUGHT: Getting to the root may be only part of the problem.

Broadmoor San Clemente Homeowners Association v. Nelson (1994) 25 Cal.App.4th 1.

A homeowners' association brought a CC&R enforcement action against an owner to prohibit the operation of a residential care facility for the elderly in violation of a CC&Rs provision prohibiting any business or commercial activity within a home. The court held that the CC&R provision was not enforceable because it violated both the California Fair Employment & Housing Act (Government Code § 12955) and the Federal Fair Housing Act of 1968 (42 United States Code § 3604(f)(1)), both of which extend special protections to those who provide residential housing for the elderly and disabled.

LESSON: When dealing with protected classes of people, you must research in depth the implications of an enforcement action or risk the possibility of an embarrassing result.

California Riviera Homeowners Association v. Superior Court (1994) 24 Cal.App.4th 146.

A homeowners' association in the Pacific Palisades area of Los Angeles recorded a "notice of violation" of the CC&Rs against a parcel after the owner violated a 10-foot setback requirement of the CC&Rs during remodeling. The owner sued the association to clear title claiming that no statute or other legal authority authorized recording a "notice of violation". The court held that since the CC&Rs specifically allowed recording of a notice of violation, no statutory authority was necessary. But the court warned that it would have difficulty in finding legal justification for recording a notice of violation absent a CC&R provision authorizing recordation.

QUOTE: "Because recordation of a document may be accomplished for a nominal fee, a notice of violation is viewed as an efficient and economical method for a homeowners' association to enforce its CC&Rs." But be sure there is proper authority before recording a notice of violation.

Fidelity Mortgage Trustee Service, Inc. v. Ridgegate East Homeowners Association (1994) 27 Cal.App.4th 503.

Fidelity Mortgage Trustee Service, Inc. (formerly Condominium Trustee Service) sued Ridgegate East Homeowners Association and its property management company to recover attorney fees it incurred in defending another lawsuit brought by a foreclosed condominium unit owner. Fidelity, as well as Ridgegate and the property manager, were found to have acted properly in the related foreclosure proceeding. The issue in this case was simply whether the professional trustee service could recover its legal expense from the homeowners' association and the property manager. The court ruled that in the absence of an agreement to the contrary, the trustee could recover its legal expense if it could prove that it was acting as the "agent" of the association and the property manager in conducting the foreclosure.

CAUTION: The association, the property manager and the trustee service may wish to work this out in advance by a written contract.

Heather Farms Homeowners Association v. Robinson (1994) 21 Cal.App.4th 1568.

Heather Farms Homeowners' Association, a planned development in Walnut Creek, California, brought a CC&R enforcement action against an owner. It developed into a war of attrition that lasted more than 5 years and spawned a complex series of cross-complaints and related actions entangling the association, the association's attorneys, real estate agents, the purchasers of a unit and others in various lawsuits. Ultimately, the case was "settled" under court supervision by mutual dismissals. Then the owner attempted to recover $479,000 in attorney fees as the "prevailing party" under Civil Code § 1354. The court held that there was no "prevailing party" in this messy litigation and that no one was entitled to attorney fees.

WARNING: CC&R enforcement actions can become economic black holes if rationality gets lost in a battle over principle.

Koll-Irvine Center Property Owners Association v. County of Orange (1994) 24 Cal.App.4th 1036.

A commercial property owners' association at the Koll-Irvine Center near John Wayne Airport in Orange County brought an action for nuisance against a jet fuel supplier that built fuel storage tanks in the proximity of an industrial park alleging extreme risk to people and property from the potential for an aircraft accident or other rupture of the tanks. The court dismissed the action ruling that the "fear of a catastrophic accident" was insufficient interference with the use and enjoyment of property to constitute a nuisance or support a claim for diminution in value, loss of use of property or mental anguish.

CONSIDER: Commercial property owners may have trouble establishing "mental anguish" from a fear of flying.

Marina Green Homeowners Association v. State Farm Fire & Casualty Co. (1994) 25 Cal.App.4th 200.

The Marina Green Homeowners Association in San Francisco brought an action against its insurance carrier in an effort to secure coverage for damage suffered in the Loma Prieta earthquake of 1989. At issue was whether an insurance company owed a duty to the homeowners' association, or only the individual condominium owners, to offer earthquake coverage when issuing a policy covering residential property. The court ruled that there was no duty on the part of the insurer to offer earthquake coverage to the association - as distinct from the owners - because the statute (Insurance Code § 10087) requiring an insurer of residential property to offer such coverage extends only to "individually owned condominium units" and residential structures of not more than 4 units.

COMMENT: The association found little sympathy in court when it did not buy earthquake coverage, did not pay for earthquake coverage and presumably did not even want earthquake coverage until after a loss occurred.

Pamela W. v. Millsom (1994) 25 Cal.App.4th 950; but see Pamela B. v. Hayden (1994) 25 Cal.App.4th 785.

A tenant of a condominium unit sued the unit owner and the homeowners' association for personal injuries she suffered as a victim of criminal assault and rape she suffered when an assailant gained entry to her unit at a Pacific Beach complex. The court dismissed the action against the association without trial on the basis that the criminal activity was not foreseeable to the degree that would have imposed a duty upon the association to protect residents against criminal conduct. The association had no notice of prior similar incidents on the premises and therefore no reason to know such activities might occur. But see Pamela B. v. Hayden, where a jury awarded $1.2 million to a female rape victim assaulted in an apartment parking lot, apportioning fault 95% to the landlord and property management company, 4% to the assailant and 1% to an aider and abettor. The appellate court ordered a new trial base upon the jury's "blatantly unfair" apportionment of fault.

SIGNIFICANCE: Assault cases are emotionally charged and must be handled very, very carefully.

Park Place Estates Homeowners Association, Inc. v. Naber (1994) 29 Cal.App.4th 42.

A condominium unit owner refused to pay regular monthly assessments because he claimed the Park Place Estates Homeowners Association failed to maintain the common area. The association recorded an assessment lien against the owner's unit and then brought suit to foreclose the lien. The owner defended on the ground that he had a right to "offset" damages to the value of his property resulting from the association's failure to maintain the common area against his obligation to pay assessments. The court disagreed and awarded the association $6,500 in unpaid assessments and related penalties, and an additional $47,403.05 in attorney fees. The owner appealed. The appellate court upheld both awards on the grounds that provisions of the Davis-Stirling Common Interest Development Act (i.e. Civil Code §§ 1366, 1366(a), 1367, 1367(a), 1367(b), 1367(d)) establish a strong public policy against allowing an owner to offset assessments against claims he or she may have for monetary damage against an association.

NOTABLE QUOTE: "Because homeowner associations would cease to exist without regular payment of assessment fees, the Legislature has created procedures for associations to quickly and efficiently seek relief against a non-paying owner. Permitting an owner to broadly assert the homeowners association's conduct as a defense or setoff to such enforcement action would seriously undermine these rules."

Swan v. Olivier (1994) 22 Cal.App.4th 1324.

A non-owner guest brought an action against an owner and the Cyprus Shore Community Association in San Clemente for injuries he suffered in the ocean surf just off a private beach owned by the association. He alleged that they failed to warn him of riptides, submerged rocks and other hazardous conditions. The court dismissed the action ruling that the association did not own or control the ocean, did not derive any commercial benefit from the use of the beach and did not create the hazards. The association published rules and regulations warning against the hazards and the absence of lifeguards, and notifying swimmers that they assumed the risk for their own personal safety. Under the circumstances the association had no further legal duty to warn of unsafe conditions.

QUERY: Would the result have been the same if the hazards were known and the association had failed to warn?

LEGISLATIVE HIGHLIGHTS OF 1994

Civil Code § 1363.5 has been added to require the articles of incorporation of an incorporated association filed with the California Secretary of State after January 1,

1995, to contain specified information identifying the association, its location, business address, the name and address of its managing agent and stating that it was formed under the Davis-Stirling Common Interest Development Act. The same information must be provided with each annual statement of officers filed with the Secretary of State.

Civil Code § 1365.5(c) and (d) has been amended to alter the requirements for temporary borrowing from reserves to meet short-term cash flow requirements or other authorized expenses. The amendment requires the board to make a written finding, recorded in the minutes, explaining the reasons that the transfer is needed and describing when and how the money will be repaid to the reserves.

Civil Code § 1365.9 has been added to provide that any tort claim for personal injury or property damage existing against an owner in a common interest development solely by reason of that owner's having an ownership interest in common area shall not be brought against the owner provided that the association maintains specified levels of general liability insurance. For associations with 100 units or fewer, the minimum level is $2,000,000 in liability coverage; for those with more than 100 units the minimum level is $3,000,000 in liability coverage. The association must notify the owners at least annually of the amount and type of liability insurance it carries. Nothing in the statute affect the right of an injured party to sued the association as distinct from an innocent owner.

Civil Code § 1374 has been added to provide the Davis-Stirling Common Interest Development Act (Civil Code §§ 1350-1373) does not apply to common interest developments where there is no common area responsibility and such associations do not have standing to bring a lawsuit on behalf of the owners. The statute states that it is merely declaratory of existing law, but some legal authorities are concerned about the status of master associations, etc. that only indirectly manage common area.

Civil Code § 1102.6, which specifies the form and content of a Real Estate Transfer Disclosure Statement that must be given by the seller of residential property of one to four dwelling units to prospective purchasers, has been amended to require disclosure of any lawsuits by, or against, the seller affecting the property, "including any lawsuits alleging a defect or deficiency in this real property or "common areas" (facilities such as pools, tennis courts, walkways, or other areas co-owned in undivided interests with others.)" Any waiver of these disclosure requirements is now void as against public policy.

Code of Civil Procedure § 415.21 has been added to authorize licensed process servers and other specified persons to have unimpeded access to a gated community staffed by security personnel for a reasonable period of time to perform lawful service of process. The process server must present specified identification and name the person to be served.

11 United States Code § 523(a)(16) of the federal Bankruptcy Act has been amended to make a fee or assessment that accrues after an order for relief from stay is entered in favor of an association a non-dischargeable debt if (1) the debtor physically occupies the unit, or (2) the debtor rents the unit and is receiving rent from a tenant. Thus, an association may now petition the Bankruptcy Court for relief from the automatic stay against enforcement of a debt and continue to receive on-going fees and assessments despite the pendency of bankruptcy. But fees and assessments that accrued <u>prior</u> to the relief from stay remain dischargeable and are unaffected by this amendment.

CHAPTER 3

DAVIS-STIRLING COMMON INTEREST DEVELOPMENT ACT

(Civil Code §§ 1350-1373)

Civ. C. § 1350. Title.

This title shall be known and may be cited as the Davis-Stirling Common Interest Development Act.

Civ. C. § 1351. Definitions.

As used in this title, the following terms have the following meanings:

(a) "**Association**" means a nonprofit corporation or unincorporated association created for the purpose of managing a common interest development.

(b) "**Common area**" means the entire common interest development except the separate interests therein. The estate in the common area may be a fee, a life estate, an estate for years, or any combination of the foregoing. However, the common area for a planned development specified in paragraph (2) of subdivision (k) may consist of mutual or reciprocal easement rights appurtenant to the separate interests.

(c) "**Common interest development**" means any of the following:

(1) A community apartment project.

(2) A condominium project.

(3) A planned development.

(4) A stock cooperative.

(d) "**Community apartment project**" means a development in which an undivided interest in land is coupled with the right of exclusive occupancy of any apartment located thereon.

(e) "**Condominium plan**" means a plan consisting of (1) a description or survey map of a condominium project, which shall refer to or show monumentation on the ground, (2) a three-dimensional description of a condominium project, one or more dimensions of which may extend for an indefinite distance upwards or downwards, in sufficient detail to identify the common areas and each separate interest, and (3) a certificate consenting to the recordation of the condominium plan pursuant to this title signed and acknowledged by the record owner of fee title to that property included in the condominium project. In the case of a condominium project which will terminate upon the termination of an estate for years, the certificate shall be signed and acknowledged by all lessors and lessees of the estate for years and, in the case of a condominium project subject to a life estate, the certificate shall be signed and acknowledged by all life tenants and remainder interests. The certificate shall also be signed and acknowledged by either the trustee or the beneficiary of each recorded deed of trust, and the mortgagee of each recorded mortgage encumbering the property. Owners of mineral rights, easements, rights-of-way, and other nonpossessory interests do not need to sign the condominium plan. A condominium plan may be amended or revoked by a subsequently acknowledged recorded instrument executed by all the persons whose signatures would be required to record a condominium plan pursuant to this subdivision.

(f) A "**condominium project**" means a development consisting of condominiums. A condominium consists of an undivided interest in common in a portion of real property coupled with a separate interest in space called a unit, the boundaries of which are described on a recorded final map, parcel map, or condominium plan in sufficient detail to locate all boundaries thereof. The area within these boundaries may be filled with air, earth, or water, or any combination thereof, and need not be physically attached to land except by easements for access and, if necessary, support. The description of the unit may refer

est" means an individual unit, as specified in subdivision (f).

(3) In a planned development, "separate interest" means a separately owned lot, parcel, area, or space.

(4) In a stock cooperative, "separate interest" means the exclusive right to occupy a portion of the real property, as specified in subdivision (m).

Unless the declaration or condominium plan, if any exists, otherwise provides, if walls, floors, or ceilings are designated as boundaries of a separate interest, the interior surfaces of the perimeter walls, floors, ceilings, windows, doors, and outlets located within the separate interest are part of the separate interest and any other portions of the walls, floors, or ceilings are part of the common areas.

The estate in a separate interest may be a fee, a life estate, an estate for years, or any combination of the foregoing.

(m) "**Stock cooperative**" means a development in which a corporation is formed or availed of primarily for the purpose of holding title to, either in fee simple or for a term of years, improved real property, and all or substantially all of the shareholders of the corporation receive a right of exclusive occupancy in a portion of the real property, title to which is held by the corporation. The owners' interest in the corporation, whether evidenced by a share of stock, a certificate of membership, or otherwise, shall be deemed to be an interest in a common interest development and a real estate development for purposes of subdivision (f) of Section 25100 of the Corporations Code.

A "stock cooperative" includes a limited equity housing cooperative which is a stock cooperative that meets the criteria of Section 33007.5 of the Health and Safety Code.

Civ. C. § 1352. Requirements For Creation Of Common Interest Development.

This title applies and a common interest development is created whenever a separate interest coupled with an interest in the common area or membership in the association is, or has been, conveyed, provided, all of the following are recorded:

(a) A declaration.

(b) A condominium plan, if any exists.

(c) A final map or parcel map, if Division 2 (commencing with Section 66410) of Title 7 of the Government Code requires the recording of either a final map or parcel map for the common interest development.

Civ. C. § 1353. Contents Of Declaration.

(a) A declaration, recorded on or after January 1, 1986, shall contain a legal description of the common interest development, and a statement that the common interest development is a community apartment project, condominium project, planned development, stock cooperative, or combination thereof. The declaration shall additionally set forth the name of the association and the restrictions on the use or enjoyment of any portion of the common interest development that are intended to be enforceable equitable servitudes.

(b) The declaration may contain any other matters the original signator of the declaration or the owners consider appropriate.

Civ. C. § 1354. Covenants And Restrictions In Declaration; Enforcement.

(a) The covenants and restrictions in the declaration shall be enforceable equitable servitude, unless unreasonable, and shall inure to the benefit of and bind all owners of separate interests in the development. Unless the declaration states otherwise, these servitudes may be enforced by any owner of a separate interest or by the association, or by both.

(b) Unless the applicable time limitation for commencing the action would run within 120 days, prior to the filing of a civil action by either an association or an owner or a member of a common interest development solely for declaratory relief or injunctive relief, or for declaratory relief or injunctive relief in conjunction with a claim for monetary damages, other than association assessments, not in excess of five thousand dollars ($5,000), related to the enforcement of the governing documents, the parties shall endeavor, as provided in this subdivision, to submit their dispute to a form of alternative dispute resolution such as mediation or arbitration. The form of alternative dispute resolution chosen may be binding or nonbinding at the option of the parties. Any party to such a dispute may initiate this process by serving on another party to the dispute a Request for Resolution. The Request for Resolution shall include (1) a brief description of the dispute between the parties, (2) a request for alternative dispute resolution, and (3) a notice that the party receiving the Request for Resolution is required to respond thereto within 30 days of receipt or it will be deemed rejected. Service of the Request for Resolution shall be in the same manner as prescribed for service in a small claims action as provided in Section 116.340 of the Code of Civil Procedure. Parties receiving a Request for Resolution shall have 30 days following service of the Request for Resolution to accept or reject alternative dispute resolution and, if not accepted within the 30-day period by a party, shall be deemed rejected by that party. If alternative dispute resolution is accepted by the party upon whom the Request for Resolution is served, the alternative dispute resolution shall be completed within 90 days of receipt of the acceptance by the party initiating the Request for Resolution, unless extended by written stipulation signed by both parties. The costs of the alternative dispute resolution shall be borne by the parties.

(c) At the time of filing a civil action by either an association or an owner or a member of a common interest development solely for declaratory relief or injunctive relief, or for declaratory relief or injunctive relief in conjunction with a claim for monetary damages, other than association assessments, not in excess of five thousand dollars ($5,000), related to the enforcement of the governing documents, the party filing the action shall file with the complaint a certificate stating that alternative dispute resolution has been completed in compliance with subdivision (b). The failure to file a certificate as required by subdivision (b) shall be grounds for a demurrer pursuant to Section 430.10 of the Code of Civil Procedure or a motion to strike pursuant to Section 435 of the Code of Civil Procedure unless the filing party certifies in writing that one of the other parties to the dispute refused alternative dispute resolution prior to the filing of the complaint, that preliminary or temporary injunctive relief is necessary, or that alternative dispute resolution is not required by subdivision (b), because the limitation period for bringing the action would have run within the 120-day period next following the filing of the action, or the court finds that dismissal of the action for failure to comply with subdivision (b) would result in substantial prejudice to one of the parties.

(d) Once a civil action specified in subdivision (a) to enforce the governing documents has been filed by either an association or an owner or member of a common interest development, upon written stipulation of the parties the matter may be referred to alternative dispute resolution and stayed. The costs of the alternative dispute resolution shall be borne by the parties. During this referral, the action shall not be subject to the rules implementing subdivision (c) of Section 68603 of the Government Code.

(e) The requirements of subdivisions (b) and (c) shall not apply to the filing of a cross-complaint.

(f) In any action specified in subdivision (a) to enforce the governing documents, the prevailing party shall be awarded reasonable attorney's fees and costs. Upon motion by any party for attorney's fees and costs to be awarded to the prevailing party in these actions, the court, in determining the amount of the award, may consider a party's refusal to participate in alternative dispute resolution prior to the filing of the action.

(g) Unless consented to by both parties to alternative dispute resolution that is initiated by a Request for Resolution under subdivision (b), evidence of anything said or of admissions made in the course of the alternative dispute resolution process shall not be admissible in evidence, and testimony or disclosure of such a statement or admission may not be compelled, in any civil action in which, pursuant to law, testimony can be compelled to be given.

(h) Unless consented to by both parties to alternative dispute resolution that is initiated by a Request for Resolution under subdivision (b), documents prepared for the purpose or in the course of, or pursuant to, the alternative dispute resolution shall not be admissible in evidence, and disclosure of these documents may not be compelled, in any civil action in which, pursuant to law, testimony can be compelled to be given.

(i) Members of the Association shall annually be provided a summary of the provisions of this section, which specifically references this section. The summary shall include the following language:

> "Failure by any member of the association to comply with the prefiling requirements of Section 1354 of the Civil Code may result in the loss of your rights to sue the association or another member of the association regarding enforcement of the governing documents."

The summary shall be provided either at the time the *pro forma* budget required by Section 1365 is distributed or in the manner specified in Section 5016 of the Corporations Code.

(j) Any Request for Resolution sent to the owner of a separate interest pursuant to subdivision (b) shall include a copy of this section.

Civ. C. § 1355. Amendment Of Declaration.

(a) The declaration may be amended pursuant to the governing documents or this title. Except as provided in Section 1356, an amendment is effective after (1) the approval of the percentage of owners required by the governing documents has been given, (2) that fact has been certified in a writing executed and acknowledged by the officer designated in the declaration or by the association for that purpose, or if no one is designated, by the president of the association, and (3) that writing has been recorded in each county in which a portion of the common interest development is located.

(b) Except to the extent that a declaration provides by its express terms that it is not amendable, in whole or in part, a declaration which fails to include provisions permitting its amendment at all times during its existence may be amended at any time. For purposes of this subdivision, an amendment is only effective after

(1) the proposed amendment has been distributed to all of the owners of separate interests in the common interest development by first-class mail postage prepaid or personal delivery not less than 15 days and not more than 60 days prior to any approval being solicited;

(2) the approval of owners representing more than 50 percent, or any higher percentage required by the declaration for the approval of an amendment to the declaration, of the separate interests in the common interest development has been given, and that fact has been certified in a writing, executed and acknowledged by an officer of the association; and

(3) the amendment has been recorded in each county in which a portion of the common interest development is located. A copy of any amendment adopted pursuant to this subdivision shall be distributed by first-class mail

postage prepaid or personal delivery to all of the owners of separate interest immediately upon its recordation.

Civ. C. § 1355.5. Amendment of Declaration; Deletion of Developer Provisions.

(a) Notwithstanding any provision of the governing documents of a common interest development to the contrary, the board of directors of the association may after the developer of the common interest development has completed construction of the development, has terminated construction activities, and has terminated his or her marketing activities for the sale, lease, or other disposition of separate interests within the development, adopt an amendment deleting from any of the governing documents any provision which is unequivocally designed and intended, or which by its nature can only have been designed or intended, to facilitate the developer in completing the construction or marketing of the development. However, provisions of the governing documents relative to a particular construction or marketing phase of the development may not be deleted under the authorization of this subdivision until that construction or marketing phase has been completed.

(b) The provisions which may be deleted by action of the board shall be limited to those which provide for access by the developer over or across the common area for the purposes of (a) completion of construction of the development, and (b) the erection, construction, or maintenance of structures or other facilities designed to facilitate the completion of construction or marketing of separate interests.

(c) At least 30 days prior to taking action pursuant to subdivision (a), the board of directors of the association shall mail to all owners of the separate interests, by first-class mail, (1) a copy of all amendments to the governing documents proposed to be adopted under subdivision (a) and (2) a notice of the time, date, and place the board of directors will consider adoption of the amendments. The board of directors of an association may consider adoption of amendments to the governing documents pursuant to subdivision (a) only at a meeting which is open to all owners of the separate interests in the common interest development, who shall be given opportunity to make comments thereon. All deliberations of the board of directors on any action proposed under subdivision (a) shall only be conducted in such an open meeting.

(d) The board of directors of the association may not amend the governing documents pursuant to this section without the approval of the owners, casting a majority of the votes at a meeting or election of the association constituting a quorum and conducted in accordance with Chapter 5 (commencing with Section 7510) of Part 3 of Division 2 of Title 1 of, and Section 7613 of, the Corporations Code. For the purposes of this section, "quorum" means more than 50 percent of the owners who own no more than two separate interests in the development.

Civ. C. § 1356. Amendment Of Declaration; Petition; Contents; Filing, Findings By Court, Power Of Court To Approve Amendment; Recording Amendment; Mailing.

(a) If in order to amend a declaration, the declaration requires owners having more than 50 percent of the votes in the association, in a single class voting structure, or owners having more than 50 percent of the votes in more than one class in a voting structure with more than one class, to vote in favor of the amendment, the association, or any owner of a separate interest, may petition the superior court of the county in which the common interest development is located for an order reducing the percentage of the affirmative votes necessary for such an amendment. The petition shall describe the effort that has been made to solicit approval of the association members in the manner provided in the declaration, the number of affirmative and negative votes actually received, the number or percentage of affirmative votes required to effect the amendment in accordance with the existing declaration, and other matters the petitioner considers relevant to the court's determination. The petition shall also contain, as exhibits thereto, copies of all of the following:

(1) The governing documents.
(2) A complete text of the amendment.
(3) Copies of any notice and solicitation materials utilized in the solicitation of owner approvals.
(4) A short explanation of the reason for the amendment.
(5) Any other documentation relevant to the court's determination.

(b) Upon filing the petition, the court shall set the matter for hearing and issue an *ex parte* order setting forth the manner in which notice shall be given.

(c) The court may, but shall not be required to, grant the petition if it finds all of the following:

(1) The petitioner has given not less than 15 days written notice of the court hearing to all members of the association, to any mortgagee of a mortgage or beneficiary of a deed of trust who is entitled to notice under the terms of the declaration, and to the city, county, or city and county in which the common interest development is located that is entitled to notice under the terms of the declaration.
(2) Balloting on the proposed amendment was conducted in accordance with all applicable provisions of the governing documents.
(3) A reasonably diligent effort was made to permit all eligible members to vote on the proposed amendment.
(4) Owners having more than 50 percent of the votes, in a single class voting structure, voted in favor of the amendment. In a voting structure with more than one class, where the declaration requires a majority of more than one class to vote in favor of the amendment,

owners having more than 50 percent of the votes of each class required by the declaration to vote in favor of the amendment voted in favor of the amendment.

(5) The amendment is reasonable.

(6) Granting the petition is not improper for any reason stated in subdivision (e).

(d) If the court makes the findings required by subdivision (c), any order issued pursuant to this section may confirm the amendment as being validly approved on the basis of the affirmative votes actually received during the balloting period or the order may dispense with any requirement relating to quorums or to the number or percentage of votes needed for approval of the amendment that would otherwise exist under the governing documents.

(e) Subdivisions (a) to (d) inclusive, not withstanding, the court shall not be empowered by this section to approve any amendment to the declaration that:

(1) Would change provisions in the declaration requiring the approval of owners having more than 50 percent of the votes in more than one class to vote in favor of an amendment, unless owners having more than 50 percent of the votes in each affected class approved the amendment.

(2) Would eliminate any special rights, preferences, or privileges designated in the declaration as belonging to the declarant, without the consent of the declarant.

(3) Would impair the security interest of a mortgagee of a mortgage or the beneficiary of a deed of trust without the approval of the percentage of the mortgagees and beneficiaries specified in the declaration, if the declaration requires the approval of a specified percentage of the mortgagees and beneficiaries.

(f) An amendment is not effective pursuant to this section until the court order and amendment have been recorded in every county in which a portion of the common interest development is located. The amendment may be acknowledged by, and the court order and amendment may be recorded by, any person designated in the declaration or by the association for that purpose, or if no one is designated for that purpose, by the president of the association. Upon recordation of the amendment and court order, the declaration, as amended in accordance with this section, shall have the same force and effect as if the amendment were adopted in compliance with every requirement imposed by the governing documents.

(g) Within a reasonable time after the amendment is recorded the association shall mail a copy of the amendment to each member of the association, together with a statement that the amendment has been recorded.

Civ. C. § 1357. Extension Of Term Of Declaration.

(a) The Legislature finds that there are common interest developments that have been created with deed restrictions which do not provide a means for the property owners to extend the term of the declaration. The Legislature further finds that covenants and restrictions, contained in the declaration, are an appropriate method for protecting the common plan of developments and to provide for a mechanism for financial support for the upkeep of common areas including, but not limited to, roofs, roads, heating systems, and recreational facilities. If declarations terminate prematurely, common interest developments may deteriorate and the housing supply of affordable units could be impacted adversely.

The Legislature further finds and declares that it is in the public interest to provide a vehicle for extending the term of the declaration if owners having more than 50 percent of the votes in the association choose to do so.

(b) A declaration which specifies a termination date, but which contains no provision for extension of the termination date, may be extended by the approval of owners having more than 50 percent of the votes in the association or any greater percentage specified in the declaration for an amendment thereto. If the approval of owners having more than 50 percent of the votes in the association is required to amend the declaration, the term of the declaration may be extended in accordance with Section 1356.

(c) Any amendment to a declaration made in accordance with subdivision (b) shall become effective upon recordation in accordance with Section 1355.

(d) No single extension of the terms of the declaration made pursuant to this section shall exceed the initial term of the declaration or 20 years, whichever is less. However, more than one extension may occur pursuant to this section.

Civ. C. § 1358. Interests Included In Conveyance, Judicial Sale Or Transfer Of Separate Interests; Transfers Of Exclusive Use Areas; Restrictions Upon Severability Of Component Interests.

(a) In a community apartment project, any conveyance, judicial sale, or other voluntary or involuntary transfer of the separate interest includes the undivided interest in the community apartment project. Any conveyance, judicial sale, or other voluntary or involuntary transfer of the owner's entire estate also includes the owner's membership interest in the association.

(b) In a condominium project, the common areas are not subject to partition, except as provided in Section 1359. Any conveyance, judicial sale, or other voluntary or involuntary transfer of the separate interest includes the undivided interest in the common areas. Any conveyance, judicial sale, or other voluntary or involuntary transfer of the owner's entire estate also includes the owner's membership interest in the association.

(c) In a planned development, any conveyance, judicial sale, or other voluntary or involuntary transfer of the separate interest includes the undivided interest in the common areas, if any exist. Any conveyance, judicial sale, or other voluntary or involuntary transfer of the owner's entire estate also includes the owner's membership interest in the association.

(d) In a stock cooperative, any conveyance, judicial sale, or other voluntary or involuntary transfer of the separate interest includes the ownership interest in the corporation, however evidenced. Any conveyance, judicial sale, or other voluntary or involuntary transfer of the owner's entire estate also includes the owner's membership interest in the association.

Nothing in this section prohibits the transfer of exclusive use areas, independent of any other interest in a common interest subdivision, if authorization to separately transfer exclusive use areas is expressly stated in the declaration and the transfer occurs in accordance with the terms of the declaration.

Any restrictions upon the severability of the component interests in real property which are contained in the declaration shall not be deemed conditions repugnant to the interest created within the meaning of Section 711 of the Civil Code. However, these restrictions shall not extend beyond the period in which the right to partition a project is suspended under Section 1359.

Civ. C. § 1359. Restrictions On Partition.

(a) Except as provided in this section, the common areas in a condominium project shall remain undivided, and there shall be no judicial partition thereof. Nothing in this section shall be deemed to prohibit partition of a cotenancy in a condominium.

(b) The owner of a separate interest in a condominium project may maintain a partition action as to the entire project as if the owners of all of the separate interests in the project were tenants in common in the entire project in the same proportion as their interests in the common areas. The court shall order partition under this subdivision only by sale of the entire condominium project and only upon a showing of one of the following:

(1) More than three years before the filing of the action, the condominium project was damaged or destroyed, so that a material part was rendered unfit for its prior use, and the condo-

minium project has not been rebuilt or repaired substantially to its state prior to the damage or destruction.

(2) Three-fourths or more of the project is destroyed or substantially damaged and owners of separate interests holding in the aggregate more than a 50-percent interest in the common areas oppose repair or restoration of the project.

(3) The project has been in existence more than 50 years, is obsolete and uneconomic, and owners of separate interests holding in the aggregate more than a 50-percent interest in the common area oppose repair or restoration of the project.

(4) The conditions for such a sale, set forth in the declaration, have been met.

Civ. C. § 1360. Modification Of Unit By Owner; Facilitation Of Access For Handicapped; Approval By Project Associations.

(a) Subject to the provisions of the governing documents and other applicable provisions of law, if the boundaries of the separate interest are contained within a building, the owner of the separate interest may do the following:

(1) Make any improvements or alterations within the boundaries of his or her separate interest that do not impair the structural integrity or mechanical systems or lessen the support of any portions of the common interest development.

(2) Modify a unit in a condominium project, at the owner's expense, to facilitate access for persons who are blind, visually handicapped, deaf, or physically disabled, or to alter conditions which could be hazardous to these persons. These modifications may also include modifications of the route from the public way to the door of the unit for the purposes of this

paragraph if the unit is on the ground floor or already accessible by an existing ramp or elevator. The right granted by this paragraph is subject to the following conditions:

(A) The modifications shall be consistent with applicable building code requirements.

(B) The modifications shall be consistent with the intent of otherwise applicable provisions of the governing documents pertaining to safety or aesthetics.

(C) Modifications external to the dwelling shall not prevent reasonable passage by other residents, and shall be removed by the owner when the unit is no longer occupied by persons requiring those modifications who are blind, visually handicapped, deaf or physically disabled.

(D) Any owner who intends to modify a unit pursuant to this paragraph shall submit his or her plans and specifications to the association of the condominium project for review to determine whether the modifications will comply with the provisions of this paragraph. The association shall not deny approval of the proposed modifications under this paragraph without good cause.

(b) Any change in the exterior appearances of a separate interest shall be in accordance with the governing documents and applicable provisions of law.

Civ. C. § 1361. Rights And Easements Of Ingress, Egress, and Support.

Unless the declaration otherwise provides:

(a) In a community apartment project and condominium project, and in those planned developments with common areas owned in common by the owners of the separate interests, there are appurtenant to each separate interest nonexclusive rights of ingress, egress, and support, if necessary, through the common areas. The common areas are subject to these rights.

(b) In a stock cooperative, and in a planned development with common areas owned by the association, there is an easement for ingress, egress, and support, if necessary, appurtenant to each separate interest. The common areas are subject to these easements.

Civ. C. § 1362. Ownership Of Common Areas.

Unless the declaration otherwise provides, in a condominium project, or in a planned development in which the common areas are owned by the owners of the separate interests, the common areas are owned as tenants in common, in equal shares, one for each unit or lot.

Civ. C. § 1363. Management; Powers Of Association; Reference To As Community Association; Meetings; Access To Records; Consolidated Association Membership Rights; Copies Of Minutes; Proposed Minutes, Or Summaries.

(a) A common interest development shall be managed by an association which may be incorporated or unincorporated. The association may be referred to as a community association.

(b) An association, whether incorporated or unincorporated, shall prepare a budget pursuant to Section 1365 and disclose information, if requested, in accordance with Section 1368.

(c) Unless the governing documents provide otherwise, and regardless of whether the association is incorporated or unincorporated, the association may exercise the powers granted to a nonprofit mutual benefit corporation, as enumerated in Section 7140 of the Corporations Code, except that an unincorporated association may not adopt or use a corporate seal or issue membership certificates in accordance with Section 7313 of the Corporations Code.

The association, whether incorporated or unincorporated, may exercise the powers granted to an association by Section 383 of the Code of Civil Procedure and the powers granted to the association in this title.

(d) Meetings of the membership of the association shall be conducted in accordance with a recognized system of parliamentary procedure or such parliamentary procedures as the association may adopt.

(e) Notwithstanding any other provision of law, notice of meetings of the members shall specify those matters the board intends to present for action by the members, but, except as otherwise provided by law, any proper matter may be presented at the meeting for action.

(f) Members of the association shall have access to association records in accordance with Article 3 (commencing with Section 8330) of Chapter 13 of Part 3 of Division 2 of Title 1 of the Corporations Code.

(g) Any member of the association may attend meetings of the board of directors of the association, except when the board adjourns to executive session to consider litigation, matters that relate to the formation of contracts with third parties, or personnel matters.

(h) Any matter discussed in executive session shall be generally noted in the minutes of the board of directors.

(i) If an association adopts or has adopted a policy imposing any monetary penalty, including any fee, on any association member for a violation of the governing documents or rules of the association, including any monetary penalty relating to the activities of a guest or invitee of a member, the board of directors shall adopt and distribute to each member, by personal delivery or first-class mail, a schedule of the monetary penalties that may be assessed for those violations, which shall be in accordance with authorization for members discipline contained in the governing documents. The board of directors shall not be required to distribute any additional schedules of monetary penalties unless there are changes from the schedule that was adopted and distributed to the members pursuant to this subdivision. The board of directors of the association shall meet in executive session if requested by the member being disciplined, and the member shall be entitled to attend the executive session.

(j) Whenever two or more associations have consolidated any of their functions under a joint neighborhood association or similar organization, members of each participating association shall be entitled to attend all meetings of the joint association other than executive sessions, (1) shall be given reasonable opportunity for participation in those meetings and (2) shall be entitled to the same access to the joint association's records as they are to the participating association's records.

(k) The minutes, minutes proposed for adoption that are marked to indicate draft status, or a summary of the minutes, of any meeting of the board of directors of an association, other than an executive session, shall be available to members within 30 days of the meeting. The minutes, proposed minutes, or summary of minutes shall be distributed to any member of the association upon request and upon reimbursement of the association's costs in making that distribution.

(l) Members of the association shall be notified in writing at the time that the *pro forma* budget required in Section 1365 is distributed or at the time of any general mailing to the entire membership of the association of their right to have copies of the minutes of meetings of the board of directors and how and where those minutes may be obtained.

(m) Nothing in this section shall be construed to create, expand, or reduce the authority of the board of directors of an association to impose monetary penalties on an association member for a violation of the governing documents or rules of the association.

Civ. C. § 1363.1. Prospective Managing Agent; Written Disclosures; Duration of Section.

(a) A prospective managing agent of a common interest development shall provide a written statement to the board of directors of the association of a common interest development as soon as practicable, but in no event more than 90 days, before entering into a management agreement which shall contain all of the following information concerning the managing agent:

(1) The names and business addresses of the owners or general partners of the managing agent. If the managing agent is a corporation, the written statement shall include the names and business addresses of the directors and officers and shareholders holding greater than 10 percent of the shares of the corporation.

(2) Whether or not any relevant licenses such as architectural design, construction, engineering, real estate, or accounting have been issued by this state and are currently held by the persons specified in paragraph (1). If a license is currently held by any of those persons, the statement shall contain the following information:

(A) What license is held.

(B) The status of that license.

(C) The name of the licensee appearing on that license.

(3) Whether or not any relevant professional certifications or designations such as architectural design, construction, engineering, real property management, or accounting are currently held by any of the persons specified in paragraph (1), including, but not limited to, certified property manager or professional association manager. If any certification or designation is held, the statement shall include the following information:

(A) What the certification or designation is and what entity issued it.

(B) The status of that certification of designation.

(C) The names in which the certification or designation is held.

(b) As used in this section, a "managing agent" is a person or entity, who for compensation or, in expectation of compensation, exercises control over the assets of a common interest development. A "managing agent" does not include any of the following:

(1) A full-time employee of the association.

(2) Any regulated financial institution operating within the normal course of its regulated business practice.

(c) This section shall remain in effect only until January 1, 1997, and as of that date is repealed unless a later enacted statute which is chaptered before January 1, 1997, deletes or extends that date.

Civ. C. § 1363.2. Managing Agent; Deposit Of Funds Received; Requirements; Separate Record; Commingling Of Funds.

(a) A managing agent of a common interest development who accepts or receives funds belonging to the association shall deposit all such funds that are not placed into an escrow account with a bank, savings association, or credit union, or into an account under the control of the association, into a trust fund account maintained by the managing agent in a bank, savings association, or credit union in this state. All funds deposited by the managing agent in the trust fund account shall be kept in this state in a financial institution, as defined in Section 31041 of the Financial Code, which is insured by the federal government, and shall be maintained there until dispersed in accordance with written instructions from the association entitled to the funds.

(b) At the written request of the board of directors of the association, the funds the managing agent accepts or receives on behalf of the association shall be deposited into an interest-bearing account in a bank, savings association, or credit union in this state, provided all of the following requirements are met:

(1) The account is in the name of the managing agent as trustee for the association or in the name of the association.

(2) All of the funds in the account are covered by insurance provided by an agency of the federal government.

(3) The funds in the account are kept separate, distinct, and apart from the funds belonging to the managing agent or to any other person or entity for whom the managing agent holds funds in trust except that the funds of various associations may be commingled as permitted pursuant to subdivision (d).

(4) The managing agent discloses to the board of directors of the association the nature of the account, how interest will be calculated and paid, whether service charges will be paid to the depository and by whom, and any notice requirements or penalties for withdrawal of funds from the account.

(5) No interest earned on funds in the account shall inure directly or indirectly to the benefit of the managing agent for his or her employees.

(c) The managing agent shall maintain a separate record of the receipt and disposition of all funds described in this section, including any interest earned on the funds.

(d) The managing agent shall not commingle the funds of the association with his or her own money or with the money of others that he or she receives or accepts, unless all of the following requirements are met:

(1) The managing agent commingled the funds of various associations on or before February 26, 1990, and has retained a written agreement with the board of directors of each association that he or she will maintain a fidelity and surety bond in an amount that provides adequate protection to the associations as agreed upon by the managing agent and the board of directors of each association.

(2) The managing agent discloses in a written agreement whether he or she is deriving benefits from the commingled account or the bank,

credit union, or savings institution where the monies will be on deposit.

(3) The written agreement provided pursuant to this subdivision includes, but is not limited to, the name and address of the bonding companies, the amount of the bonds, and the expiration dates of the bonds.

(4) If there are any changes in the bond coverage or the companies providing the coverage, the managing agent discloses that fact to the board of directors of each affected association as soon as practical, but in no event more than 10 days after the change.

(5) The bonds assure the protection of the association and provide the association at least 10 days notice prior to cancellation.

(6) Completed payments on the behalf of the association are deposited within 24 hours or the next business day and do not remain commingled for more than 10 calendar days.

(e) The prevailing party in an action to enforce this section shall be entitled to recover reasonable legal fees and court costs.

(f) As used in this section, a "managing agent" is a person or entity, who for compensation or, in expectation of compensation, exercises control over the assets of the association. However, a "managing agent" does not include a full-time employee of the association or a regulated financial institution operating within the normal course of business, or an attorney at law acting within the scope of his or her license.

(g) As used in this section, "completed payment" means funds received which clearly identify the account to which the funds are to be credited.

Civ. C. 1363.5. Filing Requirement With The Secretary Of State.

(a) The articles of incorporation of any common interest development association filed with the Secretary of State

on or after January 1, 1995, shall include a statement that shall be in addition to the statement of purposes of the corporation, and that

(1) identifies the corporation as an association formed to manage a common interest development under the Davis-Stirling Common Interest Development Act,

(2) states the business or corporate office of the association, if any, and, if the office is not on the site of the common interest development, states the nine-digit ZIP Code, front street, and nearest cross street for the physical location of the common interests development, and

(3) states the name and address of the association's managing agent, as defined in Section 1363.1, if any.

(b) The statement of principal business activity contained in the annual statement filed by an incorporated association with the Secretary of State pursuant to Section 1502 of the Corporations Code shall also contain the statement specified in subdivision (a).

Civ. C. § 1364. Responsibility For Repair, Replacement, Or Maintenance; Damage By Wood-Destroying Pests Or Organisms; Cost Allocation; Notice of Repair Requirements; Access For Maintenance Of Telephone Wiring.

(a) Unless otherwise provided in the declaration of a common interest development, the association is responsible for repairing, replacing, or maintaining the common areas, other than exclusive use common area, and the owner of each separate interest is responsible for maintaining that separate interest and any exclusive use common area appurtenant to the separate interest.

(b) (1) In a community apartment project, condominium project, or stock cooperative, as defined in Section 1351, unless otherwise provided in the declaration, the association is responsible for the repair and maintenance of the common area occasioned by the presence of wood-destroying pests or organisms.

(2) In a planned development as defined in Section 1351, unless a different maintenance scheme is provided in the declaration, each owner of a separate interest is responsible for the repair and maintenance of that separate interest as may be occasioned by the presence of wood-destroying pests or organisms. Upon approval of the majority of all members of the association, the responsibility for such repair and maintenance may be delegated to the association, which shall be entitled to recover the cost thereof as a special assessment.

(c) The costs of temporary relocation during the repair and maintenance of the areas within the responsibility of the association shall be borne by the owner of the separate interest affected.

(d) (1) The association may cause the temporary, summary removal of any occupant of a common interest development for such periods and at such times as may be necessary for prompt, effective treatment of wood-destroying pests or organisms.

(2) The association shall give notice of the need to temporarily vacate a separate interest to the occupants and to the owners, not less than 15 days nor more than 30 days prior to the date of the temporary relocation. The notice shall state the reason for the temporary relocation, the date and time of the beginning of treatment, the anticipated date and time of termination of treatment, and that the occupants will be responsible for their own accommodations during the temporary relocation.

(3) Notice by the association shall be deemed complete upon either:

(A) Personal delivery of a copy of the notice to the occupants, and sending a copy of the notice to the owners, if different than the occupants, by first-class mail, postage prepaid at the most current address shown on the books of the association.

(B) By sending a copy of the notice to the occupants at the separate interest address and a copy of the notice to the owners, if different than the occupants, by first-class mail, postage prepaid, at the most current address shown on the books of the association.

(e) For purposes of this section, "occupant" means an owner, resident, guest, invitee, tenant, lessee, sublessee, or other person in possession of the separate interest.

(f) Notwithstanding the provisions of the declaration, the owner of a separate interest is entitled to reasonable access to the common areas for the purpose of maintaining the internal and external telephone wiring made part of the exclusive use common areas of a separate interest pursuant to paragraph (2) of subdivision (i) of Section 1351. The access shall be subject to the consent of the association, whose approval shall not be unreasonably withheld, and which may include the association's approval of telephone wiring upon the exterior of the common areas, and other conditions as the association determines reasonable.

Civ. C. § 1365. Financial Documents.

Unless the declaration imposes more stringent standards, the association shall prepare and distribute to all its members the following documents:

(a) A *pro forma* operating budget, which shall include all of the following:

(1) The estimated revenue and expenses on an accrual basis.

(2) A summary of the association's reserves based upon the most recent review or study conducted pursuant to Section 1365.5, which shall be printed in bold type and include all of the following:

(A) The current estimated replacement cost, estimated remaining life, and estimated useful life of each major component.

(B) As of the end of the fiscal year for which the study is prepared:

(i) The current estimate of the amount of cash reserves necessary to repair, replace, restore, or maintain the major components.

(ii) The current amount of accumulated cash reserves actually set aside to repair, replace, restore, or maintain major components.

(C) The percentage that the amount determined for purposes of clause (ii) of subparagraph (B) is of the amount determined for purposes of clause (i) of subparagraph (B).

(3) A statement as to whether the board of directors of the association has determined or anticipates that the levy of one or more special assessments will be required to repair, replace, or restore any major component or to provide adequate reserves therefor.

(4) A general statement addressing the procedures used for the calculation and establishment of those reserves to defray the future repair, replacement, or additions to those major components that the association is obligated to maintain.

The summary of the association's reserves disclosed pursuant to paragraph (2) shall not be admissible in evidence to show improper financial management of an association, provided that other relevant and competent evidence of the financial condition of the association is not made inadmissible by this provision.

A copy of the operating budget shall be annually distributed not less than 45 days nor more than 60 days prior to the beginning of the association's fiscal year.

(b) A review of the financial statement of the association shall be prepared in accordance with generally accepted accounting principles by a licensee of the California State Board of Accountancy for any fiscal year in which the gross income to the association exceeds seventy-five thousand dollars ($75,000). A copy of the review of the financial statement shall be distributed within 120 days after the close of each fiscal year.

(c) In lieu of the distribution of the *pro forma* operating budget required by subdivision (a), the board of directors may elect to distribute a summary of the *pro forma* operating budget to all its members with a written notice that the *pro forma* operating budget is available at the business office of the association or at another suitable location within the boundaries of the development and that copies will be provided upon request and at the expense of the association. If any member requests that a copy of the *pro forma* operating budget required by subdivision (a) be mailed to the member, the association shall provide the copy to the member by first-class United States mail at the expense of the association and delivered within five days. The written notice that is distributed to each of the association members shall be in at least 10-point bold type on the front page of the summary of the budget.

(d) A statement describing the association's policies and practices in enforcing lien rights or other legal remedies for default in payment of its assessments against its members shall be annually delivered to the members during the 60-day period immediately preceding the beginning of the association's fiscal year.

Civ. C. § 1365.5 Board Of Directors; Duties.

(a) Unless the governing documents impose more stringent standards, the board of directors of the association shall do all of the following:

(1) Review a current reconciliation of the association's operating accounts on at least a quarterly basis.

(2) Review a current reconciliation of the association's reserve accounts on at least a quarterly basis.

(3) Review, on at least a quarterly basis, the current year's actual reserve revenues and expenses compared to the current year's budget.

(4) Review the latest account statements prepared by the financial institutions where the association has its operating and reserve accounts.

(5) Review an income and expense statement for the association's operating and reserve accounts on at least a quarterly basis.

(b) The signatures of at least two persons, who shall be members of the association's board of directors, or one officer who is not a member of the board of directors and a member of the board of directors, shall be required for the withdrawal of moneys from the association's reserve accounts.

(c) (1) The board of directors shall not expend funds designated as reserve funds for any purpose other than the repair, restoration, replacement, or maintenance of, or litigation involving the repair, restoration, replacement, or maintenance of, major components which the association is obligated to repair, restore, replace, or maintain and for which the reserve fund was established.

(2) However, the board may authorize the temporary transfer of money from a reserve fund to the association's general operating fund to meet short-term cash-flow requirements or other expenses, provided the board has made a written

finding, recorded in the board's minutes, explaining the reasons that the transfer is needed, and describing when and how the money will be repaid to the reserve fund. The transferred funds shall be restored to the reserve fund within one year of the date of the initial transfer, except that the board may, upon making a finding supported by documentation that a temporary delay would be in the best interests of the common interest development, temporarily delay the restoration. The board shall exercise prudent fiscal management in delaying restoration of these funds and in restoring the expended funds to the reserve account, and shall, if necessary, levy a special assessment to recover the full amount of the expended funds within the time limits required by this section. This special assessment is subject to the limitation imposed by Section 1366, unless the special assessment is to pay for legal costs associated with litigation involving the repair, restoration, replacement, or maintenance of, major components which the association is obligated to repair, restore, replace, or maintain. The board may, at its discretion, extend the date the payment on the special assessment is due. Any extension shall not prevent the board from pursuing any legal remedy to enforce the collection of an unpaid special assessment.

(d) When the decision is made to use reserve funds or to temporarily transfer money from the reserve fund to pay for litigation, the association shall notify the members of the association of that decision in the next available mailing to all members pursuant to Section 5016 of the Corporations Code, and of the availability of an accounting of those expenses. Unless the governing documents impose more stringent standards, the association shall make an accounting of expenses related to the litigation on at last a quarterly basis. The accounting shall be made available for inspection by members of the association at the association's office.

(e) At least once every three years the board of directors shall cause a study of the reserve account requirements of the common interest development to be conducted if the current replacement value of the major components which the association is obligated to repair, replace, restore, or maintain is equal to or greater than one-half of the gross budget of the association for any fiscal year. The board shall review this study annually and shall consider and implement necessary adjustments to the board's analysis of the reserve account requirements as a result of that review.

The study required by this subdivision shall at a minimum include:

(1) Identification of the major components which the association is obligated to repair, replace, restore, or maintain which, as of the date of the study, have a remaining useful life of less than 30 years.

(2) Identification of the probable remaining useful life of the components identified in paragraph (1) as of the date of the study.

(3) An estimate of the cost of repair, replacement, restoration, or maintenance of the components identified in paragraph (1) during and at the end of their useful life.

(4) An estimate of the total annual contribution necessary to defray the cost to repair, replace, restore, or maintain the components identified in paragraph (1) during and at the end of their useful life, after subtracting total reserve funds as of the date of the study.

(f) As used in this section, "reserve accounts" means moneys that the association's board of directors has identified for use to defray the future repair or replacement of, or additions to, those major components which the association is obligated to maintain.

(g) As used in this section, "reserve account requirements" means the estimated funds which the association's board of directors has determined are required to be available at a specified point in time to repair, replace, or restore those major components which the association is obligated to maintain.

(h) This section does not apply to an association that does not have a "common area" as defined in Section 1351.

Civ. C. § 1365.7 Tortious Act Or Omission Of Volunteer Officer Or Director Of Association Managing Residential Development; Liability; Criteria; Limitations.

(a) A volunteer officer or volunteer director of an association, as defined in subdivision (a) of Section 1351, which manages a common interest development that is exclusively residential, shall not be personally liable in excess of the coverage of insurance specified in paragraph (4) to any person who suffers injury, including, but not limited to, bodily injury, emotional distress, wrongful death, or property damage or loss as a result of the tortious act or omission of the volunteer officer or volunteer director if all of the following criteria are met:

(1) The act or omission was performed within the scope of the officer's or director's association duties.

(2) The act or omission was performed in good faith.

(3) The act or omission was not willful, wanton, or grossly negligent.

(4) The association maintained and had in effect at the time the act or omission occurred and at the time a claim is made one or more policies of insurance which shall include coverage for (A) general liability of the association and (B) individual liability of officers and directors of the association for negligent acts or omissions in that capacity; provided, that both types of coverage are in the following minimum amount:

(A) At least five hundred thousand dollars ($500,000) if the common interest development consists of 100 or fewer separate interests.

(B) At least one million dollars ($1,000,000) if the common interest development consists of more than 100 separate interests.

(b) The payment of actual expenses incurred by a director or officer in the execution of the duties of that position does not affect the director's or officer's status as a volunteer within the meaning of this section.

(c) An officer or director who at the time of the act or omission was a declarant, as defined in subdivision (g) of Section 1351, or who received either direct or indirect compensation as an employee from the declarant, or from a financial institution that purchased a separate interest, as defined in subdivision (l) of Section 1351, at a judicial or nonjudicial foreclosure of a mortgage or deed of trust on real property, is not a volunteer for the purposes of this section.

(d) Nothing in this section shall be construed to limit the liability of the association for its negligent act or omission or for any negligent act or omission of an officer or director of the association.

(e) This section shall only apply to a volunteer officer or director who is a tenant of a separate interest in the common interest development or is an owner of no more than two separate interests in the common interest development.

Civ. C. 1365.9. Tort Actions Against Association; Limits Of Insurance For Officers.

Any cause of action in tort against any person arising solely by reason of an ownership interest in the common area of a common interest development shall be brought against the association and not against the individual owners of the separate interests, as defined in subdivision (l) of Section 1351, provided that all of the following insurance requirements are met:

(a) The association maintained and had in effect at the time the alleged act or omission occurred and at the time a claim is made, one or more policies of insurance which include coverage for (1) general liability of the association and (2) individual liability of officers and directors of the association for negligent acts or omissions of those persons acting in their capacity as officers and directors.

(b) Both types of coverage described in paragraphs (1) and (2) of subdivision (a) are in the following minimum amounts:

> *(1) At least two million dollars ($2,000,000) per occurrence if the common interest development consists of 100 or fewer separate interests.*
>
> *(2) At least three million dollars ($3,000,000) per occurrence if the common interest development consists of more than 100 separate interests.*

(c) The association shall, upon issuance or renewal of insurance, but no less than annually, notify its homeowners as to the amount and type of insurance carried by the association, and it shall accompany this notification with statements to the effect that the association is or is not insured to the levels specified by this section, and that if not so insured, owners may be individually liable for the entire amount of a judgment, and if the association is insured to the levels specified in this section, then owners may be individually liable only for their proportional share of assessments levied to pay the amount of any judgment which exceeds the limits of the association's insurance.

Civ. C. § 1366. Levy of Assessments; Limitation on Increases; Delinquent Assessments; Interest.

(a) Except as provided in this section, the association shall levy regular and special assessments sufficient to perform its obligations under the governing documents and this title. However, annual increases in regular assessments for any fiscal year, as authorized by subdivision (b), shall not be imposed unless the board has complied with subdivision (a) of Section 1365 with respect to that fiscal year, or has obtained the approval of owners, constituting a quorum, casting a majority of the votes at a meeting or election of the association conducted in accordance with Chapter 5 (commencing with Section 7510) of Part 3 of Division 2 of Title 1 of the Corporations Code, and Section 7613 of the Corporations Code. For the purposes of this section, "quorum" means more than 50 percent of the owners of an association.

(b) Notwithstanding more restrictive limitations placed on the board by the governing documents, the board of directors may not impose a regular assessment that is more than 20 percent greater than the regular assessment for the association's preceding fiscal year or impose special assessments which in the aggregate exceed 5 percent of the budgeted gross expenses of the association for that fiscal year without the approval of owners, constituting a quorum, casting a majority of the votes at a meeting or election of the association conducted in accordance with Chapter 5 (commencing with Section 7510) of Part 3 of Division 2 of Title 1 of the Corporations Code and Section 7613 of the Corporations Code. For the purposes of this section, quorum means more than 50 percent of the owners of an association. This section does not limit assessment increases necessary for emergency situations. For purposes of this section, an emergency situation is any one of the following:

(1) An extraordinary expense required by an order of a court.

(2) An extraordinary expense necessary to repair or maintain the common interest development or any part of it for which the association is responsible where a threat to personal safety on the property is discovered.

(3) An extraordinary expense necessary to repair or maintain the common interest development or any part of it for which the association is responsible that could not have been reasonably foreseen by the board in preparing and distributing the *pro forma* operating budget under Section 1365. However,

prior to the imposition or collection of an assessment under this subdivision, the board shall pass a resolution containing written findings as to the necessity of the extraordinary expense involved and why the expense was not or could not have been reasonably foreseen in the budgeting process, and the resolution shall be distributed to the members with the notice of assessment.

(4) An extraordinary expense in making the first payment of the earthquake insurance surcharge pursuant to Section 5003 of the Insurance Code.

(c) The association shall provide notice by first-class mail to the owners of the separate interests of any increase in the regular or special assessments of the association, not less than 30 nor more than 60 days prior to the increased assessment becoming due.

(d) Regular and special assessments levied pursuant to the governing documents are delinquent 15 days after they become due. If an assessment is delinquent, the association may recover all of the following:

(1) Reasonable costs incurred in collecting the delinquent assessment, including reasonable attorneys' fees.

(2) A late charge not exceeding 10 percent of the delinquent assessment or ten dollars ($10), whichever is greater, unless the declaration specifies a late charge in a smaller amount, in which case any late charge imposed shall not exceed the amount specified in the declaration.

(3) Interest on all sums imposed in accordance with this section, including the delinquent assessment, reasonable costs of collection, and late charges, at an annual percentage rate not to exceed 12 percent interest, commencing 30 days after the assessment becomes due.

(e) Associations are hereby exempted from interest-rate limitations imposed by Article XV of the California Constitution, subject to the limitations of this section.

Civ. C. § 1366.1. Imposition Or Collection Of Assessments, Penalties Or Fees; Limit On Amount.

An association shall not impose or collect an assessment or fee that exceeds the amount necessary to defray the costs for which it is levied.

Civ. C. § 1367. Assessments; Debt Of Owner; Lien; Notice; Enforcement Of Lien; Application Of Section.

(a) A regular or special assessment and any late charges, reasonable costs of collection, and interest, as assessed in accordance with Section 1366, shall be a debt of the owner of the separate interest at the time the assessment or other sums are levied.

(b) The amount of the assessment, plus any costs of collection, late charges, and interest assessed in accordance with Section 1366, shall be a lien on the owner's interest in the common interest development from and after the time the association causes to be recorded with the county recorder of the county in which the separate interest is located, a notice of delinquent assessment, which shall state the amount of the assessment and other sums imposed in accordance with Section 1366, a description of the owner's interest in the common interest development against which the assessment and other sums are levied, the name of the record owner of the owner's interest in the common interest development against which the lien is imposed, and, in order for the lien to be enforced by nonjudicial foreclosure as provided in subdivision (d) the name and address of the trustee authorized by the association to enforce the lien by sale. The notice of delinquent assessment shall be signed by the person designated in the declaration or by the association for that purpose, or if no one is designated, by the president of the association. Upon payment of the sums specified in the notice of delinquent assessment, the association shall cause to be recorded a further notice stating the satisfaction and release of the lien thereof.

(c) A lien created pursuant to subdivision (b) shall be prior to all other liens recorded subsequent to the notice of assessment, except that the declaration may provide for the subordination thereof to any other liens and encumbrances.

(d) A lien created pursuant to subdivision (b) may be enforced in any manner permitted by law, including sale by the court, sale by the trustee designated in the notice of delinquent assessment, or sale by a trustee substituted pursuant to Section 2934a. Any sale by the trustee shall be conducted in accordance with the provisions of Sections 2924, 2924b and 2924c applicable to the exercise of powers of sale in mortgages and deeds of trusts.

(e) Nothing in this section or in subdivision (a) of Section 726 of the Code of Civil Procedure prohibits actions against the owner of a separate interest to recover sums for which a lien is created pursuant to this section or prohibits an association from taking a deed in lieu of foreclosure.

(f) This section only applies to liens recorded on or after January 1, 1986.

Civ. C. § 1368. Sale Or Title Transfer; Provision Of Specified Items To Prospective Purchasers; Copies; Fees; Violations; Penalty And Attorney Fees; Validity Of Title Transferred In Violation; Additional Requirements.

(a) The owner of a separate interest, other than an owner subject to the requirements of Section 11018.6 of the Business and Professions Code, shall, as soon as practicable before transfer of title to the separate interest or execution of a real property sales contract therefor, as defined in Section 2985, provide the following to the prospective purchaser:

(1) A copy of the governing documents of the common interest development.

(2) If there is a restriction in the governing documents limiting the occupancy, residency, or use of a separate interest on the basis of age in a manner different from that provided in Section 51.3, a statement that the restriction is only enforceable to the extent permitted by Section 51.3 and a statement specifying the applicable provisions of Section 51.3.

(3) A copy of the most recent financial statement distributed pursuant to Section 1365.

(4) A true statement in writing from an authorized representative of the association as to the amount of the association's current regular and special assessments and fees, as well as any assessments levied upon the owner's interest in the common interest development which are unpaid on the date of the statement. The statement shall also include true information on late charges, interest, and costs of collection which, as of the date of the statement, are or may be made a lien upon the owner's interest in a common interest development pursuant to Section 1367.

(5) Any change in the association's current regular and special assessments and fees which have been approved by the association's board of directors, but have not become due and payable as of the date disclosure is provided pursuant to this subdivision.

(b) Upon written request, an association shall, within 10 days of the mailing or delivery of the request, provide the owner of a separate interest with a copy of the requested items specified in paragraphs (1), (2), (3), and (4) of subdivision (a). The association may charge a fee for this service, which shall not exceed the association's reasonable cost to prepare and reproduce the requested items.

(c) An association shall not impose or collect any assessment, penalty, or fee in connection with a transfer of title or any other interest except the association's actual costs to change its records and that authorized by subdivision (b).

(d) Any person or entity who willfully violates this section shall be liable to the purchaser of a separate interest which is subject to this section for actual damages occasioned thereby and, in addition, shall pay a civil penalty in an amount not to exceed five hundred dollars ($500). In an action to enforce this liability, the prevailing party shall be awarded reasonable attorneys' fees.

(e) Nothing in this section affects the validity of title to real property transferred in violation of this section.

(f) In addition to the requirements of this section, an owner transferring title to a separate interest shall comply with applicable requirements of Sections 1133 and 1134.

Civ. C. § 1369. Liens For Labor And Materials.

In a condominium project, no labor performed or services or materials furnished with the consent of, or at the request of, an owner in the condominium project or his or her agent or his or her contractor shall be the basis for the filing of a lien against any other property of any other owner in the condominium project unless that other owner has expressly consented to or requested the performance of the labor or furnishing of the materials or services. However, express consent shall be deemed to have been given by the owner of any condominium in the case of emergency repairs thereto. Labor performed or services or materials furnished for the common areas, if duly authorized by the association, shall be deemed to be performed or furnished with the express consent of each condominium owner. The owner of any condominium may remove his or her condominium from a lien against two or more condominiums or any part thereof by payment to the holder of the lien of the fraction of the total sum secured by the lien which is attributable to his or her condominium.

Civ. C. § 1370. Liberal Construction Of Instruments.

Any deed, declaration, or condominium plan for a common interest development shall be liberally construed to facilitate the operation of the common interest development, and its provision shall be presumed to be independent and severable. Nothing in Article 3 (commencing with Section 715) of Chapter 2 of Title 2 of Part 1 of this division shall operate to invalidate any provisions of the governing documents of a common interest development.

Civ. C. § 1371. Boundaries Of Units; Presumption.

In interpreting deeds and condominium plans, the existing physical boundaries of a unit in a condominium project, when the boundaries of the unit are contained within a building, or of a unit reconstructed in substantial accordance with the original plans thereof, shall be conclusively presumed to be its boundaries rather than the metes and bounds expressed in the deed or condominium plan, if any exists, regardless of settling or lateral movement of the building and regardless of minor variance between boundaries shown on the plan or in the deed and those of the building.

Civ. C. § 1372. Construction Of Zoning Ordinances.

Unless a contrary intent is clearly expressed, local zoning ordinances shall be construed to treat like structures, lots, parcels, areas, or spaces in like manner regardless of whether the common interest development is a community apartment project, condominium project, planned development, or stock cooperative.

Civ. C. § 1373. Developments Expressly Zoned As Industrial Or Commercial And Limited To Such Purposes; Exclusions.

Sections 1356, 1365, 1365.5, 1366.1 and 1368, and subdivision (b) of Section 1363 and subdivision (b) of Section 1366 are not applicable to common interest developments that are expressly zoned as industrial developments and limited in use to industrial purposes or expressly zoned as commercial developments and limited in use to commercial purposes.

The Legislature finds that those aforementioned provisions may be appropriate to protect purchasers in residential common interest developments, however, the provisions are not necessary to protect purchasers in commercial or industrial developments since the application of those provisions results in unnecessary burdens and costs for these types of developments.

Civ. C. 1374. Application Of Law In An Association With No Common Area.

Nothing in this title may be construed to apply to a development wherein there does not exist a common area as defined in subdivision (b) of Section 1351, nor may this title be construed to confer standing pursuant to Section 383 of the Code of Civil Procedure to an association created for the purpose of managing a development wherein there does not exist a common area.

This section is declaratory of existing law.

CHAPTER 4

RESTRAINT ON ALIENATION; REGULATION OF SIGNS ADVERTISING SALE OF PROPERTY

(Civil Code §§ 711-714.5)

Civ. C. § 711. Restraining Alienation.

Conditions restraining alienation, when repugnant to the interest created, are void.

Civ. C. § 712. Real Estate Sales; Prohibitions Of Signs Void; Permissible Displays.

(a) Every provision contained in or otherwise affecting a grant of a fee interest in, or purchase money security instrument upon, real property in this state heretofore or hereafter made, which purports to prohibit or restrict the right of the property owner or his or her agent to display or have displayed on the real property, or on real property owned by others with their consent, or both, signs which are reasonably located, in plain view of the public, are of reasonable dimensions and design, and do not adversely affect public safety, including traffic safety, and which advertise the property for sale, lease, or exchange, or advertise directions to the property, by the property owner or his or her agent is void as an unreasonable restraint upon the power of alienation.

(b) This section shall operate retrospectively, as well as prospectively, to the full extent that it may constitutionally operate retrospectively.

(c) A sign which conforms to the ordinance adopted in conformity with Section 713 shall be deemed to be of reasonable dimension and design pursuant to this section.

Civ. C. § 713. Display Of Signs.

(a) Notwithstanding any provision of any ordinance, an owner of real property or his or her agent may display or have displayed on the owner's real property, and on real property owned by others with their consent, signs which are reasonably located, in plain view of the public, are of reasonable dimensions and design, and do not adversely affect public safety, including traffic safety, as determined by the city, county or city and county, advertising the following:

(1) That the property is for sale, lease or exchange by the owner or his or her agent.

(2) Directions to the property.

(3) The owner's or agent's name.

(4) The owner's or agent's address and telephone number.

(b) Nothing in this section limits any authority which a person or local governmental entity may have to limit or regulate the display or placement of a sign on a private or public right-of-way.

Civ. C. § 714. Voidability of Covenants Restricting Solar Energy Systems; Application for Approval; Penalties.

(a) Any covenant, restriction, or condition contained in any deed, contract, security instrument, or other instrument affecting the transfer or sale of, or any interest in, real property *that* effectively prohibits or restricts the installation or use of a solar energy system is void and unenforceable.

(b) This section shall not apply to provisions which impose reasonable restrictions on solar energy systems. However, it is the policy of the state to promote and encourage the use of solar energy systems and to remove obstacles thereto. Accordingly, reasonable restrictions on a solar energy system are those restrictions *that* do not significantly increase the cost of the system or significantly decrease its efficiency or specified performance, or *that* allow for an alternative system of comparable cost, efficiency, and energy conservation benefits.

(c) For the purposes of this section:

(1) *"Significantly" means an amount exceeding 20 percent of the cost of the system or decreasing the efficiency of the solar energy system by an amount exceeding 20 percent, as originally specified and proposed. Solar collectors shall meet applicable standards and requirements imposed by state and local permitting authorities. Specifically, solar energy systems shall be certified by the Solar Rating Certification Corporation (SRCC) or other nationally recognized certification agencies. SRCC is a nonprofit third-party supported by the United States Department of Energy. The certification shall be for the entire solar energy system and installation.*

(2) "Solar energy system" has the same meaning as defined in Section 801.5.

(d) Whenever approval is required for the installation or use of a solar energy system, the application for approval shall be processed and approved by the appropriate approving entity in the same manner as an application for approval of an architectural modification to the property, and shall not be willfully avoided or delayed.

(e) Any entity, other than a public entity, that willfully violates this section shall be liable to the applicant or other party for actual damages occasioned thereby, and shall pay a civil penalty to the applicant or other party in an amount not to exceed one thousand dollars ($1,000).

(f) In any action to enforce compliance with this section, the prevailing party shall be awarded reasonable attorney's fees.

Civ. C. § 714.1. Restrictions by Common Interest Development on Installation of Solar Energy Systems in Common Areas.

Notwithstanding Section 714, any association, as defined in Section 1351, may impose reasonable provisions which:

(a) Restrict the installation of solar energy systems installed in common areas, as defined in Section 1351, to those systems approved by the association.

(b) Require the owner of a separate interest, as defined in Section 1351 to obtain the approval of the association for the installation of a solar energy system in a separate interest owned by another.

(c) Provide for the maintenance, repair, or replacement of roofs or other building components.

(d) Require installers of solar energy systems to indemnify or reimburse the association or its members for loss or damage caused by the installation, maintenance, or use of the solar energy system.

Civ. C. § 714.5. Covenants Restricting Use of Structures Constructed in Offsite Facility are Void.

The covenants, conditions, and restrictions or other management documents shall not prohibit the sale, lease, rent, or use of real property on the basis that the structure intended for occupancy on the real property is constructed in an offsite facility or factory, and subsequently moved or transported in sections or modules to the real property. Nothing herein shall preclude the governing instruments from being uniformly applied to all structures subject to the covenants, conditions, and restrictions or other management documents.

This section shall apply to covenants, conditions, and restrictions or other management documents adopted on and after the effective date of this section.

CHAPTER 5

DISCLOSURE REQUIREMENTS UPON TRANSFER OF RESIDENTIAL PROPERTY

(Civil Code §§ 1102-1102.15)

Civ. C. § 1102. Application Of Article.

(a) Except as provided in Section 1102.1, this article applies to any transfer by sale, exchange, installment land sale contract, as defined in Section 2985, lease with an option to purchase, any other option to purchase, or ground lease coupled with improvements, of real property, or residential stock cooperative, improved with or consisting of not less than one nor more than four dwelling units.

(b) *Any waiver of the requirements of this article is void as against public policy.*

Civ. C. § 1102.1. Nonapplication of Article.

The provisions of this article do not apply to the following:

(a) Transfers which are required to be preceded by the furnishing to a prospective transferee of a copy of a public report pursuant to Section 11018.1 of the Business and Professions Code and transfers which can be made without a public report pursuant to Section 11010.4 of the Business and Professions Code.

(b) Transfers pursuant to court order, including, but not limited to, transfers ordered by a probate court in administration of an estate, transfers pursuant to a writ of execution, transfers by any foreclosure sale, transfers by a trustee in bankruptcy, transfers by eminent domain, and transfers resulting from a decree for specific performance.

(c) Transfers to a mortgagee by a mortgagor or successor in interest who is in default, transfers to a beneficiary of a deed of trust by a trustor or successor in interest who is in default, transfers by any foreclosure sale after default, in an obligation secured by a mortgage, transfers by a sale under a power of sale or any foreclosure sale under a decree of foreclosure after default in an obligation secured by a deed of trust or secured by any other instrument containing a power of sale, or transfers by a mortgagee or a beneficiary under a deed of trust who has acquired the real property at a sale conducted pursuant to a power of sale under a mortgage or deed of trust or a sale pursuant to a decree of foreclosure or has acquired the real property by a deed in lieu of foreclosure.

(d) Transfers by a fiduciary in the course of the administration of a decedent's estate, guardianship, conservatorship, or trust.

(e) Transfers from one co-owner to one or more other co-owners.

(f) Transfers made to a spouse, or to a person or persons in the lineal line of consanguinity of one or more of the transferors.

(g) Transfers between spouses resulting from a decree of dissolution of marriage or a decree of legal separation or from a property settlement agreement incidental to such a decree.

(h) Transfers by the Controller in the course of administering Chapter 7 (commencing with Section 1500) of Title 10 of Part 3 of the Code of Civil Procedure.

(i) Transfers under Chapter 7 (commencing with Section 3691) or Chapter 8 (commencing with Section 3771) of Part 6 of Division 1 of the Revenue and Taxation Code.

(j) Transfers or exchanges to or from any governmental entity.

Civ. C. § 1102.2. Delivery Of Required Written Statement From Transferor To Prospective Transferee; Indication Of Compliance With Article; Disclosures Delivered After Offer To Purchase; Time To Terminate.

The transferor of any real property subject to this article shall deliver to the prospective transferee the written statement required by this article, as follows:

(a) In the case of a sale, as soon as practicable before transfer of title.

(b) In the case of transfer by a real property sales contract, as defined in Section 2985, or by a lease together with an option to purchase, or a ground lease coupled with improvements, as soon as practicable before execution of the contract. For the purpose of this subdivision, "execution" means the making or acceptance of an offer.

With respect to any transfer subject to subdivision (a) or (b), the transferor shall indicate compliance with this article either on the receipt for deposit, the real property sales contract, the lease, or any addendum attached thereto or on a separate document.

If any disclosure, or any material amendment of any disclosure, required to be made by this article, is delivered after the execution of an offer to purchase, the transferee shall have three days after delivery in person or five days after delivery by deposit in the mail, to terminate his or her offer by delivery of a written notice of termination to the transferor or the transferor's agent.

Civ. C. § 1102.4. Errors, Inaccuracies, Or Omissions Of Information Delivered; Liability Of Transferor; Delivery Of Information By Public Agency; Delivery Of Reports Or Opinions Prepared By Experts.

(a) Neither the transferor nor any listing or selling agent shall be liable for any error, inaccuracy, or omission of any information delivered pursuant to this article if the error, inaccuracy, or omission was not within the personal knowledge of the transferor or that listing or selling agent, was based on information timely provided by public agencies or by other persons providing information as specified in subdivision (c) that is required to be disclosed pursuant to this article, and ordinary care was exercised in obtaining and transmitting it.

(b) The delivery of any information required to be disclosed by this article to a prospective transferee by a public agency or other person providing information required to be disclosed pursuant to this article shall be deemed to comply with the requirements of this article and shall relieve the transferor or any listing or selling agent of any further duty under this article with respect to that item of information.

(c) The delivery of a report or opinion prepared by a licensed engineer, land surveyor, geologist, structural pest control operator, contractor, or other expert, dealing with matters within the scope of the professional's license or expertise, shall be sufficient compliance for application of the exemption provided by subdivision (a) if the information is provided to the prospective transferee pursuant to a request therefor, whether written or oral. In responding to such a request, an expert may indicate, in writing, an understanding that the information provided will be used in fulfilling the requirements of Section 1102.6 and, if so, shall indicate the required disclosures, or parts thereof, to which the information being furnished is applicable. Where such a statement is furnished, the expert shall not be responsible for any items of information, or parts thereof, other than those expressly set forth in the statement.

Civ. C. § 1102.5. Information Subsequently Rendered Inaccurate; Required Information Unknown Or Not Available.

If information disclosed in accordance with this article is subsequently rendered inaccurate as a result of any act, occurrence, or agreement subsequent to the delivery of the required disclosures, the inaccuracy resulting therefrom does not constitute a violation of this article. If at the time the disclosures are required to be made, an item of information required to be disclosed is unknown or not available to the transferor, and the transferor or his or her agent has made a reasonable effort to ascertain it, the transferor may use an approximation of the information, provided the approximation is clearly identified as such, is reasonable, is based on the best information available to the transferor or his or her agent, and is not used for the purpose of circumventing or evading this article.

Civ. C. § 1102.6. Disclosure Form.

The disclosures required by this article pertaining to the property proposed to be transferred are set forth in, and shall be made on a copy of, the following disclosure form:

REAL ESTATE TRANSFER DISCLOSURE STATEMENT

THIS DISCLOSURE STATEMENT CONCERNS THE REAL PROPERTY SITUATED IN THE CITY OF __________, COUNTY OF __________, STATE OF CALIFORNIA, DESCRIBED AS _________. THIS STATEMENT IS A DISCLOSURE OF THE CONDITION OF THE ABOVE DESCRIBED PROPERTY IN COMPLIANCE WITH Section 1102 OF THE CIVIL CODE AS OF _________, 19__. IT IS NOT A WARRANTY OF ANY KIND BY THE SELLER(S) OR ANY AGENT(S) REPRESENTING ANY PRINCIPAL(S) IN THIS TRANSACTION, AND IS NOT A SUBSTITUTE FOR ANY INSPECTIONS OR WARRANTIES THE PRINCIPAL(S) MAY WISH TO OBTAIN.

I.

COORDINATION WITH OTHER DISCLOSURE FORMS

This Real Estate Transfer Disclosure Statement is made pursuant to Section 1102 of the Civil Code. Other statutes require disclosures, depending upon the details of the particular real estate transaction (for example: special study zone and purchase-money liens on residential property).

Substituted Disclosures: The following disclosures have or will be made in connection with this real estate transfer, and are intended to satisfy the disclosure obligations on this form, where the subject matter is the same:

☐ *Inspection reports completed pursuant to the contract of sale or receipt for deposit.*
☐ *Additional inspection reports or disclosure:*

____
____
____

SELLER'S INFORMATION

The Seller discloses the following information with the knowledge that even though this is not a warranty, prospective Buyers may rely on this information in deciding whether and on what terms to purchase the subject property. Seller hereby authorizes any agent(s) representing any principal(s) in this transaction to provide a copy of this statement to any person or entity in connection with any actual or anticipated sale of the property.

THE FOLLOWING ARE REPRESENTATIONS MADE BY THE SELLER(S) AND ARE NOT THE REPRESENTATIONS OF THE AGENT(S), IF ANY. THIS INFORMATION IS A DISCLOSURE AND IS NOT INTENDED TO BE A PART OF ANY CONTRACT BETWEEN THE BUYER AND SELLER.

Seller ___is ___is not occupying the property.

A. The subject property has the items checked below (read across):

___ Range	___ Oven	___ Microwave
___ Dishwasher	___ Trash Compactor	___ Garbage Disposal
___ Wshr/Dry Hokups	___ Window Screens	___ Rain Gutters
___ Burglar Alarms	___ Smoke Detector(s)	___ Fire Alarm
___ T.V. Antenna	___ Satellite Dish	___ Intercom
___ Central Heating	___ Central Air Con	___ Evaporator Cooler(s)
___ Wall/Wind Air	___ Sprinklers	___ Public Sewer Sys
___ Septic Tank	___ Sump Pump	___ Water Softener
___ Patio/Decking	___ Built-in-Barbecue	___ Gazebo
___ Sauna	___ Pool	___ Spa___ Hot Tub
___ Security Gate(s)	___ Auto Garage Door Opener	___ Number Remote Controls

Garage: ___ Attached ___ Not Attached ___ Carport
Pool/Spa Heater:___ Gas ___ Solar ___ Electric
Water Heater:___ Gas
Water Supply:___ City___Well Private Utililty or Other______________
Gas supply:___ Utility___Bottled

Exhaust Fan(s) in_______ 220 volt wiring in_______ Fireplace(s) in_______
Gas Starter___ Roof(s): Type:___________ Age:_____(approx.)
Other:____

Are there, to the best of your (Seller's) knowledge, any of the above that are not in operating condition? ___ Yes ___ No. If yes, then describe.

(Attach additional sheets if necessary.):__________________________________
____
____

B. Are you (Seller) aware of any significant defects/malfunctions in any of the following?
___ Yes ___ No.

If yes, check appropriate space(s) below.

___ Interior Walls ___ Ceilings ___ Floors ___ Exterior Walls ___ Insulation ___ Roof(s)
___ Windows ___ Doors ___ Foundation ___ Slab(s) ___ Driveways ___ Sidewalks
___ Walls/Fences ___ Electrical Systems ___ Plumbing/Sewers/Septics ___ Other

StructuralComponents(Describe:____
____

If any of the above is checked, explain. (Attach additional sheets if necessary):
____
____

* This garage door opener may not be in compliance with the safety standards relating to automatic reversing devices as set forth in Chapter 12.5 (commencing with Section 19890) of Part 3 of Division 13 of the Health and Safety Code.

C. Are you (Seller) aware of any of the following:

Chapt. 5 Disclosure Requirements

1. Substances, materials, or products which may be an environmental hazard such as, but not limited to, asbestos, formaldehyde, radon gas, lead-based paint, fuel or chemical storage tanks, and contaminated soil or water on the subject property ___ Yes ___ No

2. Features of the property shared in common with adjoining landowners, such as walls, fences, and driveways, whose use or responsibility for maintenance may have an effect on the subject property
___ Yes ___ No

3. Any encroachments, easements or similar matters that may affect your interest in the subject property
___ Yes ___ No

4. *Room* additions, structural modifications, or other alterations or repairs made without necessary permits
___ Yes ___ No

5. *Room* additions, structural modifications, or other alterations or repairs not in compliance with building codes
___ Yes ___ No

6. Fill (compacted or otherwise) on the property or any portion thereof
___ Yes ___ No

7. Any settling from any cause or slippage, sliding, or other soil problems
___ Yes ___ No

8. Flooding, drainage or grading problems
___ Yes ___ No

9. Major damage to the property or any of the structures from fire, earthquake, floods, or landslides
___ Yes ___ No

10. Any zoning violations, nonconforming uses, violations of "setback" requirements
___ Yes ___ No

11. Neighborhood noise problems or other nuisances
___ Yes ___ No

12. CC&R's or other deed restrictions or obligations
___ Yes ___ No

13. Homeowners' Association which has any authority over the subject property
___ Yes ___ No

14. Any "common area" (facilities such as pools, tennis courts, walkways, or other areas co-owned in undivided interest with others)
___ Yes ___ No

15. Any notices of abatement or citations against the property
___ Yes ___ No

16. *Any lawsuits by or against the seller threatening to or affecting this real property, including any lawsuits alleging a defect or deficiency in this real property or "common areas" (facilities such as pools, tennis courts, walkways, or other areas co-owned in undivided interest with others)*
___ Yes ___ No

If the answer to any of these is yes, explain. (Attach additional sheets if necessary):

____

____

Seller certifies that the information herein is true and correct to the best of the Seller's knowledge as of the date signed by the Seller.

Seller ________________ Date ___________

Seller ________________ Date ___________

III

AGENT'S INSPECTION DISCLOSURE

(To be completed only if the Seller is represented by an agent in this transaction.)

THE UNDERSIGNED, BASED ON THE ABOVE INQUIRY OF THE SELLER(S) AS TO THE CONDITION OF THE PROPERTY AND BASED ON A REASONABLY COMPETENT AND DILIGENT VISUAL INSPECTION OF THE ACCESSIBLE AREAS OF THE PROPERTY IN CONJUNCTION WITH THAT INQUIRY, STATES THE FOLLOWING:

☐ *Agent notes no items for disclosure.*
☐ *Agent notes the following items:*

____

____

____

____

Agent (Broker obtaining the Offer)______________________ (Please Print) By__________________________ (Associate Licensee or Broker-Signature) Date________

IV

AGENT'S INSPECTION DISCLOSURE

(To be completed only if the agent who has obtained the offer is other than the agent above.)

THE UNDERSIGNED, BASED ON A REASONABLY COMPETENT AND DILIGENT VISUAL INSPECTION OF THE ACCESSIBLE AREAS OF THE PROPERTY, STATES THE FOLLOWING:

☐ *Agent notes no items for disclosure.*
☐ *Agent notes the following items:*

____

____

____

____

Agent (Broker obtaining the Offer)______________________ (Please Print) By__________________________ (Associate Licensee or Broker-Signature) Date________

V

BUYER(S) AND SELLER(S) MAY WISH TO OBTAIN PROFESSIONAL ADVICE AND/OR INSPECTIONS OF THE PROPERTY AND TO PROVIDE FOR APPROPRIATE PROVISIONS IN A CONTRACT BETWEEN BUYER AND SELLER(S) WITH RESPECT TO ANY ADVICE/INSPECTIONS/DEFECTS.

I/WE ACKNOWLEDGE RECEIPT OF A COPY OF THIS STATEMENT.

Seller __________ Date _______ Buyer __________ Date _______
Seller __________ Date _______ Buyer __________ Date _______

Agent (Broker Representing Seller)____________________ By________________________ Date_______
(Associate Licensee or Broker-Signature)

Agent (Broker Obtaining the Offer)____________________ By________________________ Date_______
(Associate Licensee or Broker-Signature)

SECTION 1102.2 OF THE CIVIL CODE PROVIDES A BUYER WITH THE RIGHT TO RESCIND A PURCHASE CONTRACT FOR AT LEAST THREE DAYS AFTER THE DELIVERY OF THIS DISCLOSURE IF DELIVERY OCCURS AFTER THE SIGNING OF AN OFFER TO PURCHASE. IF YOU WISH TO RESCIND THE CONTRACT, YOU MUST ACT WITHIN THE PRESCRIBED PERIOD.

A REAL ESTATE BROKER IS QUALIFIED TO ADVISE ON REAL ESTATE, IF YOU DESIRE LEGAL ADVICE, CONSULT YOUR ATTORNEY.

Civ. C. § 1102.6a. Disclosure Form.

(a) On or after July 1, 1990, any city or county may elect to require disclosures on the form set forth in subdivision (b) in addition to those disclosures required by Section 1102.6. However, this section does not affect or limit the authority of a city or county to require disclosures on a different disclosure form in connection with transactions subject to this article pursuant to an ordinance adopted prior to July 1, 1990. Such an ordinance adopted prior to July 1, 1990, may be amended thereafter to revise the disclosure requirements of the ordinance, in the discretion of the city council or county board of supervisors.

(b) Disclosures required pursuant to this section pertaining to the property proposed to be transferred, shall set forth in, and shall be made on a copy of, the following disclosure form:

LOCAL OPTION
REAL ESTATE TRANSFER DISCLOSURE STATEMENT

THIS DISCLOSURE STATEMENT CONCERNS THE REAL PROPERTY SITUATED IN THE CITY OF _________, COUNTY OF _________, STATE OF CALIFORNIA, DESCRIBED AS __________. THIS STATEMENT IS A DISCLOSURE OF THE CONDITION OF THE ABOVE-DESCRIBED PROPERTY IN COMPLIANCE WITH ORDINANCE NO._____ OF THE _________ CITY OR COUNTY CODE AS OF _____, 19___. IT IS NOT A WARRANTY OF ANY KIND BY THE SELLER(S) OR ANY AGENT(S) REPRESENTING ANY PRINCIPAL(S) IN THIS TRANSACTION, AND IS NOT A SUBSTITUTE FOR ANY INSPECTIONS OR WARRANTIES THE PRINCIPAL(S) MAY WISH TO OBTAIN.

I.

SELLERS INFORMATION

The Seller discloses the following information with the knowledge that even though this is not a warranty, prospective buyers may rely on this information in deciding whether and on what terms to purchase the subject property. Seller hereby authorizes any agent(s) representing any principal(s) in this transaction to provide a copy of this statement to any person or entity in connection with any actual or anticipated sale of the property.

THE FOLLOWING ARE REPRESENTATIONS MADE BY THE SELLER(S) AS REQUIRED BY THE CITY OR COUNTY OF _________, AND ARE NOT THE REPRESENTATIONS OF THE AGENT(S), IF ANY, THIS INFORMATION IS A DISCLOSURE AND IS NOT INTENDED TO BE PART OF ANY CONTRACT BETWEEN THE BUYER AND SELLER.

1. ____
2. ____

(Example: Adjacent land is zoned for timber production which may be subject to harvest.)

Seller certifies that the information herein is true and correct to the best of the Seller's knowledge as of the date signed by the Seller.

Seller: ___________________________ Date________________
Seller: ___________________________ Date________________

II.

BUYER(S) AND SELLER(S) MAY WISH TO OBTAIN PROFESSIONAL ADVICE AND/OR INSPECTIONS OF THE PROPERTY AND TO PROVIDE FOR APPROPRIATE PROVISIONS IN A CONTRACT BETWEEN BUYER AND SELLER(S) WITH RESPECT TO ANY ADVICE/INSPECTIONS/DEFECTS.

I/WE ACKNOWLEDGE RECEIPT OF A COPY OF THIS STATEMENT.

Seller___________________________Date________________
Buyer___________________________Date________________
Seller___________________________Date________________
Buyer___________________________Date________________
AGENT (Broker Representing SELLER) ___________________
BY (Assoc. Licensee or Broker Signature) _________________
DATE ____

AGENT (Broker Obtaining Offer) ______________________
BY (Assoc. Licensee or Broker Signature) _________________
DATE ____

A REAL ESTATE BROKER IS QUALIFIED TO ADVISE ON REAL ESTATE. IF YOU DESIRE LEGAL ADVICE, CONSULT YOUR ATTORNEY.

(c) This section does not preclude the use of addenda to the form specified in subdivision (b) to facilitate the required disclosures. This section does not preclude a city or county from using the disclosure form specified in subdivision (b) for a purpose other than that specified in this section.

Civ. C. § 1102.7. Good Faith Required.

Each disclosure required by this article and each act which may be performed in making the disclosure, shall be made in good faith. For purposes of this article, "good faith" means honesty in fact in the conduct of the transaction.

Civ. C. § 1102.8. Specification Of Items For Disclosure Not Limitation On Other Disclosure Obligations.

The specification of items for disclosure in this article does not limit or abridge any obligation for disclosure created by any other provision of law or which may exist in order to avoid fraud, misrepresentation, or deceit in the transfer transaction.

Civ. C. § 1102.9. Amendment of Disclosures.

Any disclosure made pursuant to this article may be amended in writing by the transferor or his or her agent, but the amendment shall be subject to the provisions of Section 1102.2.

Civ. C. § 1102.10. Delivery Of Disclosures; Personal Delivery Of Mail.

Delivery of disclosures required by this article shall be by personal delivery to the transferee or by mail to the prospective transferee. For the purposes of this article, delivery to the spouse of a transferee shall be deemed delivery to the transferee, unless otherwise provided by contract.

Civ. C. § 1102.11. Escrow Agents Not Deemed Agent For Purposes Of Disclosure; Exception.

Any person or entity, other than a real estate licensee licensed pursuant to Part 1 (commencing with Section 10000) of Division 4 of the Business and Professions Code, acting in the capacity of an escrow agent for the transfer of real property subject to this article shall not be deemed the agent of the transferor or transferee for purposes of the disclosure requirements of this article, unless the person or entity is empowered to so act by an express written agreement to that effect. The extent of such an agency shall be governed by the written agreement.

Civ. C. § 1102.12. Licensed Real Estate Brokers As Agents In Transaction; Delivery Of Disclosure; Advising Transferee Of Rights To Disclosure; Record.

(a) If more than one licensed real estate broker is acting as an agent in a transaction subject to this article, the broker who has obtained the offer made by the transferee shall, except as otherwise provided in this article, deliver the disclosure required by this article to the transferee, unless the transferor has given other written instructions for delivery.

(b) If a licensed real estate broker responsible for delivering the disclosures under this section cannot obtain the disclosure document required and does not have written assurance from the transferee that the disclosure has been received, the broker shall advise the transferee in writing of his or her rights to the disclosure. A licensed real estate broker responsible for delivering disclosures under this section shall maintain a record of the action taken to effect compliance in accordance with Section 10148 of the Business and Professions Code.

Civ. C. § 1102.13. Failure To Comply With Article; Transfer Not Invalidated; Damages.

No transfer subject to this article shall be invalidated solely because of the failure of any person to comply with any provision of this article. However, any person who willfully or negligently violates or fails to perform any duty prescribed by any provision of this article shall be liable in the amount of actual damages suffered by a transferee.

Civ. C. § 1102.14. Definitions.

(a) As used in this article, "listing agent" means listing agent as defined in subdivision (f) of Section 1086.

(b) As used in this article, "selling agent" means selling agent as defined in subdivision (g) of Section 1086, exclusive of the requirement that the agent be a participant in a multiple listing service as defined in Section 1087.

Civ. C. § 1102.15. Former Federal Or State Ordinance Locations; Definition.

The seller of residential real property subject to this article who has actual knowledge of any former federal or state ordinance locations within the neighborhood area shall give written notice of that knowledge as soon as practicable before transfer of title.

For purposes of this section, "former federal or state ordinance locations" means an area identified by an agency or instrumentality of the federal or state government as an area once used for military training purposes which may contain potentially explosive munitions. "Neighborhood area" means within one mile of the residential real property.

The disclosure required by this section does not limit or abridge any obligation for disclosure created by any other law or that may exist in order to avoid fraud, misrepresentation, or deceit in the transfer transaction.

CHAPTER 6

EFFECT OF TRANSFER
(Civil Code §§ 1104-1134)

Civ. C. § 1104. Easements Passing With Property.

A transfer of real property passes all easements attached thereto, and creates in favor thereof an easement to use other real property of the person whose estate is transferred in the same manner and to the same extent as such property was obviously and permanently used by the person whose estate is transferred, for the benefit thereof, at the time when the transfer was agreed upon or completed.

Civ. C. § 1105. Fee Simple Title; Presumption.

A fee simple title is presumed to be intended to pass by a grant of real property, unless it appears from the grant that a lesser estate was intended.

Civ. C. § 1106. Subsequently Acquired Title; Passage By Operation Of Law.

Where a person purports by proper instrument to grant real property in fee simple, and subsequently acquires any title, or claim of title thereto, the same passes by operation of law to the grantee, or his successors.

Civ. C. § 1107. Persons Concluded Or Bound.

Every grant of an estate in real property is conclusive against the grantor, also against everyone subsequently claiming under him, except a purchaser or encumbrancer who in good faith and for a valuable consideration acquires a title or a lien by an instrument that is first duly recorded.

Civ. C. § 1133. Property Subject To Blanket Encumbrance But Exempt From Compliance With § 11013.2; Notice To Prospective Purchaser Or Lessee; Civil And Criminal Liability.

(a) If a lot, parcel, or unit of a subdivision is subject to a blanket encumbrance, as defined in Section 11013 of the Business and Professions Code, but is exempt from a requirement of compliance with Section 11013.2 of the Business and Professions Code, the subdivider, his or her agent, or representative, shall not sell, or lease for a term exceeding five years, the lot, parcel, or unit, nor cause it to be sold, or leased for a term exceeding five years, until the prospective purchaser or lessee of the lot, parcel, or unit has been furnished with and has signed a true copy of the following notice:

BUYER/LESSEE IS AWARE OF THE FACT THAT THE LOT, PARCEL, OR UNIT WHICH HE OR SHE IS PROPOSING TO PURCHASE OR LEASE IS SUBJECT TO A DEED OF TRUST, MORTGAGE, OR OTHER LIEN KNOWN AS A "BLANKET ENCUMBRANCE".

IF BUYER/LESSEE PURCHASES OR LEASES THIS LOT, PARCEL, OR UNIT, HE OR SHE COULD LOSE THAT INTEREST THROUGH FORECLOSURE OF THE BLANKET ENCUMBRANCE OR OTHER LEGAL PROCESS EVEN THOUGH BUYER/LESSEE IS NOT DELINQUENT IN HIS OR HER PAYMENTS OR OTHER OBLIGATIONS UNDER THE MORTGAGE, DEED OF TRUST, OR LEASE.

Date ________________

____
Signature of Buyer or Lessee

(b) "Subdivision", as used in subdivision (a), means improved or unimproved land that is divided or proposed to be divided for the purpose of sale, lease, or financing, whether immediate or future, into two or more lots, parcels, or units and includes a condominium project, as defined in subdivision (f) of Section 1351, a community apartment project, as defined in subdivision (d) of Section 1351, a stock cooperative, as defined in subdivision (m) of Section 1351, and a limited equity housing cooperative, as defined in subdivision (m) of Section 1351.

(c) The failure of the buyer or lessee to sign the notice shall not invalidate any grant, conveyance, lease, or encumbrance.

(d) Any person or entity who willfully violates the provisions of this section shall be liable to the purchaser of a lot or unit which is subject to the provisions of this section, for actual damages, and in addition thereto, shall be guilty of a public offense punishable by a fine in an amount not to exceed five hundred dollars ($500). In an action to enforce such liability or fine, the prevailing party shall be awarded reasonable attorneys' fees.

Civ. C. § 1134. Statement Of Defects Or Disclaimer; Termination Of Purchase Agreement; Definitions.

(a) As soon as practicable before transfer of title for the first sale of a unit in a residential condominium, community apartment project, or stock cooperative which was converted from an existing dwelling to a condominium project, community apartment project, or stock cooperative, the owner or subdivider, or agent of the owner or subdivider, shall deliver to a prospective buyer a written statement listing all substantial defects or malfunctions in the major systems in the unit and common areas of the premises, or a written statement disclaiming knowledge of any such substantial defects or malfunctions. The disclaimer may be delivered only after the owner or subdivider has inspected the unit and the common areas and has not discovered a substantial defect or malfunction which a reasonable inspection would have disclosed.

(b) If any disclosure required to be made by this section is delivered after the execution of an agreement to purchase, the buyer shall have three days after delivery in person or five days after delivery by deposit in the mail, to terminate his or her agreement by delivery of a written notice of that termination to the owner, subdivider, or agent. Any disclosure delivered after the execution of an agreement to purchase shall contain a statement describing the buyer's right, method and time to rescind as prescribed by this subdivision.

(c) For the purposes of this section:

(1) "Major Systems" includes, but is not limited to, the roof, walls, floors, heating, air con-

ditioning, plumbing, electrical systems or components of a similar or comparable nature, and recreational facilities.

(2) Delivery to a prospective buyer of the written statement required by this section shall be deemed effected when delivered personally or by mail to the prospective buyer or to an agent thereof, or to a spouse unless the agreement provides to the contrary. Delivery shall also be made to additional prospective buyers who have made a request therefore in writing.

(3) "Prospective buyer" includes any person who makes an offer to purchase a unit in the condominium, community apartment project, or stock cooperative.

(d) Any person who willfully fails to carry out the requirements of this section shall be liable in the amount of actual damages suffered by the buyer.

(e) Nothing in this section shall preclude the injured party from pursuing any remedy available under any other provision of law.

(f) No transfer of title to a unit subject to the provisions of this chapter shall be invalid solely because of the failure of any person to comply with the requirements of this section.

(g) The written statement required by this section shall not abridge or limit any other obligation of disclosure created by any other provision of law or which is or may be required to avoid fraud, deceit, or misrepresentation in the transaction.

CHAPTER 7

ARBITRATION & MEDIATION PROCEDURES

(Evidence Code § 1152.5)
(Code of Civil Procedure §§ 1280-1288.8)

1. GENERAL PROVISIONS

Evid. C. § 1152.5. Communications During Mediation Proceedings.

(a) When persons agree to conduct and participate in a mediation for the purpose of compromising, settling, or resolving a dispute in whole or in part:

(1) Except as otherwise provided in this section, evidence of anything said or of any admission made in the course of the mediation is not admissible in evidence or subject to discovery, and disclosure of this evidence shall not be compelled, in any civil action or proceeding in which, pursuant to law, testimony can be compelled to be given.

(2) Except as otherwise provided in this section, unless the document otherwise provides, no document prepared for the purpose of, or in the course of, or pursuant to, the mediation, or copy thereof, is admissible in evidence or subject to discovery, and disclosure of such a document shall not be compelled, in any civil action or proceeding in which, pursuant to law, testimony can be compelled to be given.

(3) When persons agree to conduct or participate in mediation for the sole purpose of compromising, settling, or resolving a dispute, in whole or in part, all communications, negotiations, or settlement discussions by and between participants or mediators in the mediation shall remain confidential.

(4) All or part of a communication or document which may be otherwise privileged or confidential may be disclosed if all parties who conduct or otherwise participate in a mediation so consent.

(5) A written settlement agreement, or part thereof, is admissible to show fraud, duress, or illegality if relevant to an issue in dispute.

(6) Evidence otherwise admissible or subject to discovery outside of mediation shall not be or become inadmissible or protected from disclosure solely by reason of its introduction or use in a mediation.

(b) *This section does not apply where the admissibility of the evidence is governed by Section 1818 or 3177 of the Family Code.*

(c) Nothing in this section makes admissible evidence that is inadmissible under Section 1152 or any other statutory provision, including, but not limited to, the sections listed in subdivision (d). Nothing in this section limits the confidentiality provided pursuant to Section 65 of the Labor Code.

(d) If the testimony of a mediator is sought to be compelled in any action or proceeding as to anything said or any admission made in the course of the mediation that is inadmissible and not subject to disclosure under this section, the court shall award reasonable attorney's fees and costs to the mediator against the person or persons seeking that testimony.

(e) Paragraph (2) of subdivision (a) does not limit the effect of an agreement not to take a default in a pending civil action.

CCP § 1280. Definitions.

(a) "Agreement" includes but is not limited to agreements providing for valuations, appraisals and similar proceedings and agreements between employers and employees or between their respective representatives.

(b) "Award" includes but is not limited to an award made pursuant to an agreement not in writing.

(c) "Controversy" means any questions arising between parties to an agreement whether such question is one of law or of fact or both.

(d) "Neutral arbitrator" means an arbitrator who is

(1) Selected jointly by the parties or by the arbitrators selected by the parties; or

(2) Appointed by the court when the parties or the arbitrators selected by the parties fail to select an arbitrator who was to be selected jointly by them.

(e) "Party to the arbitration" means a party to the arbitration agreement:

(1) Who seeks to arbitrate a controversy pursuant to the agreement;

(2) Against whom such arbitration is sought pursuant to the agreement; or

(3) Who is made a party to such arbitration by order of the neutral arbitrator upon such party's application, upon the application of any other party to the arbitration or upon the neutral arbitrator's own determination.

(f) "Written agreement" shall be deemed to include a written agreement which has been extended or renewed by an oral or implied agreement.

CCP § 1280.1. Immunity of Arbitrator From Civil Liability.

An arbitrator has the immunity of a judicial officer from civil liability when acting in the capacity of arbitrator under any statute or contract. The immunity afforded by this section shall supplement, and not supplant, any otherwise applicable common law or statutory immunity. This section shall remain in effect only until January 1,

1996, and as of that date is repealed, unless a later enacted statute, which is enacted before January 1, 1996, deletes or extends that date.

CCP § 1280.2. Reference to Portion of Title or of Any Other Law.

Whenever reference is made in this title to any portion of the title or of any other law of this State, the reference applies to all amendments and additions thereto now or here after made.

2. ENFORCEMENT OF ARBITRATION AGREEMENTS

CCP § 1281. Requisites and Validity.

A written agreement to submit to arbitration an existing controversy or a controversy thereafter arising is valid, enforceable and irrevocable, save upon such grounds as exist for the revocation of any contract.

CCP § 1281.2. Order to Arbitrate; Determination of Other Issues.

On petition of a party to an arbitration agreement alleging the existence of a written agreement to arbitrate a controversy and that a party thereto refuses to arbitrate such controversy, the court shall order the petitioner and the respondent to arbitrate the controversy if it determines that an agreement to arbitrate the controversy exists, unless it determines that:

(a) The right to compel arbitration has been waived by the petitioner; or

(b) Grounds exist for the revocation of the agreement.

(c) A party to the arbitration agreement is also a party to a pending court action or special proceeding with a third party, arising out of the same transaction or series of related transactions and there is a possibility of conflicting rulings on a common issue of law or fact. For purposes of this section, a pending court action or special proceeding includes an action or proceeding initiated by the party refusing to arbitrate after the petition to compel arbitration has been filed, but on or before the date of the hearing on the petition. This subdivision shall not be applicable to an agreement to arbitrate disputes as to the professional negligence of a health care provider made pursuant to Section 1295. If the court determines that a written agreement to arbitrate a controversy exists, an order to arbitrate such controversy may not be refused on the ground that the petitioner's contentions lack substantive merit. If the court determines that there are other issues between the petitioner and the respondent which are not subject to arbitration and which are the subject of a pending action or special proceeding between the petitioner and the respondent and that a determination of such issues may make the arbitration unnecessary, the court may delay its order to arbitrate until the determination of such other issues or until such earlier time as the court specifies. If the court determines that a party to the arbitration is also a party to litigation in a pending court action or special proceeding with a third party as set forth under subdivision (c) herein, the court

(1) may refuse to enforce the arbitration agreement and may order intervention or joinder of all parties in a single action or special proceeding;

(2) may order intervention or joinder as to all or only certain issues;

(3) may order arbitration among the parties who have agreed to arbitration and stay the pending court action or special proceeding pending the outcome of the

arbitration proceeding; or

(4) may stay arbitration pending the outcome of the court action or special proceeding.

CCP § 1281.3. Petition to Consolidate Separate Arbitration Proceedings.

A party to an arbitration agreement may petition the court to consolidate separate arbitration proceedings, and the court may order consolidation of separate arbitration proceedings when:

(1) Separate arbitration agreements or proceedings exist between the same parties; or one party is a party to a separate arbitration agreement or proceeding with a third party; and

(2) The disputes arise from the same transactions or series of related transactions; and

(3) There is common issue or issues of law or fact creating the possibility of conflicting rulings by more than one arbitrator or panel of arbitrators. If all of the applicable arbitration agreements name the same arbitrator, arbitration panel, or arbitration tribunal, the court, if it orders consolidation, shall order all matters to be heard before the arbitrator, panel, or tribunal agreed to by the parties. If the applicable arbitration agreements name separate arbitrators, panels, or tribunals, the court, if it orders consolidation, shall, in the absence of an agreed method of selection by all parties to the consolidated arbitration, appoint an arbitrator in accord with the procedures set forth in Section 1281.6. In the event that the arbitration agreements in consolidated proceedings contain inconsistent provisions, the court shall resolve such conflicts and determine the rights and duties of the various parties to achieve substantial justice under all the circumstances. The court may exercise its discretion under this section to deny consolidation of separate arbitration proceed-

ings or to consolidate separate arbitration proceedings only as to certain issues, leaving other issues to be resolved in separate proceedings. This section shall not be applicable to an agreement to arbitrate disputes as to the professional negligence of a health care provider made pursuant to Section 1295.

CCP § 1281.4. Arbitration of Issue Involved in Pending Action or Proceeding.

If a court of competent jurisdiction, whether in this State or not, has ordered arbitration of a controversy which is an issue involved in an action or proceeding pending before a court of this State, the court in which such action or proceeding is pending shall, upon motion of a party to such action or proceeding, stay the action or proceeding until an arbitration is had in accordance with the order to arbitrate or until such earlier time as the court specifies. If an application has been made to a court of competent jurisdiction, whether in this State or not, for an order to arbitrate a controversy which is an issue involved in an action or proceeding pending before a court of this State and such application is undetermined, the court in which such action or proceeding is pending shall, upon motion of a party to such action or proceeding, stay the action or proceeding until the application for an order to arbitrate is determined and, if arbitration of such controversy is ordered, until an arbitration is had in accordance with the order to arbitrate or until such earlier time as the court specifies. If the issue which is the controversy subject to arbitration is severable, the stay may be with respect to that issue only.

CCP § 1281.5. Action to Enforce Lien as Waiver of Arbitration Right.

(a) Any person, who proceeds to record and enforce a claim of lien by commencement of an action pursuant to Title 15 (commencing with Section 3082) of Part 4 of Division 3 of the Civil Code, shall not thereby waive any right of arbitration which that person may have pursuant to a written agreement to arbitrate, if, in filing an action to enforce the claim of lien, the claimant at the same time presents to the court an application that the action be stayed pending the arbitration of any issue, question, or dispute which is claimed to be arbitrable under the agreement and which is relevant to the action to enforce the claim of lien. The applicant may join with the application for the stay, pending arbitration, a claim of lien otherwise within the jurisdiction of the municipal court.

(b) The failure of a defendant to file a petition pursuant to Section 1281.2 at or before the time he or she answers the complaint filed pursuant to subdivision (a) shall constitute a waiver of that party's right to compel arbitration.

CCP § 1281.6. Appointment of Arbitrator.

If the arbitration agreement provides a method of appointing an arbitrator, such method shall be followed. If the arbitration agreement does not provide a method for appointing an arbitrator, the parties to the agreement who seek arbitration and against whom arbitration is sought may agree on a method of appointing an arbitrator and that method shall be followed. In the absence of an agreed method, or if the agreed method fails or for any reason cannot be followed, or when an arbitrator appointed fails to act and his successor has not been appointed, the court, on petition of a party to the arbitration agreement, shall appoint the arbitrator.

When a petition is made to the court to appoint a neutral arbitrator, the court shall nominate five persons from lists of persons supplied jointly by the parties to the arbitration or obtained from a governmental agency concerned with arbitration or private disinterested association concerned with arbitration. The parties to the agreement who seek arbitration and against whom arbitration is sought may within five days of receipt of notice of such nominees from the court jointly select the arbitrator whether or not such arbitrator is among the nominees. If such parties fail to select an arbitrator within the five-day period, the court shall appoint the arbitrator from the nominees.

All neutral arbitrators shall comply with the requirements of Section 1297.121, which requirements shall apply to every agreement to arbitrate pursuant to this title.

CCP § 1281.7. Petition in Lieu of Answer to Complaint.

A petition pursuant to Section 1281.2 may be filed in lieu of filing an answer to a complaint. The petitioning defendant shall have 15 days after any denial of the petition to plead to the complaint.

CCP § 1281.8. "Provisional Remedy".

(a) As used in this section, "provisional remedy" includes the following:

(1) Attachments and temporary protective orders issued pursuant to Title 6.5 (commencing with Section 481.010) of Part 2.

(2) Writs of possession issued pursuant to Article 2 (commencing with Section 512.010) of Chapter 2 of Title 7 of Part 2.

(3) Preliminary injunctions and temporary restraining orders issued pursuant to Section 527.

(4) Receivers appointed pursuant to Section 564.

(b) A party to an arbitration agreement may file in the court in the county in which an arbitration proceeding is pending, or if an arbitration proceeding has not commenced, in any proper court, an application for a provisional remedy in connection with an arbitrable controversy, but only upon the ground that the award to which the applicant may be entitled may be rendered ineffectual without provisional relief. The application shall be accompanied by a complaint or by copies of the demand for arbitration and any response thereto. If accompanied by a complaint, the application shall also be accompanied by a statement stating whether the party is or is not reserving the party's right to arbitration.

(c) A claim by the party opposing issuance of a provisional remedy, that the controversy is not subject to arbitration, shall not be grounds for denial of any provisional remedy.

(d) An application for a provisional remedy under subdivision (b) shall not operate to waive any right of arbitration which the applicant may have pursuant to a written agreement to arbitrate, if, at the same time as the application for a provisional remedy is presented, the applicant also presents to the court an application that all other proceedings in the action be stayed pending the arbitration of any issue, question, or dispute which is claimed to be arbitrable under the agreement and which is relevant to the action pursuant to which the provisional remedy is sought.

CCP § 1281.9. Disclosure By Arbitrator Of All Prior And Pending Arbitrations; Disqualification For Failure to File Notice; Disqualification Of Court Appointed Arbitrator; Statute Of Limitations.

(a) In any arbitration pursuant to an arbitration agreement involving a claim for damages, when a person is proposed for nomination by all parties or all party arbitrators to serve as a neutral arbitrator, or is proposed for appointment by the court to serve as a neutral arbitrator in response to any petition brought pursuant to Section 1281.6, the proposed nominee or appointee shall disclose, within 10 days of serve of notice of the proposed nomination or appointment, to all parties, both of the following:

> *(1) The names of any prior or pending cases in which the proposed neutral arbitrator served or is serving as a party arbitrator for any party to the arbitration agreement, or for a lawyer for a party, and the results of each case arbitrated to conclusion, including the date of the arbitration*

award, identification of the prevailing party, the names of the parties' attorneys, if known, and the amount of monetary damages awarded, if any. (2) The names of any prior or pending cases involving any party to the arbitration agreement or the lawyer for a party for which the proposed neutral arbitrator served or is serving as neutral arbitrator, and the results of each case arbitrated to conclusion, including the date of the arbitration award, identification of the prevailing party, the names of the parties' attorneys, if known, and the amount of monetary damages awarded, if any.

(b) A proposed nominee or appointee shall be disqualified as a neutral arbitrator if the proposed nominee or appointee fails to comply with subdivision (a) and any party entitled to receive the disclosure serves a notice of disqualification within 15 days after the proposed nominee or appointee fails to comply with subdivision (a). A proposed nominee or appointee shall be deemed to have complied with subdivision (a) with respect to any arbitration commenced prior to January 1, 1995, if the person declares that he or she has disclosed all required information pertaining to those arbitrations within his or her knowledge or possession and has made a good faith effort to obtain the required information from any arbitration service serving in that prior case.

(c) (1) If the proposed nominee or appointee complies with subdivision (a), the proposed nominee or appointee shall be disqualified as a neutral arbitrator on the basis of the disclosure statement after any party entitled to receive the disclosure serves a notice of disqualification within 15 days after service of the disclosure statement.

(2) A party shall have the right to disqualify one court-appointed arbitrator without cause in any one arbitration, and may petition the court to dis-

qualify a subsequent appointee only upon a showing of cause.

(d) The right of a party to disqualify a proposed nominee or appointee shall be waived if the party fails to serve the notice pursuant to the times set forth in this section, unless the proposed nominee or appointee makes a material omission or material misrepresentation in his or her disclosure. In no event shall the notice of disqualification be made after a hearing of any contested issue of fact relating the merits of the claim. Nothing in this section shall limit the right of a party to vacate an award or to disqualify an arbitrator pursuant to subdivision (e) of Section 1282, Section 1286.2, or any other law or statute.

(e) For purposes of this section, "lawyer for a party" includes any lawyer or law firm associated in the practice of law with the lawyer hired to represent a party.

(f) For purposes of this section, "prior cases" means cases in which an arbitration award was rendered within one of the following time periods:

(1) Three years prior to the date of the proposed nomination or appointment if the proposed nomination or appointment occurs on or between January 1, 1995, and December 31, 1995.

(2) Four years prior to the date of the proposed nomination or appointment if the proposed nomination or appointment occurs on or between January 1, 1996, and December 31, 1996.

(3) Five years prior to the date of the proposed nomination or appointment if the proposed nomination or appointment occurs on or after January 1, 1997.

(g) For purposes of this section, "claim for damages" does not include a grievance or other claim brought pursuant to the terms of a public or private sector collective bargaining agreement, even where the object of the grievance or other claim is a monetary award.

CCP § 1281.95. Provisions For Dismissal Of Arbitrator.

(a) In a binding arbitration of any claim for more than three thousand dollars ($3,000) pursuant to a contract for the construction or improvement of residential property consisting of one to four units, the arbitrator shall, within 10 days following his or her appointment, provide to each party a written declaration under penalty of perjury. This declaration shall disclose

(1) whether the arbitrator or his or her employer or arbitration service had or has a personal or professional affiliation with either party, and

(2) whether the arbitrator or his or her employer or arbitration service has been selected or designated as an arbitrator by either party in another transaction.

(b) If the arbitrator discloses an affiliation with either party, discloses that the arbitrator has been selected or designated as an arbitrator by either party in another arbitration, or fails to comply with this section, he or she may be disqualified from the arbitration by either party.

(c) A notice of disqualification shall be served within 15 days after the arbitrator makes the required disclosures or fails to comply. The right of a party to disqualify an arbitrator shall be waived if the party fails to serve the notice of disqualification pursuant to this subdivision unless the arbitration makes a material omission or material misrepresentation in his or her disclosure. Nothing in this section shall limit the right of a party to vacate an award or to disqualify an arbitrator pursuant to subdivision (e) of Section 1282, Section 1286.2, or any other law or statute.

3. CONDUCT OF ARBITRATION PROCEEDINGS

CCP § 1282. Exercise of Powers and Duties of Arbitrator(s).

Unless the arbitration agreement otherwise provides, or unless the parties to the arbitration otherwise provide by an agreement which is not contrary to the arbitration agreement as made or as modified by all of the parties thereto:

(a) The arbitration shall be by a single neutral arbitrator.

(b) If there is more than one arbitrator, the powers and duties of the arbitrators, other than the powers and duties of a neutral arbitrator, may be exercised by a majority of them if reasonable notice of all proceedings has been given to all arbitrators.

(c) If there is more than one neutral arbitrator:

(1) The powers and duties of a neutral arbitrator may be exercised by a majority of the neutral arbitrators.

(2) By unanimous agreement of the neutral arbitrators, such powers and duties may be delegated to one of their number but the power to make or correct the award may not be so delegated.

(d) If there is no neutral arbitrator, the powers and duties of a neutral arbitrator may be exercised by a majority of the arbitrators.

(e) An arbitrator shall disqualify himself or herself, upon demand of any party to the arbitration agreement made before the conclusion of the arbitration proceedings, on any of the grounds specified in Section 170.1 for disqualification of a judge. However this subdivision does not apply to arbitration proceedings conducted under a collective agreement between employers and employees or between their respective representatives.

CCP § 1282.2. Hearing Proceedings, and Incidental Procedure.

Unless the arbitration agreement otherwise provides, or unless the parties to the arbitration otherwise provide by an agreement which is not contrary to the arbitration agreement as made or as modified by all the parties thereto:

(a) (1) The neutral arbitrator shall appoint a time and place for the hearing and cause notice thereof to be served personally or by registered or certified mail on the parties to the arbitration and on the other arbitrators not less than seven days before the hearing. Appearance at the hearing waives the right to notice.

(2) With the exception of matters arising out of collective-bargaining agreements, those described in Section 1283.05, actions involving personal injury or death, or as provided in the parties' agreement to arbitrate, in the event the aggregate amount in controversy exceeds fifty thousand dollars ($50,000) and the arbitrator is informed thereof by any party in writing by personal service, registered or certified mail, prior to designating a time and place of hearing pursuant to paragraph (1), the neutral arbitrator by the means prescribed in paragraph (1) shall appoint a time and place for hearing not less than 60 days before the hearing, and the following provisions shall apply:

(A) Either party shall within 15 days of receipt of the notice of hearing have the right to demand in writing, served personally or by registered or certified mail, that the other party provide a list of witnesses it intends to call designating which will be called as expert witnesses and a list of documents it intends to introduce at the hearing provided that the demanding party provides such lists at the time of its demand. A copy of such demand and the demanding party's lists shall be served on the arbitrator.

(B) Such lists shall be served personally or by registered or certified mail on the requesting party 15 days thereafter. Copies thereof shall be served on the arbitrator.

(C) Listed documents shall be made available for inspection and copying at reasonable times prior to the hearing.

(D) Time limits provided herein may be waived by mutual agreement of the parties if approved by the arbitrator.

(E) The failure to list a witness or a document shall not bar the testimony of an unlisted witness or the introduction of an undesignated document at the hearing, provided that good cause for omission from the requirements of subparagraph (A) is shown, as determined by the arbitrator.

(F) The authority of the arbitrator to administer and enforce this paragraph shall be as provided in subdivisions (b) to (e), inclusive, of Section 1283.05.

(b) The neutral arbitrator may adjourn the hearing from time to time as necessary. On request of a party to the arbitration for good cause, or upon his own determination, the neutral arbitrator may postpone the hearing to a time not later than the date fixed by the agreement for making the award, or to a later date if the parties to the arbitration consent thereto.

(c) The neutral arbitrator shall preside at the hearing, shall rule on the admission and exclusion of evidence and on questions of hearing procedure and shall exercise all powers relating to the conduct of the hearing.

(d) The parties to the arbitration are entitled to be heard, to present evidence and to cross-examine witnesses appearing at the hearing, but rules of evidence and rules of judicial procedure need not be observed. On request of any party to the arbitration, the testimony of witnesses shall be given under oath.

(e) If a court has ordered a person to arbitrate a controversy, the arbitrators may hear and determine the controversy upon the evidence produced notwithstanding the failure of a party ordered to arbitrate, who has been duly notified, to appear.

(f) If an arbitrator, who has been duly notified, for any reason fails to participate in the arbitration, the arbitration shall continue but only the remaining neutral arbitrator or neutral arbitrators may make the award.

(g) If a neutral arbitrator intends to base an award upon information not obtained at the hearing, he shall disclose the information to all parties to the arbitration and give the parties an opportunity to meet it.

CCP § 1282.4. Right to Counsel.

A party to the arbitration has the right to be represented by an attorney at any proceeding or hearing in arbitration under this title. A waiver of this right may be revoked; but if a party revokes such waiver, the other party is entitled to a reasonable continuance for the purpose of procuring an attorney.

CCP § 1282.6. Attendance of Witnesses and Production of Evidence; Subpoenas.

(a) A subpoena requiring the attendance of witnesses, and a subpoena duces tecum for the production of books, records, documents and other evidence, at an arbitration proceeding or a deposition under Section 1283, and if Section 1283.05 is applicable, for the purposes of discovery, shall be issued as provided in this section. In addition, the neutral arbitrator upon his own determination may issue subpoenas for the attendance of witnesses and subpoenas duces tecum for the production of books, records, documents and other evidence.

(b) Subpoenas shall be issued, as of course, signed but otherwise in blank, to the party requesting them, by a neutral association, organization, governmental agency, or office if the arbitration agreement provides for administration of the arbitration proceedings by, or under the rules of, a neutral association, organization, governmental agency or office or by the neutral arbitrator.

(c) The party serving the subpoena shall fill it in before service. Subpoenas shall be served and enforced in accordance with Chapter 2 (commencing with Section 1985) of Title 3 of Part 4 of this code.

CCP § 1282.8. Authority to Administer Oaths.

The neutral arbitrator may administer oaths.

CCP § 1283. Depositions For Use as Evidence.

On application of a party to the arbitration the neutral arbitrator may order the deposition of a witness to be taken for use as evidence and not for discovery if the witness cannot be compelled to attend the hearing or if such exceptional circumstances exist as to make it desirable, in the interest of justice and with due regard to the importance of presenting the testimony of witnesses orally at the hearing, to allow the deposition to be taken. The deposition shall be taken in the manner prescribed by law for the taking of depositions in civil actions. If the neutral arbitrator orders the taking of the deposition of a witness who resides outside the state, the party who applied for the taking of the deposition shall obtain a commission therefor from the superior court in accordance with Sections 2024 to 2028, inclusive, of this code.

CCP § 1283.05. Depositions for Discovery.

To the extent provided in Section 1283.1, depositions may be taken and discovery obtained in arbitration proceedings as follows:

(a) After the appointment of the arbitrator or arbitrators, the parties to the arbitration shall have the right to take depositions and to obtain discovery regarding the subject matter of the arbitration, and, to that end, to use and exercise all of the same rights, remedies, and procedures, and be subject to all of the same duties, liabilities, and obligations in the arbitration with respect to the subject matter thereof, as provided in Chapter 2 (commencing with Section 1985) of, and Article 3 (commencing with Section 2016) of Chapter 3 of, Title 3 of Part 4 of this code, as if the subject matter of the arbitration were pending in a civil action before a superior court of this state, subject to the limitations as to depositions set forth in subdivision (e) of this section.

(b) The arbitrator or arbitrators themselves shall have power, in addition to the power of determining the merits of the arbitration, to enforce the rights, remedies, procedures, duties, liabilities, and obligations of discovery by the imposition of the same terms, conditions, consequences, liabilities, sanctions, and penalties as can be or may be imposed in like circumstances in a civil action by a superior court of this state under the provisions of this code, except the power to order the arrest or imprisonment of a person.

(c) The arbitrator or arbitrators may consider, determine, and make such orders imposing such terms, conditions, consequences, liabilities, sanctions, and penalties, whenever necessary or appropriate at any time or stage in the course of the arbitration, and such orders shall be as conclusive, final, and enforceable as an arbitration award on the merits, if the making of any such order that is equivalent to an award or correction of an award is subject to the same conditions, if any, as are applicable to the making of an award or correction of an award.

(d) For the purpose of enforcing the duty to make discovery, to produce evidence or information, including books and records, and to produce persons to testify at a deposition or at a hearing, and to impose terms, conditions, consequences, liabilities, sanctions, and penalties upon a party for violation of any such duty, such party shall be deemed to include every affiliate of such party as defined in this section. For such purpose:

(1) The personnel of every such affiliate shall be deemed to be the officers, directors, managing agents, agents, and employees of such party to the same degree as each of them, respectively, bears such status to such affiliate; and

(2) The files, books, and records of every such affiliate shall be deemed to be in the possession and control of, and capable of production by, such party. As used in this section, "affiliate" of

the party to the arbitration means and includes any party or person for whose immediate benefit the action or proceeding is prosecuted or defended, or an officer, director, superintendent, member, agent, employee, or managing agent of such party or person.

(e) Depositions for discovery shall not be taken unless leave to do so is first granted by the arbitrator or arbitrators.

CCP § 1283.1. Discovery Provisions Incorporated Into Arbitration Agreement.

(a) All of the provisions of Section 1283.05 shall be conclusively deemed to be incorporated into, made a part of, and shall be applicable to, every agreement to arbitrate any dispute, controversy, or issue arising out of or resulting from any injury to, or death of, a person caused by the wrongful act or neglect of another.

(b) Only if the parties by their agreement so provide, may the provisions of Section 1283.05 be incorporated into, made a part of, or made applicable to, any other arbitration agreement.

CCP § 1283.2. Witnesses' Fees and Mileage.

Except for the parties to the arbitration and their agents, officers and employees, all witnesses appearing pursuant to subpoena are entitled to receive fees and mileage in the same amount and under the same circumstances as prescribed by law for witnesses in civil actions in the superior court. The fee and mileage of a witness subpoenaed upon the application of a party to the arbitration shall be paid by such party. The fee and mileage of a witness subpoenaed solely upon the determination of the neutral arbitrator shall be paid in the manner provided for the payment of the neutral arbitrator's expenses.

CCP § 1283.4. Requisites and Sufficiency of Award.

The award shall be in writing and signed by the arbitrators concurring therein. It shall include a determination of all the questions submitted to the arbitrators the decision of which is necessary in order to determine the controversy.

CCP § 1283.6. Service of Award.

The neutral arbitrator shall serve a signed copy of the award on each party to the arbitration personally or by registered or certified mail or as provided in the agreement.

CCP § 1283.8. Time of Making Award.

The award shall be made within the time fixed therefor by the agreement or, if not so fixed, within such time as the court orders on petition of a party to the arbitration. The parties to the arbitration may extend the time either before or after the expiration thereof. A party to the arbitration waives the objection that an award was not made within the time required unless he gives the arbitrators written notice of his objection prior to the service of a signed copy of the award on him.

CCP § 1284. Correction of Award.

The arbitrators, upon written application of a party to the arbitration, may correct the award upon any of the grounds set forth in subdivisions (a) and (c) of Section 1286.6 not later than 30 days after service of a signed copy of the award on the applicant. Application for such correction shall be made not later than 10 days after service of a signed copy of the award on the applicant. Upon or before making such application, the applicant shall deliver or mail a copy of the application to all of the other parties to the arbitration. Any party to the arbitration may make written objection to such application. The objection shall be made not later than 10 days after the application is delivered or mailed to the objector. Upon or before making such objection, the objector shall deliver or mail a copy of the objection to the applicant and all the other parties to the arbitration. The arbitrators shall either deny the application or correct the award. The denial of the application or the correction of the award shall be in writing and signed by the arbitrators concurring therein, and the neutral arbitrator shall serve a signed copy of such denial or correction on each party to the arbitration personally or by registered or certified mail or as provided in the agreement. If no denial of the application or correction of the award is served within the 30 day period provided in this section, the application for correction shall be deemed denied on the last day thereof.

CCP § 1284.2. Payment of Expenses and Fees.

Unless the arbitration agreement otherwise provides or the parties to the arbitration otherwise agree, each party to the arbitration shall pay his *pro rata* share of the expenses and fees of the neutral arbitrator, together with other expenses of the arbitration incurred or approved by the neutral arbitrator, not including counsel fees or witness fees or other expenses incurred by a party for his own benefit.

4. ENFORCEMENT OF THE AWARD

CCP § 1285. Petition for Confirmation, Correction or Vacation of Award.

Any party to an arbitration in which an award has been made may petition the court to confirm, correct or vacate the award. The petition shall name as respondents all parties to the arbitration and may name as respondents any other persons bound by the arbitration award.

CCP § 1285.2. Response to Petition.

A response to a petition under this chapter may request the court to dismiss the petition or to confirm, correct or vacate the award.

CCP § 1285.4. Petition's Contents.

A petition under this chapter shall:

(a) Set forth the substance of or have attached copy of the agreement to arbitrate unless the petitioner denies the existence of such an agreement.

(b) Set forth the names of the arbitrators.

(c) Set forth or have attached a copy of the award and the written opinion of the arbitrators, if any.

CCP § 1285.6. Response's Contents.

Unless a copy thereof is set forth in or attached to the petition, a response to a petition under this chapter shall:

(a) Set forth the substance of or have attached a copy of the agreement to arbitrate unless the respondent denies the existence of such an agreement.

(b) Set forth the names of the arbitrators.

(c) Set forth or have attached a copy of the award and the written opinion of the arbitrators, if any.

CCP § 1285.8. Statement of Grounds for Relief.

A petition to correct or vacate an award, or a response requesting such relief, shall set forth the grounds on which the request for such relief is based.

CCP § 1286. Extent of Relief.

If a petition or response under this chapter is duly served and filed, the court shall confirm the award as made, whether rendered in this state or another state, unless in accordance with this chapter it corrects the award and confirms it as corrected, vacates the award or dismisses the proceeding.

CCP § 1286.2. Grounds for Vacation of Award.

Subject to Section 1286.4, the court shall vacate the award if the court determines any of the following:

(a) The award was procured by corruption, fraud or other undue means.

(b) There was corruption in any of the arbitrators.

(c) The rights of the party were substantially prejudiced by misconduct of a neutral arbitrator.

(d) The arbitrators exceeded their powers and the award cannot be corrected without affecting the merits of the decision upon the controversy submitted.

(e) The rights of such party were substantially prejudiced by the refusal of the arbitrators to postpone the hearing upon sufficient cause being shown therefor or by the refusal of the arbitrators to hear evidence material to the controversy or by other conduct of the arbitrators contrary to the provisions of this title.

(f) An arbitrator making the award was subject to disqualification upon grounds specified in subdivision (e) of Section 1282, but failed upon receipt of timely demand to disqualify himself or herself as required by those provisions. However, this subdivision does not apply to arbitration proceedings conducted under a collective agreement between employers and employees or between their respective representatives.

CCP § 1286.4. Prerequisites to Vacation of Award.

The court may not vacate an award unless:

(a) A petition or response requesting that the award be vacated has been duly served and filed; or

(b) A petition or response requesting that the award be corrected has been duly served and filed and:

> (1) All petitioners and respondents are before the court; or
>
> (2) All petitioners and respondents have been given reasonable notice that the court will be requested at the hearing to vacate the award or that the court on its own motion has determined to vacate the award and all petitioners and respondents have been given an opportunity to show why the award should not be vacated.

CCP § 1286.6. Correction of Award.

Subject to Section 1286.8, the court, unless it vacates the award pursuant to Section 1286.2, shall correct the award and confirm it as corrected if the court determines that:

(a) There was an evident miscalculation of figures or an evident mistake in the description of any person, thing, or property referred to in the award;

(b) The arbitrators exceeded their powers but the award may be corrected without affecting the merits of the decision upon the controversy submitted; or

(c) The award is imperfect in a matter of form, not affecting the merits of the controversy.

CCP § 1286.8. Prerequisites to Correction of Award.

The court may not correct an award unless:

(a) A petition or response requesting that the award be corrected has been duly served and filed; or

(b) A petition or response requesting that the award be vacated has been duly served and filed and;

(1) All petitioners and respondents are before the court; or

(2) All petitioners and respondents have been given reasonable notice that the court will be requested at the hearing to correct the award or that the court on its own motion has determined to correct the award and all petitioners and respondents have been given an opportunity to show why the award should not be corrected.

CCP § 1287. Rehearing Before Arbitrators.

If the award is vacated, the court may order a rehearing before new arbitrators. If the award is vacated on the grounds set forth in subdivision (d) or (e) of Section 1286.2, the court with the consent of the parties to the court proceeding may order a rehearing before the original arbitrators. If the arbitration agreement requires that the award be made within a specified period of time, the rehearing may nevertheless be held and the award made within an equal period of time beginning with the date of the order for rehearing but only if the court determines that the purpose of the time limit agreed upon by the parties to the arbitration agreement will not be frustrated by the application of this provision.

CCP § 1287.2. Dismissal of Proceeding.

The court shall dismiss the proceeding under this chapter as to any person named as a respondent if the court determines that such person was not bound by the arbitration award and was not a party to the arbitration.

CCP § 1287.4. Entry, Effect, and Enforcement of Judgement on Confirmation.

If an award is confirmed, judgment shall be entered in conformity therewith. The judgment so entered has the same force and effect as, and is subject to all the provisions of law relating to, a judgment in a civil action; and it may be enforced like any other judgment of the court in which it is entered.

CCP § 1287.6. Award as Contract.

An award that has not been confirmed or vacated has the same force and effect as a contract in writing between the parties to the arbitration.

CCP § 1288. Service of Petitions.

A petition to confirm an award shall be served and filed not later than four years after the date of service of a signed copy of the award on the petitioner. A petition to vacate an award or to correct an award shall be served and filed not later than 100 days after the date of the service of a signed copy of the award on the petitioner.

CCP § 1288.2. Service of Response.

A response requesting that an award be vacated or that an award be corrected shall be served and filed not later than 100 days after the date of service of a signed copy of the award upon:

(a) The respondent if he was a party to the arbitration; or

(b) The respondent's representative if the respondent was not a party to the arbitration.

CCP § 1288.4. Service of Petition After Service of Award.

No petition may be served and filed under this chapter until at least 10 days after service of the signed copy of the award upon the petitioner.

CCP § 1288.6. Petition After Application for Arbitrators to Correct Award.

If an application is made to the arbitrators for correction of the award, a petition may not be served and filed under this chapter until the determination of that application.

CCP § 1288.8. Dates For Service of Award After Application For Correction.

If an application is made to the arbitrators for correction of the award, the date of the service of the award for the purposes of this article shall be deemed to be whichever of the following dates is the earlier:

(a) The date of service upon the petitioner of a signed copy of the correction of the award or of the denial of the application.

(b) The date that such application is deemed to be denied under Section 1284.

CHAPTER 8

CIVIL RIGHTS

(Civil Code §§ 51, 51.3, 434.5)

Civ. C. § 51. Unruh Civil Rights Act; Equal Rights; Business Establishments.

This section shall be known, and may be cited, as the Unruh Civil Rights Act.

All persons within the jurisdiction of this state are free and equal, and no matter what their sex, race, color, religion, ancestry, national origin, or disability are entitled to the full and equal accommodations, advantages, facilities, privileges, or services in all business establishments of every kind whatsoever.

This section shall not be construed to confer any right or privilege on a person which is conditioned or limited by law or which is applicable alike to persons of every sex, color, race, religion, ancestry, national origin, or disability.

Nothing in this section shall be construed to require any construction, alteration, repair, structural or otherwise, or modification of any sort whatsoever to any new or existing establishment, facility, building, improvement, or any other structure, or to augment, restrict, or alter in any way the authority of the State Architect to require construction, alteration, repair, or modifications that the State Architect otherwise possesses pursuant to other provisions of the law.

A violation of the right of any individual under the Americans with Disabilities Act of 1990 (Public Law 101-336) shall also constitute a violation of this section.

Civ. C. § 51.3. Housing; Age Limitations; Necessity for Senior Citizen Housing.

(a) The Legislature finds and declares that this section is essential to establish and preserve specially designed accessible housing for senior citizens. There are senior citizens who need special living environments and services, and find that there is an inadequate supply of this type of housing in the state.

(b) The Legislature finds and declares that different age limitations for senior citizen housing are appropriate in recognition of the size of a development in relationship to the community in which it is located.

(c) For the purposes of this section, the following definitions apply:

(1) "Qualifying resident" or "senior citizen" means a person 62 years of age or older, or 55 years of age or older in a senior citizen housing development.

(2) "Qualified permanent resident" means a person who meets all of the following requirements:

(A) Was residing with the qualifying resident or senior citizen prior to the death, hospitalization, or other prolonged absence of, or the dissolution of marriage with, the qualifying resident or senior citizen.

(B) Was 45 years of age or older, or was a spouse, cohabitant, or person providing primary physical or economic support to the qualifying resident or senior citizen.

(C) Has an ownership interest in, or is in expectation of an ownership interest in, the dwelling unit within the housing development that limits occupancy, residency, or use on the basis of age.

(3) *"Senior citizen housing development" means a residential development developed, substantially rehabilitated, or substantially renovated for, sen-*

ior citizens that meets any of the following requirements:

(A) At least 150 dwelling units in a metropolitan statistical area, as defined by the Federal Committee on Metropolitan Statistical Areas, with a population of at least 1,000 residents per square mile or 1,000,000 total residents, based on the 1990 census.

(B) At least 100 dwelling units in a metropolitan statistical area, as defined by the Federal Committee on Metropolitan Statistical Areas, with a population not to exceed 999 residents per square mile and not to exceed 399,999 total residents, based on the 1990 census.

(C) At least 35 dwelling units in any other area.

The number of dwelling units within a development includes all dwelling units developed, whether in single or multiple phases. Developments commenced after July 1, 1986, shall be required to have been issued a public report as a senior citizen housing development under Section 11010.05 of the Business and Professions Code.

(4) "Dwelling unit" or "housing" means any residential accommodation other than a mobilehome.

(5) "Cohabitant" refers to persons who live together as husband and wife.

(6) "Permitted health care resident" means a person hired to provide live-in, long-term, or terminal health care to a qualifying resident.

(d) The covenants, conditions, and restrictions or other documents or written policy shall not limit occupancy, residency, or use on the basis of age more proscriptively than to require that one person in residence in each dwelling unit may be required to be a senior citizen and that each other resident in the same dwelling unit may be required tobe a qualified permanent resident.

(e) The covenants, conditions, and restrictions or other documents or written policy shall permit temporary residencey, as a guest of a senior citizen or qualified permanent resident, by a person of less than 45 years of age for periods of time, not less than 60 days in any year, *that* are specified in the covenants, conditions, and restrictions or other documents or written policy.

(f) Upon the death or dissolution of marriage, or upon hospitalization, or other prolonged absence of the qualifying resident, any qualified permanent resident shall be entitled to continue his or her occupancy, residency, or use of the dwelling unit as a permitted resident.

(g) The condominium, stock cooperative, limited-equity housing cooperative, planned development, or multiple-family residential rental property shall have been developed for, and initially been put to use as, housing for senior citizens, or shall have been substantially rehabilitated or renovated for, and immediately afterward put to use as, housing for senior citizens, as provided in this section.

(h) The covenants, conditions and restrictions or the documents or written policies applicable to any condominium stock cooperative, limited-equity housing cooperative, planned development or multiple-family residential property *that* contained age restrictions on January 1, 1984, shall be enforceable only to the extent permitted by this section, notwithstanding lower age restrictions contained in those documents or policies.

(i) Any person who has the right to reside in, occupy, or use the housing or an unimproved lot subject to this section on January 1, 1985, shall not be deprived of the right to continue that residency, occupancy, or use as the result of the enactment of this section.

(j) The covenants, conditions, and restrictions or other documents or written policy of the senior citizen housing development shall permit the occupancy of a dwelling unit by a permitted health care resident during any period that the person is actually providing live-in, long-term, or hospice health care to a qualifying resident for compensation.

Gov. C. § 434.5. Restrictions On Legal Right To Display U.S. Flag.

(a) No Person, private entity, or governmental agency shall adopt rules, regulations, or ordinances, or enter into any agreement or covenant, which prevents any person or private entity which would otherwise have the legal right to display a Flag of the United States on private property from exercising that right, unless it is used as, or in conjunction with, an advertising display.

(b) As used in this section, "legal right" means the freedom of use and enjoyment generally exercised by owners and occupiers of land.

(c) Nothing in this section shall be construed to prevent a city, county, or city and county from imposing reasonable restrictions as to the time, place, and manner of placement or display of a Flag of the United States when necessary for the preservation of the public's health, safety, or order. However, no restrictions solely to promote aesthetic considerations may be imposed.

CHAPTER 9

NONPROFIT MUTUAL BENEFIT CORPORATIONS FORMATION & POWERS

(Corporations Code §§ 7110-7160)

Corp. C. § 7110. Title Of Part.

This part shall be known and may be cited as the Nonprofit Mutual Benefit Corporation Law.

Corp. C. § 7111. Lawful Purposes Of Nonprofit Mutual Benefit Corporations.

Subject to any other provision of law of this state applying to the particular class of corporation or line of activity, a corporation may be formed under this part for any lawful purpose; provided that a corporation all of the assets of which are irrevocably dedicated to charitable, religious, or public purposes and which as a matter of law or according to its articles or bylaws must, upon dissolution, distribute its assets to a person or persons carrying on a charitable, religious, or public purpose or purposes may not be formed under this part.

Corp. C. § 7120. Corporation Formed By Execution And Filing Of Articles; Signatures Required.

(a) One or more persons may form a corporation under this part by executing and filing articles of incorporation.

(b) If initial directors are named in the articles, each director named in the articles shall sign and acknowledge the articles; if initial directors are not named in the articles, the articles shall be signed by one or more persons who thereupon are the incorporators of the corporation.

(c) The corporate existence begins upon the filing of the articles and continues perpetually, unless otherwise expressly provided by law or in the articles.

Corp. C. § 7121. Change Of Unincorporated Association To Corporation.

(a) In the case of an existing unincorporated association, the association may change its status to that of a corporation upon a proper authorization for such by the association in accordance with its rules and procedures.

(b) In addition to the matters required to be set forth in the articles pursuant to Section 7130, the articles in the case of an incorporation authorized by subdivision (a) shall set forth that an existing unincorporated association, stating its name, is being incorporated by the filing of the articles.

(c) The articles filed pursuant to this section shall be accompanied by a verified statement of any two officers or governing board members of the association stating that the incorporation of the association by means of the articles to which the verified statement is attached has been approved by the association in accordance with its rules and procedures.

(d) Upon the change of status of an unincorporated association to a corporation pursuant to subdivision (a), the property of the association becomes the property of the corporation and the members of the association who had any voting rights of the type referred to in Section 5056 become members of the corporation.

(e) The filing for record in the office of the county recorder of any county in this state in which any of the real property of the association is located, of a copy of the articles of incorporation filed pursuant to this section, certified by the Secretary of State, shall evidence record ownership in the corporation of all interests of the association in and to the real property located in that county.

(f) All rights of creditors and all liens upon the property of the association shall be preserved unimpaired. Any action or proceeding pending by or against the unincorporated association may be prosecuted to judgment, which shall bind the corporation, or the corporation may be proceeded against or substituted in its place.

(g) If a corporation is organized by a person who is or was an officer, director or member of an unincorporated association and such corporation is not organized pursuant to subdivision (a), the unincorporated association may continue to use its name and the corporation may not use a name which is the same as or similar to the name of the unincorporated association.

Corp. C. § 7122. Prohibited Names; Reservation Of Names.

(a) The Secretary of State shall not file articles setting forth a name in which "bank," "trust," "trustee" or related words appear, unless the certificate of approval of the Superintendent of Banks is attached thereto.

(b) The Secretary of State shall not file articles pursuant to this part setting forth a name which may create the impression that the purpose of the corporation is public, charitable or religious or that it is a charitable foundation.

(c) The Secretary of State shall not file articles which set forth a name which is likely to mislead the public or which is the same as, or resembles so closely as to tend to deceive, the name of a domestic corporation, the name of a foreign corporation which is authorized to transact intrastate business or has registered its name pursuant to Section 2101, a name which a foreign corporation has assumed under subdivision (b) of Section 2106, a name which will become the record name of a domestic or foreign corporation upon the effective date of a filed corporate instrument where there is a delayed effective date pursuant to subdivision (c) of Section 110, or subdivision (c) of Section 5008, or a name which is under reservation pursuant to this section, Section 201, Section 5122, or Section 9122 except that a corporation may adopt a name that is substantially the same as an existing domestic or foreign corporation which is authorized to transact intrastate business or has registered its name pursuant to Section 2101, upon proof of consent by such corporation and a finding by the Secretary of State that under the circumstances the public is not likely to be misled.

The use by a corporation of a name in violation of this section may be enjoined notwithstanding the filing of its articles by the Secretary of State.

(d) Any applicant may, upon payment of the fee prescribed therefor in the Government Code, obtain from the Secretary of State a certificate of reservation of any name not prohibited by subdivision (c), and upon the issuance of the certificate the name stated therein shall be reserved for a period of 60 days. The Secretary of State shall not, however, issue certificates reserving the same name for two or more consecutive 60-day periods to the same applicant or for the use or benefit of the same person; nor shall consecutive reservations be made by or for the use or benefit of the same person of names so similar as to fall within the prohibitions of subdivision (c).

Corp. C. § 7130. Required Provisions.

The articles of incorporation of a corporation formed under this part shall set forth:

(a) The name of the corporation.

(b) The following statement:

> "This corporation is a nonprofit mutual benefit corporation organized under the Nonprofit Mutual Benefit Corporation Law. The purpose of this corporation is to engage in any lawful act or activity for which a corporation may be organized under such law."

[The articles may include a further description of the corporation's purposes.]

(c) The name and address in this state of the corporation's initial agent for service of process in accordance with subdivision (b) of Section 8210.

Corp. C. § 7131. Statement Limiting Purposes Or Powers.

The articles of incorporation may set forth a further statement limiting the purposes or powers of the corporation.

Corp. C. § 7132. Optional Provisions.

(a) The articles of incorporation may set forth any or all of the following provisions, which shall not be effective unless expressly provided in the articles:

(1) A provision limiting the duration of the corporation's existence to a specified date.

(2) A provision conferring upon the holdings of any evidences of indebtedness, issued or to be issued by a corporation the right to vote in the election of directors and on any other matters on which members may vote under this part even if the corporation does not have members.

(3) A provision conferring upon members the right to determine the consideration for which memberships shall be issued.

(4) In the case of a subordinate corporation instituted or created under the authority of a head organization, a provision setting forth either or both of the following:

(i) That the subordinate corporation shall dissolve whenever its charter is surrendered to, taken away by, or revoked by the head organization granting it.

(ii) That in the event of its dissolution pursuant to an article provision allowed by subdivision (a), paragraph (4), clause (i), of this section, or, in the event of its dissolution for any reason, any assets of the corporation after compliance with the applicable provisions of Chapters 15 (commencing with Section 8510), 16 (commencing with Section 8610), and 17 (commencing with Section 8710) shall be distributed to the head organization.

(b) Nothing contained in subdivision (a) shall affect the enforceability, as between the parties thereto, of any lawful agreement not otherwise contrary to public policy.

(c) The articles of incorporation may set forth any or all of the following provisions:

(1) The names and addresses of the persons appointed to act as initial directors.

(2) Provisions concerning the transfer of memberships, in accordance with Section 7320.

(3) The classes of members, if any, and if there are two or more classes, the rights, privileges, preferences, restrictions and conditions attaching to each class.

(4) A provision which would allow any member to have more or less than one vote in any election or other matter presented to the members for a vote.

(5) Any other provision, not in conflict with law, for the management of the activities and for the conduct of the affairs of the corporation, including any provision which is required or permitted by this part to be stated in the bylaws.

Corp. C. § 7133. Articles As Proof Of Corporate Existence.

For all purposes other than an action in the nature of *quo warranto*, a copy of the articles of a corporation duly certified by the Secretary of State is conclusive evidence of the formation of the corporation and *prima facie* evidence of its corporate existence.

Corp. C. § 7134. Powers of Incorporators When Directors Not Named.

If initial directors have not been named in the articles, the incorporator or incorporators, until the directors are elected, may do whatever is necessary and proper to perfect the organization of the corporation, including the adoption and amendment of bylaws of the corporation and the election of directors and officers.

Corp. C. § 7135. Sections 7130 and 7131 As Not Limiting Court Power Over Corporation.

Nothing in Sections 7130 or 7131 or in any provision of the articles of a mutual benefit corporation shall be construed to limit the equitable power of a court to impress a charitable trust upon any or all of the assets of a mutual benefit corporation or otherwise treat it as a public benefit corporation.

Corp. C. § 7140. Powers Of Corporation.

Subject to any limitations contained in the articles or bylaws and to compliance with other provisions of this division and any other applicable laws, a corporation, in carrying out its activities, shall have all of the powers of a natural person, including, without limitation, the power to:

(a) Adopt, use, and at will alter a corporate seal, but failure to affix a seal does not affect the validity of any instrument.

(b) Adopt, amend, and repeal bylaws.

(c) Qualify to conduct its activities in any other state, territory, dependency or foreign country.

(d) Issue, purchase, redeem, receive, take or otherwise acquire, own, sell, lend, exchange, transfer or otherwise dispose of, pledge, use and otherwise deal in and with its own memberships bonds, debentures, notes and debt securities.

(e) Pay pensions, and establish and carry out pension, deferred compensation, saving, thrift and other retirement, incentive and benefit plans, trusts and provisions for any or all of its directors, officers, employees and persons providing services to it or any of its subsidiary or related or associated corporations, and to indemnify and purchase and maintain insurance on behalf of any fiduciary of such plans, trusts, or provisions.

(f) Issue certificates evidencing membership in accordance with the provisions of Section 7313 and issue identity cards.

(g) Levy dues, assessments, and admission and transfer fees.

(h) Make donations for the public welfare or for community funds, hospital, charitable, educational, scientific, civic, religious or similar purposes.

(i) Assume obligations, enter into contracts, including contracts of guarantee or suretyship, incur liabilities, borrow or lend money or otherwise use its credit, and secure any of its obligations, contracts or liabilities by mortgage, pledge or other encumbrance of all or any part of its property and income.

(j) Participate with others in any partnership, joint venture or other association, transaction or arrangement of any kind whether or not such participation involves sharing or delegation of control with or to others.

(k) Act as trustee under any trust incidental to the principal objects of the corporation, and receive, hold, administer, exchange, and expend funds and property subject to such trust.

(l) Carry on a business at a profit and apply any profit that results from the business activity to any activity in which it may lawfully engage.

Corp. C. § 7141. Ultra Vires Acts; Corporation Bound By Authorized Or Ratified Contract.

Subject to Section 7142:

(a) No limitation upon the activities, purposes, or powers of the corporation or upon the powers of the members, officers, or directors, or the manner of exercise of such powers, contained in or implied by the articles or by Chapters 15 (commencing with Section 8510), 16 (commencing with Section 8610), and 17 (commencing with

Section 8710) shall be asserted as between the corporation or member, officer or director and any third person, except in a proceeding: (1) by a member or the state to enjoin the doing or continuation of unauthorized activities by the corporation or its officers, or both, in cases where third parties have not acquired rights thereby, (2) to dissolve the corporation, or (3) by the corporation or by a member suing in a representative suit against the officers or directors of the corporation for violation of their authority.

(b) Any contract or conveyance made in the name of a corporation which is authorized or ratified by the board, or is done within the scope of authority, actual or apparent, conferred by the board or within the agency power of the officer executing it, except as the board's authority is limited by law other than this part, binds the corporation, and the corporation acquires rights thereunder whether the contract is executed or wholly or in part executory.

Corp. C. § 7142. Action For Breach Of Charitable Trust; Who May Bring; Remedies.

(a) Notwithstanding Section 7141, in the case of a corporation holding assets in charitable trust, any of the following may bring an action to enjoin, correct, obtain damages for or to otherwise remedy a breach of the charitable trust:

(1) The corporation, or a member in the name of the corporation pursuant to Section 7710.

(2) An officer of the corporation.

(3) A director of the corporation.

(4) A person with a reversionary, contractual, or property interest in the assets subject to such charitable trust.

(5) The Attorney General, or any person granted relator status by the Attorney General. The Attorney General shall be given notice of any action brought by the persons

specified in paragraphs (1) through (4), and may intervene.

(b) In an action under this section, the court may not rescind or enjoin the performance of a contract unless:

(1) All of the parties to the contract are parties to the action; or

(2) No party to the contract has, in good faith, and without actual notice of the trust restriction, parted with value, under the contract or in reliance upon it; and

(3) It is equitable to do so.

Corp. C. § 7150. Adoption, Amendment Or Repeal.

(a) Except as provided in subdivision (c) and Sections 7151, 7220, 7224, 7512, 7613, and 7615, bylaws may be adopted, amended or repealed by the board unless the action would:

(1) Materially and adversely affect the rights of members as to voting, dissolution, redemption, or transfer;

(2) Increase or decrease the number of members authorized in total or for any class;

(3) Effect an exchange, reclassification or cancellation of all or part of the memberships; or

(4) Authorize a new class of membership.

(b) Bylaws may be adopted, amended or repealed by approval of the members (Section 5034); provided, however, that such adoption, amendment or repeal also requires approval by the members of a class if such action would:

(1) Materially and adversely affect the rights, privileges, preferences, restrictions or conditions of that class as to voting, dissolution, redemption, or
transfer in a manner different than such action affects another class;

(2) Materially and adversely affect such class as to voting, dissolution, redemption, or

transfer by changing the rights, privileges, preferences, restrictions or conditions of another class;

(3) Increase or decrease the number of memberships authorized for such class;

(4) Increase the number of memberships authorized for another class;

(5) Effect an exchange, reclassification or cancellation of all or part of the memberships of such class; or

(6) Authorize a new class of memberships.

(c) The articles or bylaws may restrict or eliminate the power of the board to adopt, amend or repeal any or all bylaws, subject to subdivision (e) of Section 7151.

Corp. C. § 7151. Required And Optional Provisions; Number Of Directors.

(a) The bylaws shall set forth (unless such provision is contained in the articles, in which case it may only be changed by an amendment of the articles) the number of directors of the corporation; or that the number of directors shall be not less than a stated minimum nor more than a stated maximum with the exact number of directors to be fixed, within the limits specified, by approval of the board or the members (Section 5034), in the manner provided in the bylaws, subject to subdivision (e) of Section 7151. The number or minimum number of directors may be one or more.

(b) Once members have been admitted, a bylaw specifying or changing a fixed number of directors or the maximum or minimum number or changing from a fixed to a variable board or vice versa may only be adopted by approval of the members (Section 5034).

(c) The bylaws may contain any provision, not in conflict with law or the articles, for the management of the activities and for the conduct of the affairs of the corporation, including but not limited to:

(1) Any provision referred to in subdivision (c) of Section 7132.

(2) The time, place and manner of calling, conducting and giving notice of members', directors' and committee meetings, or of conducting mail ballots.

(3) The qualifications, duties and compensation of directors; the time of their election; and the requirements of a quorum for directors' and committee meetings.

(4) The appointment of committees, composed of directors or nondirectors or both, by the board or any officer and the authority of any such committees.

(5) The appointment, duties, compensation and tenure of officers.

(6) The mode of determination of members of record.

(7) The making of reports and financial statements to members.

(8) Setting, imposing and collecting dues, assessments, and admission and transfer fees.

(d) The bylaws may provide for the manner of admission, withdrawal, suspension, and expulsion of members, consistent with the requirements of Section 7341.

(e) The bylaws may require, for any or all corporate actions (except as provided in paragraphs (1) and (2) of subdivision (a) of Section 7222, subdivision (c) of Section 7615, and Section 8610) the vote of a larger proportion of, or all of, the members or the members of any class, unit, or grouping of members or the vote of a larger proportion of, or all of, the directors, than is otherwise required by this part. Such a provision in the bylaws requiring such greater vote shall not be altered, amended or repealed except by such greater vote, unless otherwise provided in the bylaws.

(f) The bylaws may contain a provision limiting the number of members, in total or of any class, which the corporation is authorized to admit.

Corp. C. § 7152. Provisions For Delegates.

A corporation may provide in its bylaws for delegates having some or all of the authority of members. Where delegates are provided for, the bylaws shall set forth delegates' terms of office, any reasonable method for delegates' selection and removal, and any reasonable method for calling, noticing and holding meetings of delegates and may set forth the manner in which delegates may act by written ballot similar to Section 7513 for written ballot of members. Delegates may only act personally at a meeting or by written ballot and may not act by proxy. Delegates may be given a name other than "delegates."

Corp. C. § 7160. Location And Inspection Of Articles And Bylaws.

Every corporation shall keep at its principal office in this state the original or a copy of its articles and bylaws as amended to date, which shall be open to inspection by the members at all reasonable times during office hours. If the corporation has no office in this state, it shall upon the written request of any member furnish to such member a copy of the articles or bylaws as amended to date.

CHAPTER 10

DUTIES AND RESPONSIBILITIES UNDER THE CALIFORNIA NONPROFIT CORPORATION LAW

(Corporations Code §§ 7210-7125)

Corp. C. § 7210. Corporate Powers Exercised By Board; Delegation.

Subject to the provisions of this part and any limitations in the articles or bylaws relating to action required to be approved by the members (Section 5034), or by a majority of all members (Section 5033), the activities and affairs of a corporation shall be conducted and all corporate powers shall be exercised by or under the direction of the board. The board may delegate the management of the activities of the corporation to any person or persons, management company, or committee however composed, provided that the activities and affairs of the corporation shall be managed and all corporate powers shall be exercised under the ultimate direction of the board.

Corp. C. § 7211. Board Meetings; Notice; Quorum; Consent To Act Without Meeting.

(a) Unless otherwise provided in the articles or in the bylaws:

(1) Meetings of the board may be called by the chairman of the board or the president or any vice president or the secretary or any two directors.

(2) Regular meetings of the board may be held without notice if the time and place of such meetings are fixed by the bylaws or the board. Special meetings of the board shall be held upon 4 days notice by first-class mail or 48 hours notice delivered personally or by telephone or telegraph. The articles or bylaws may not dispense with notice of a special meeting. A notice, or waiver of notice, need not specify the purpose of any regular or special meeting of the board.
(3) Notice of a meeting need not be given to any director who signed a waiver of notice or a written consent to holding the meeting or an approval of the minutes thereof, whether before or after the meeting, or who attends the meeting without protesting, prior thereto or at its commencement, the lack of notice to such director. All such waivers, consents and approvals shall be filed with the corporate records or made a part of the minutes of the meetings.
(4) A majority of the directors present, whether or not a quorum is present, may adjourn any meeting to another time and place. If the meeting is adjourned for more than 24 hours, notice of any adjournment to another time and place shall be given prior to time of the adjourned meeting to the directors who were not present at the time of the adjournment.
(5) Meetings of the board may be held at any place within or without the state which has been designated in the notice of the meeting or, if not stated in the notice or if there is no notice, designated in the bylaws or by resolution of the board.

(6) Members of the board may participate in a meeting through use of conference telephone or similar communications equipment, so long as all members participating in such meeting can hear one another. Participation in a meeting pursuant to this subdivision constitutes presence in person at such meeting.

(7) A majority of the number of directors authorized in the articles or bylaws constitutes a quorum of the board for the transaction of business. The articles or bylaws may not provide that a quorum shall be less than one-fifth the number of directors authorized in the articles or bylaws, or less than two, whichever is larger, unless the number of directors authorized in the articles or bylaws is one, in which case one director constitutes a quorum.

(8) Subject to the provisions of Sections 7212, 7233, 7234, and subdivision (e) of Sections 7237 and 5233, insofar as it is made applicable pursuant to Section 7238, every act or decision done or made by a majority of the directors present at a meeting duly held at which a quorum is present is the act of the board. The articles or bylaws may not provide that a lesser vote than a majority of the directors present at a meeting is the act of the board. A meeting at which a quorum is initially present may continue to transact business notwithstanding the withdrawal of directors, if any action taken is approved by at least a majority of the required quorum for such meeting, or such greater number as is required by this division, the articles or bylaws.

(b) Any action required or permitted to be taken by the board may be taken without a meeting, if all members of the board shall individually or collectively consent in writing to such action. Such written consent or consents shall be filed with the minutes of the proceedings of the board. Such action by written consent shall have the same force and effect as a unanimous vote of such directors. For the purposes of this section only, "all members of the board" shall not include any "interested director" as defined in Section 5233, insofar as it is made applicable pursuant to Section 7238.

(c) The provisions of this section apply also to incorporators, to committees of the board, and to action by such incorporators or such committees *mutatis mutandis.*

Corp. C. § 7212. Executive Committees; Creation; Authority To Act.

(a) The board may, by resolution adopted by a majority of the number of directors then in office, provided that a quorum is present, create one or more committees, each consisting of two or more directors, to serve at the pleasure of the board. Appointments to such committees shall be by a majority vote of the directors then in office, unless the articles or bylaws require a majority vote of the number of directors authorized in the articles or bylaws. The bylaws may authorize one or more committees, each consisting of two or more directors, and may provide that a specified officer or officers who are also directors of the corporation shall be a member or members of such committee or committees. The board may appoint one or more directors as alternate members of any committee, who may replace any absent member at any meeting of the committee. Any such committee, to the extent provided in the resolution of the board or in the bylaws, shall have all of the authority of the board, except with respect to:

(1) The approval of any action for which this part also requires approval of the members (Section 5034) or approval of a majority of all members (Section 5033).

(2) The filling of vacancies on the board or in any committee which has the authority of

the board.

(3) The fixing of compensation of the directors for serving on the board or on any committee.

(4) The amendment or repeal of bylaws or the adoption of new bylaws.

(5) The amendment or repeal of any resolution of the board which by its express terms is not amendable or repealable.

(6) The appointment of committees of the board or the members thereof.

(7) The expenditure of corporate funds to support a nominee for director after there are more people nominated for director than can be elected.

(8) With respect to any assets held in charitable trust, the approval of any self-dealing transaction except as provided in paragraph (3) of subdivision (d) of Section 5233.

(b) Subdivision (a) shall not apply to any committee which does not exercise the authority of the board.

(c) Unless the bylaws otherwise provide, the board may delegate to any committee, appointed pursuant to paragraph (4) of subdivision (c) of Section 7151 or otherwise, powers as authorized by Section 7210, but may not delegate the powers set forth in paragraphs (1) through (8) of subdivision (a) of this section.

Corp. C. § 7213. Corporate Officers Required; Selection; Resignation.

(a) A corporation shall have a chairman of the board or a president or both, a secretary, a chief financial officer, and such other officers with such titles and duties as shall be stated in the bylaws or determined by the board and as may be necessary to enable it to sign instruments. The president, or if there is no president the chair of the board, is the general manager and chief executive officer of the corporation, unless otherwise provided in the articles or bylaws. Any number of offices may be held by the same person unless the articles or bylaws provide otherwise.

(b) Except as otherwise provided by the articles or bylaws, officers shall be chosen by the board and serve at the pleasure of the board, subject to the rights, if any, of an officer under any contract of employment. Any officer may resign at any time upon written notice to the corporation without prejudice to the rights, if any, of the corporation under any contract to which the officer is a party.

Corp. C. § 7214. Validity Of Instrument Signed By Officers.

Subject to the provisions of subdivision (a) of Section 7141 and Section 7142, any note, mortgage, evidence of indebtedness, contract, conveyance or other instrument in writing, and any assignment or endorsement thereof, executed or entered into between any corporation and any other person, when signed by the chairman of the board, the president or any vice president, and the secretary, any assistant secretary, the chief financial officer or any assistant treasurer of such corporation, is not invalidated as to the corporation by any lack of authority of the signing officers in the absence of actual knowledge on the part of the other person that the signing officers had no authority to execute the same.

Corp. C. § 7215. Proof of Corporate Bylaws, Resolutions, Etc.

The original or a copy of the bylaws or of the minutes of any incorporators', members', directors', committee or other meeting or of any resolution adopted by the board or a committee thereof, or members, certified to be a true copy by a person purporting to be the secretary or an assistant secretary of the corporation, is *prima facie* evidence of the adoption of such bylaws or resolution or of the due holding of such meeting and of the matters stated therein.

CHAPTER 11

SELECTION, REMOVAL AND RESIGNATION OF DIRECTORS

(Corporataion Code §§ 7220-7225)

Corp. C. § 7220. Term Of Office; Manner Of Selection.

(a) Except as provided in subdivision (d), directors shall be elected for such terms, not longer than four years, as are fixed in the articles or bylaws. However, the terms of directors of a corporation without members may be up to six years. In the absence of any provision in the articles or bylaws, the term shall be one year. No amendment of the articles or bylaws may extend the term of a director beyond that for which the director was elected, nor may any bylaw provision increasing the terms of directors be adopted without approval of the members (Section 5034).

(b) Unless the articles or bylaws otherwise provide, each director, including a director elected to fill a vacancy, shall hold office until the expiration of the term for which elected and until a successor has been elected and qualified.

(c) The articles or bylaws may provide for the election of one or more directors by the members of any class voting as a class.

(d) Subdivisions (a) through (c) notwithstanding, all or any portion of the directors authorized in the articles or bylaws of a corporation without members, and up to one-third of the directors authorized in the articles or bylaws of a corporation with members, may hold office by virtue of designation or selection as provided by the articles or bylaws rather than by election by a member or members. Such directors shall continue in office for the term prescribed by the governing article or bylaw provision, or, if there is no term prescribed, until the governing article or bylaw provision is duly amended or repealed, except as provided in subdivision (e) of Section 7222. A bylaw provision authorized by this subdivision may be adopted, amended, or repealed only by approval of the members (Section 5034).

(e) In computing the one-third limit set forth in subdivision (d) the following directors shall not be counted either as designated or selected directors or as authorized directors:

(1) Directors designated or selected by a government office, board, commission, department, agency, or political subdivision.
(2) Directors designated or selected by a person who is elected by the members as an officer of the corporation.
(3) Directors appointed to fill vacancies on the board created by the death, resignation or removal of directors.

Corp. C. § 7221. Removal Of Director For Cause.

The board may declare vacant the office of a director who has been declared of unsound mind by a final order of court, or convicted of a felony, or, in the case of a corporation holding assets in charitable trust, has been found by a final order or judgment of any court to have breached any duty arising as a result of Section 7238, or, if at the time a director is elected, the bylaws provide that a director may be removed for missing a specified number of board meetings, fails to attend the specified number of meetings.

Corp. C. § 7222. Removal Of Director Without Cause.

(a) Subject to subdivisions (b) and (f) of this section, any or all directors may be removed without cause if:

(1) In a corporation with fewer than 50 members, such removal is approved by a majority of all members (Section 5033).

(2) In a corporation with 50 or more members, such removal is approved by the members (Section 5034).

(3) In a corporation with no members, such removal is approved by a majority of the directors then in office.

(b) Except for a corporation having no members, pursuant to Section 7310:

(1) In a corporation in which the articles or bylaws authorize members to cumulate their votes pursuant to subdivision (a) of Section 7615, no director may be removed (unless the entire board is removed) when the votes cast against removal, or not consenting in writing to such removal, would be sufficient to elect such director if voted cumulatively at an election at which the same total number of votes were cast (or, if such action is taken by written ballot, all memberships entitled to vote were voted) and the entire number of directors authorized at the time of the director's most recent election were then being elected.

(2) When by the provisions of the articles or bylaws the members of any class, voting as a class, are entitled to elect one ore more directors, any director so elected may be removed only by the applicable vote of the members of that class.

(3) When by the provisions of the articles or bylaws the members within a chapter or other organizational unit, or region or other geographic grouping, voting as such, are entitled to elect one or more directors, any director so elected may be removed only by the applicable vote of the members, within

such organizational unit or geographic grouping.

(c) Any reduction of the number of directors authorized in the articles or bylaws does not remove any director prior to the expiration of such director's term of office.

(d) Except as provided in this section and Sections 7221 and 7223, a director may not be removed prior to the expiration of such director's term of office.

(e) Where a director removed under this section or Section 7221 or Section 7223 was chosen by designation pursuant to subdivision (d) of Section 7220, then:

(1) Where a different person may be designated pursuant to the governing article or bylaw provision, such new designation shall be made.

(2) Where the governing article or bylaw provision contains no provision under which a different person may be designated, the governing article or bylaw provision shall be deemed repealed.

(f) When by the provisions of the articles or bylaws a person or persons are entitled to designate one or more directors, then:

(1) Unless otherwise provided in the articles or bylaws at the time of designation, any director so designated may be removed without cause by the designating person or persons.

(2) Any director so designated may only be removed under subdivision (a) with the written consent of the designating person or persons.

Corp. C. § 7223. Removal Of Director By Director's Or Members' Suit; Role Of Attorney General.

(a) The superior court of the proper county may, at the suit of one of the parties specified in subdivision (b), remove from office any director in case of fraudulent or dishonest acts or gross abuse of authority or discretion with reference to the corporation or breach of any duty arising as a result of Section 7238 and may bar from reelection any director so removed for a period prescribed by the court. The corporation shall be made a party to such action.

(b) An action under subdivision (a) may be instituted by any of the following:

(1) A director.

(2) In the case of a corporation where the total number of votes entitled to be cast for a director is less than 5,000, twice the authorized number (Section 5036) of members, or 20 members, whichever is less.

(3) In the case of a corporation where the total number of votes entitled to be cast for a director is 5,000 or more, twice the authorized number (Section 5036) of members, or 100 members, whichever is less.

(c) In the case of a corporation holding assets in charitable trust, the Attorney General may bring an action under subdivision (a), may intervene in such an action brought by any other party and shall be given notice of any such action brought by any other party.

Corp. C. § 7224. Filling Vacancies; Resignation.

(a) Unless otherwise provided in the articles or bylaws and except for a vacancy created by the removal of a director, vacancies on the board may be filled by approval of the board (Section 5032) or, if the number of directors then in office is less than a quorum, by (1) the unanimous written consent of the directors then in office, (2) the affirmative vote of a majority of the directors then in office at a meeting held pursuant to notice or waivers of notice complying with Section 7211, or (3) a sole remaining director. Unless the articles or a bylaw approved by the members (Section 5034) provide that the board may fill vacancies occurring in the board by reason of the removal of directors, or unless the corporation has no members pursuant to Section 7310, such vacancies may be filled only by approval of the members (Section 5034).

(b) The members may elect a director at any time to fill any vacancy not filled by the directors.

(c) Any director may resign effective upon giving written notice to the chairman of the board, the president, the secretary or the board of directors of the corporation, unless the notice specifies a later time for the effectiveness of such resignation. If the resignation is effective at a future time, a successor may be elected to take office when the resignation becomes effective.

Corp. C. § 7225. Provisional Director.

(a) If a corporation has an even number of directors who are equally divided and cannot agree as to the management of its affairs, so that its activities can no longer be conducted to advantage or so that there is danger that its property, activities or business will be impaired or lost, the superior court of the proper county may, notwithstanding any provisions of the articles or bylaws and whether or not an action is pending for an involuntary winding up or dissolution of the corporation, appoint a provisional director pursuant to this section. Action for such appointment may be brought by any director or by members holding not less than 33 1/3 percent of the voting power.

(b) If a corporation has an uneven number of directors and the members are deadlocked so that they cannot elect successor directors at the time prescribed therefor, the superior court of the proper county may, notwithstanding any provisions of the articles or bylaws, upon petition of members holding 50 percent of the voting power, appoint a provisional director or directors pursuant to this section or order such other equitable relief as the court deems appropriate.

(c) In the case of a corporation holding assets in charitable trust:

(1) Any person bringing an action under subdivision (a) or (b) shall give notice to the Attorney General, who may intervene; and

(2) The Attorney General may bring an action under subdivision (a) or (b).

(d) A provisional director shall be an impartial person, who is neither a member nor a creditor of the corporation, nor related by consanguinity or affinity within the third degree according to the common law to any of the other directors of the corporation or to any judge of the court by which such provisional director is appointed. A provisional director shall have all the rights and powers of a director until the deadlock in the board or among members is broken or until such provisional director is removed by order of the court or by approval of a majority of all members (Section 5033). Such person shall be entitled to such compensation as shall be fixed by the court unless otherwise agreed with the corporation.

CHAPTER 12

STANDARDS OF CONDUCT
(Corporations Code §§ 7230-7238)

Corp. C. § 7230. Application Of Article To All Directors.

(a) Any duties and liabilities set forth in this article shall apply without regard to whether a director is compensated by the corporation.

(b) Part 4 (commencing with Section 16000) of Division 9 of the Probate Code does not apply to the directors of any corporation.

Corp. C. § 7231. Duties And Liabilities.

(a) A director shall perform the duties of a director, including duties as a member of any committee of the board upon which the director may serve, in good faith, in a manner such director believes to be in the best interests of the corporation and with such care, including reasonable inquiry, as an ordinarily prudent person in a like position would use under similar circumstances.

(b) In performing the duties of a director, a director shall be entitled to rely on information, opinions, reports or statements, including financial statements and other financial data, in each case prepared or presented by:

(1) One or more officers or employees of the corporation whom the director believes to be reliable and competent in the matters presented;

(2) Counsel, independent accountants or other persons as to matters which the director believes to be within such person's professional or expert competence; or

(3) A committee of the board upon which the director does not serve, as to matters within its designated authority, which committee the director believes to merit confidence, so long as, in any such case, the director acts in good faith, after reasonable inquiry when the need therefor is indicated by the circumstances and without knowledge that would cause such reliance to be unwarranted.

(c) A person who performs the duties of a director in accordance with subdivisions (a) and (b) shall have no liability based upon any alleged failure to discharge the person's obligations as a director, including, without limiting the generality of the foregoing, any actions or omissions which exceed or defeat a public or charitable purpose to which assets held by a corporation are dedicated.

Corp. C. § 7231.5 Liability Of Volunteer Director Or Officer Failure To Discharge Duties.

(a) Except as provided in Section 7233 or 7236, there is no monetary liability on the part of, and no cause of action for damages shall arise against, any volunteer director or volunteer executive officer of a nonprofit corporation subject to this part based upon any alleged failure to discharge the person's duties as a director or officer if the duties are performed in a manner that meets all of the following criteria:

(1) The duties are performed in good faith.

(2) The duties are performed in a manner such director or officer believes to be in the best interests of the corporation.

(3) The duties are performed with such care, including reasonable inquiry as an ordinarily prudent person in a like position would use under similar circumstances.

(b) "Volunteer" means the rendering of services without compensation. "Compensation" means remuneration whether by way of salary, fee, or other consideration for services rendered. However, the payment of per diem, mileage, or other reimbursement expenses to a director or executive officer does not affect that person's status as a volunteer within the meaning of this section.

(c) "Executive officer" means the president, vice president, secretary, or treasurer of a corporation or other individual serving in like capacity who assists in establishing the policy of the corporation.

(d) This section shall apply only to trade, professional, and labor organizations incorporated pursuant to this part which operate exclusively for fraternal, educational, and other nonprofit purposes, and under the provisions of Section 501(c) of the United States Internal Revenue Code.

(e) This section shall not be construed to limit the provisions of Section 7231.

Corp. C. § 7232. Applicability Of § 7231 To Selection Of Directors.

(a) Section 7231 governs the duties of directors as to any acts or omissions in connection with the election, selection, or nomination of directors.

(b) This section shall not be construed to limit the generality of Section 7231.

Corp. C. § 7233. Transactions Involving Director.

(a) No contract or other transaction between a corporation and one or more of its directors, or between a corporation and any domestic or foreign corporation, firm or association in which one or more of its directors has a material financial interest, is either void or voidable because such director or directors or such other corporation, business corporation, firm or association are parties or because such director or directors are present at the meeting of the board or a committee thereof which authorizes, approves or ratifies the contract or transaction, if:

(1) The material facts as to the transaction and as to such director's interest are fully disclosed or known to the members and such contract or transaction is approved by the members (Section 5034) in good faith, with any membership owned by any interested director not being entitled to vote thereon;

(2) The material facts as to the transaction and as to such director's interest are fully disclosed or known to the board or committee, and the board or committee authorizes, approves or ratifies the contract or transaction in good faith by a vote sufficient without counting the vote of the interested director or directors and the contract or transaction is just and reasonable as to the corporation at the time it is authorized, approved or ratified; or

(3) As to contracts or transactions not approved as provided in paragraph (1) or (2) of this subdivision, the person asserting the validity of the contract or transaction sustains the burden of proving that the contract or transaction was just and reasonable as to the corporation at the time it was authorized, approved or ratified.

A mere common directorship does not constitute a material financial interest within the meaning of this subdivision. A director is not interested within the meaning of this subdivision in a resolution fixing the compensation of another director as a director, officer or employee of the corporation, notwithstanding the fact that the first director is also receiving compensation from the corporation.

(b) No contract or other transaction between a corporation and any corporation, business corporation or association of which one or more of its directors are directors is either void or voidable because such director or directors are present at the meeting of the board or a committee thereof which authorizes, approves or ratifies the contract or transaction, if:

(1) The material facts as to the transaction and as to such director's other directorship are fully disclosed or known to the board or committee, and the board or committee authorizes, approves or ratifies the contract or transaction in good faith by a vote sufficient without counting the vote of the common director or directors or the contract or transaction is approved by the members (Section 5034) in good faith; or

(2) As to contracts or transactions not approved as provided in paragraph (1) of this subdivision, the contract or transaction is just and reasonable as to the corporation at the time it is authorized, approved or ratified.

This subdivision does not apply to contracts or transactions covered by subdivision (a).

Corp. C. § 7234. Quorum For Purposes Of § 7233.

Interested or common directors may be counted in determining the presence of a quorum at a meeting of the board or a committee thereof which authorizes, approves or ratifies a contract or transaction as provided in Section 7233.

Corp. C. § 7235. Corporate Loans, Guarantees, And Advances.

(a) Unless prohibited by the articles or bylaws, a corporation may loan money or property to, or guarantee the obligation of, any director or officer of the corporation or of its parent, affiliate or subsidiary, provided:

(1) The board determines the loan or guaranty may reasonably be expected to benefit the corporation.

(2) Prior to consummating the transaction or any part thereof, the loan or guaranty is either:

(A) Approved by the members (Section 5034), without counting the vote of the director or officer, if a member, or

(B) Approved by the vote of a majority of the directors then in office, without counting the vote of the director who is to receive the loan or the benefit of the guaranty.

(b) Notwithstanding subdivision (a), a corporation may advance money to a director or officer of the corporation or of its parent, affiliate or subsidiary, for any expenses reasonably anticipated to be incurred in the performance of the duties of the director or officer of the corporation or of its parent, affiliate or subsidiary, provided that in the absence of such an advance the director or officer would be entitled to be reimbursed for these expenses by the corporation, its parent, affiliate or subsidiary.

(c) The provisions of subdivisions (a) and (b) do not apply to credit unions, or to the payment of premiums in whole or in part by a corporation on a life insurance policy on the life of a director or officer, so long as repayment to the corporation of the amount paid by it is secured by the proceeds of the policy and its cash surrender value, or to loans permitted under any statute regulating any special class of corporations.

Corp. C. § 7236. Directors' Liability For Distributions, Loans And Guaranties.

(a) Subject to the provisions of Section 7231, directors of a corporation who approve any of the following corporate actions shall be jointly and severally liable to the corporation for the benefit of all of the creditors entitled to institute an action under paragraph (1) or (2) of subdivision (c) or to the corporation in an action by the head organization or members under paragraph (1) or (3) of subdivision (c):

(1) The making of any distribution contrary to Chapter 4 (commencing with Section 7410).

(2) The distribution of assets after institution of dissolution proceedings of the corporation, without paying or adequately providing for all known liabilities of the corporation, excluding any claims not filed by creditors within the time limit set by the court in a notice given to creditors under Chapter 15 (commencing with Section 8510), 16 (commencing with Section 8610), and 17 (commencing with Section 8710).

(3) The making of any loan or guaranty contrary to Section 7235.

(b) A director who is present at a meeting of the board, or any committee thereof, at which action specified in subdivision (a) is taken and who abstains from voting shall be considered to have approved the action.

(c) Suit may be brought in the name of the corporation to enforce the liability:

(1) Under paragraph (1) of subdivision (a) against any or all directors liable by the persons entitled to sue under subdivision (c) of Section 7420.

(2) Under paragraph (2) or (3) of subdivision (a) against any or all directors liable by any one or more creditors of the corporation whose debts or claims arose prior to the time of the corporate action who have not consented to the corporate action, whether or not they have reduced their claims to judgment.

(3) Under paragraph (3) of subdivision (a) against any or all directors liable by any one or more members at the time of any corporate action specified in paragraph (3) of subdivision (a) who have not consented to the corporate action, without regard to the provisions of Section 7710.

(d) The damages recoverable from a director under this section shall be the amount of the illegal distribution, or the loss suffered by the corporation as a result of the illegal loan or guaranty, but not exceeding, in the case of an action for the benefit of creditors, the liabilities of the corporation owed to nonconsenting creditors at the time of the violation.

(e) Any director sued under this section may implead all other directors liable and may compel contribution, either in that action or in an independent action against directors not joined in that action.

(f) Directors liable under this section shall also be entitled to be subrogated to the rights of the corporation:

> (1) With respect to paragraph (1) of subdivision (a), against the persons who received the distribution.
>
> (2) With respect to paragraph (2) of subdivision (a), against the persons who received the distribution.
>
> (3) With respect to paragraph (3) of subdivision (a), against the person who received the loan or guaranty.

Any director sued under this section may file a cross-complaint against the person or persons who are liable to the director as a result of the subrogation provided for in this subdivision or may proceed against them in an independent action.

Corp. C. § 7237. Indemnification Of Corporate "Agent".

(a) For the purposes of this section, "agent" means any person who is or was a director, officer, employee or other agent of the corporation, or is or was serving at the request of the corporation as a director, officer, employee or agent of another foreign or domestic corporation, partnership, joint venture, trust or other enterprise, or was a director, officer, employee or agent of a foreign or domestic corporation which was a predecessor corporation of the corporation or of another enterprise at the request of such predecessor corporation; "proceeding" means any threatened, pending or completed action or proceeding, whether civil, criminal, administrative or investigative; and "expenses" includes without limitation attorneys' fees and any expenses of establishing a right to indemnification under subdivision (d) or paragraph (3) of subdivision (e).

(b) A corporation shall have power to indemnify any person who was or is a party or is threatened to be made a party to any proceeding (other than an action by or in the right of the corporation to procure a judgment in its favor, an action brought under Section 5233 of Part 2 (commencing with Section 5110) made applicable pursuant to Section 7238, or an action brought by the Attorney General or a person granted relator status by the Attorney General for any breach of duty relating to assets held in charitable trust) by reason of the fact that such person is or was an agent of the corporation, against expenses, judgments, fines, settlements and other amounts actually and reasonably incurred in connection with such proceeding if such person acted in good faith and in a manner such person reasonably believed to be in the best interests of the corporation and, in the case of a criminal proceeding, had no reasonable cause to believe the conduct of such person was unlawful. The termination of any proceeding by judgment, order, settlement, conviction or upon a plea of *nolo contendere* or its equivalent shall not, of itself, create a presumption that the person did not act in good faith and in a manner which the person reasonably believed to be in the best interests of the corporation or that the person had reasonable cause to believe that the person's conduct was unlawful.

(c) A corporation shall have power to indemnify any person who was or is a party or is threatened to be made a party to any threatened, pending or completed action by or in the right of the corporation, or brought under Section 5233 of Part 2 (commencing with Section 5110) made applicable pursuant to Section 7238, or brought by the Attorney General or a person granted relator status by the Attorney General for breach of duty relating to assets held in charitable trust, to procure a judgment in its favor by reason of the fact that such person is or was an agent of the corporation, against expenses actually and reasonably incurred by such person in connection with the defense or settlement of such action if such person acted in good faith, in a manner such person believed to be in the best interests of the corporation and with such care, including reasonable inquiry, as an ordinarily prudent person in a like position would use under similar circumstances. No indemnification shall be made under this subdivision:

(1) In respect of any claim, issue or matter as to which such person shall have been adjudged to be liable to the corporation in the performance of such person's duty to the corporation, unless and only to the extent that the court in which such proceeding is or was pending shall determine upon application that, in view of all the circumstances of the case, such person is fairly and reasonably entitled to indemnity for the expenses which such court shall determine;

(2) Of amounts paid in settling or otherwise disposing of a threatened or pending action, with or without court approval; or

(3) Of expenses incurred in defending a threatened or pending action which is settled or otherwise disposed of without court approval unless such action concerns assets held in charitable trust and is settled with the approval of the Attorney General.

(d) To the extent that an agent of a corporation has been successful on the merits in defense of any proceeding referred to in subdivision (b) or (c) or in defense of any claim, issue or matter therein, the agent shall be indemnified against expenses actually and reasonably incurred by the agent in connection therewith.

(e) Except as provided in subdivision (d), any indemnification under this section shall be made by the corporation only if authorized in the specific case, upon a determination that indemnification of the agent is proper in the circumstances because the agent has met the applicable standard of conduct set forth in subdivision (b) or (c) by:

(1) A majority vote of a quorum consisting of directors who are not parties to such proceeding;

(2) Approval of the members (Section 5034), with the persons to be indemnified not being entitled to vote thereon; or

(3) The court in which such proceeding is or was pending upon application made by the corporation or the agent or the attorney or other person rendering services in connection with the defense, whether or not such application by the agent, attorney or other person is opposed by the corporation.

(f) Expenses incurred in defending any proceeding may be advanced by the corporation prior to the final disposition of such proceeding upon receipt of an undertaking by or on behalf of the agent to repay such amount unless it shall be determined ultimately that the agent is entitled to be indemnified as authorized in this section.

(g) No provision made by a corporation to indemnity its or its subsidiary's directors or officers for the defense of any proceeding, whether contained in the articles, bylaws, a resolution of members or directors, an agreement or otherwise, shall be valid unless consistent with this section. Nothing contained in this section shall affect any right to indemnification to which persons other than such directors and officers may be entitled by contract or otherwise.

(h) No indemnification or advance shall be made under this section, except as provided in subdivision (d) or paragraph (3) of subdivision (e), in any circumstance where it appears:

(1) That it would be inconsistent with a provision of the articles, bylaws, a resolution of the members or an agreement in effect at the time of the accrual of the alleged cause of action asserted in the proceeding in which the expenses were incurred or other amounts were paid, which prohibits or otherwise limits indemnification; or

(2) That it would be inconsistent with any condition expressly imposed by a court in approving a settlement.

(i) A corporation shall have power to purchase and maintain insurance on behalf of any agent of the corporation against any liability asserted against or incurred by the agent in such capacity or arising out of the agent's status as such whether or not the corporation would have the power to indemnify the agent against such liability under the provisions of this section.

(j) This section does not apply to any proceeding against any trustee, investment manager or other fiduciary of an employee benefit plan in such person's capacity as such, even though such person may also be an agent as defined in subdivision (a) of the employer corporation. A corporation shall have power to indemnify such trustee, investment manager or other fiduciary to the extent permitted by subdivision (f) of Section 207.

Corp. C. § 7238. Law Governing Assets In Charitable Trust.

Where a corporation holds assets in charitable trust, the conduct of its directors or of any person performing functions similar to those performed by a director, shall, in respect to the assets held in charitable trust, be governed by the standards of conduct set forth in Article 3 (commencing with Section 5230) of Chapter 2 of Part 2 for directors of nonprofit public benefit corporations. This does not limit any additional requirements which may be specifically set forth in this part regarding corporations holding assets in charitable trust.

CHAPTER 13

MEMBERSHIP: ISSUANCE, TERMINATION & NOTICES TO

(Corporations Code §§ 7312, 7341 & 5016)

Corp. C. § 7312. Multiple And Fractional Memberships.

No person may hold more than one membership, and no fractional memberships may be held, provided, however, that:

(a) Two or more persons may have an indivisible interest in a single membership when authorized by, and in such manner or under the circumstances prescribed by, the articles or bylaws subject to Section 7612.

(b) If the articles or bylaws provide for classes of membership and if the articles or bylaws permit a person to be a member of more than one class, a person may hold a membership in one or more classes.

(c) Any branch, division, or office of any person, which is not formed primarily to be a member, may hold a separate membership.

(d) In the case of membership in an owners association, (as defined in Section 11003.1 of the Business and Professions Code, and created in connection with any of the forms of development referred to in Section 11004.5 of the Business and Professions Code) the articles or bylaws may permit a person who owns an interest, or who has a right of exclusive occupancy, in more than one lot, parcel, area, apartment, or unit to hold a separate membership in the owners association for each such lot, parcel, area, apartment, or unit.

(e) In the case of membership in a mutual water company, as defined in Section 330.24 of the Civil Code, the articles or bylaws may permit a person entitled to membership by reason of the ownership, lease, or right of occupancy of more than one lot, parcel, or other service unit to hold a separate membership in the mutual water company for each such lot, parcel, or other service unit.

Corp. C. § 7341. Expulsion, Suspension or Termination; Fairness And Reasonableness; Procedure.

(a) No member may be expelled or suspended, and no membership or memberships may be terminated or suspended, except according to procedures satisfying the requirements of this section. An expulsion, termination or suspension not in accord with this section shall be void and without effect.

(b) Any expulsion, suspension, or termination must be done in good faith and in a fair and reasonable manner. Any procedure which conforms to the requirements of subdivision (c) is fair and reasonable, but a court may also find other procedures to be fair and reasonable when the full circumstances of the suspension, termination, or expulsion are considered.

(c) A prodecure is fair and reasonable when:

(1) The provisions of the procedure have been set forth in the articles or bylaws, or copies of such provisions are sent annually to all the members as required by the articles or bylaws;

(2) It provides the giving of 15 days' prior notice of the expulsion, suspension or termination and the reasons therefor;

(3) It provides an opportunity for the member to be heard, orally or in writing, not less than five days before the effective date of the expulsion, suspension or termination by a person or body authorized to decide that the proposed expulsion, termination or suspension not take place.

(d) Any notice required under this section may be given by any method reasonably calculated to provide actual notice. Any notice given by mail must be given by first-class or registered mail sent to the last address of the members shown on the corporation's records.

(e) Any action challenging an expulsion, suspension or termination of membership, including any claim alleging defective notice, must be commenced within one year after the date of the expulsion, suspension or termination. In the event such an action is successful the court may order any relief, including reinstatement, it finds equitable under the circumstances, but no vote of the members or of the board may be set aside solely because a person was at the time of the vote wrongfully excluded by virtue of the challenged expulsion, suspension or termination, unless the court finds further that the wrongful expulsion, suspension or termination was in bad faith and for the purpose, and with the effect, of wrongfully excluding the member from the vote or from the meeting at which the vote took place, so as to affect the outcome of the vote.

(f) This section governs only the procedures for expulsion, suspension or termination based upon substantive grounds which violate contractual or other rights of the member or are otherwise unlawful is not made valid by compliance with this section.

Corp. C. § 5016. Notices or Reports Mailed or Delivered as Part of Newsletter or Magazine.

A notice or report mailed or delivered as part of a newsletter, magazine or other organ regularly sent to members shall constitute written notice or report pursuant to this division when addressed and mailed or delivered to the member, or in the case of members who are residents of the same household and who have the same address on the books of the corporation, when addressed and mailed or delivered to one of such members, at the address appearing on the books of the corporation.

CHAPTER 14

MEETINGS AND VOTING

(Corporations Code §§ 7510-7516)

Corp. C. § 7510. Place, Date, And Time; Failure To Hold Meetings; Quorum; Special Meetings.

(a) Meetings of members may be held at a place within or without the state that is stated in or fixed in accordance with the bylaws. If no other place is so stated or fixed, meetings of members shall be held at the principal office of the corporation.

(b) A regular meeting of members shall be held on a date and time, and with the frequency stated in or fixed in accordance with the bylaws, but in any event in each year in which directors are to be elected at that meeting for the purpose of conducting such election, and to transact any other proper business which may be brought before the meeting.

(c) If a corporation with members is required by subdivision (b) to hold a regular meeting and fails to hold the regular meeting for a period of 60 days after the date designated therefor or, if no date has been designated, for a period of 15 months after the formation of the corporation or after its last regular meeting, or if the corporation fails to hold a written ballot for a period of 60 days after the date designated therefor, then the superior court of the proper county may summarily order the meeting to be held or the ballot to be conducted upon the application of a member, after notice to the corporation giving it an opportunity to be heard.

(d) The votes represented, either in person or by proxy, at a meeting called or by written ballot ordered pursuant to the subdivision (c) and entitled to be cast on the business to be transacted shall constitute a quorum, notwithstanding any provision of the articles or bylaws or in this part to the contrary. The court may issue such orders as may be appropriate including, without limitation, orders designating the time and place of the meeting, the record date for determination of members entitled to vote, and the form of notice of the meeting.

(e) Special meetings of members for any lawful purpose may be called by the board, the chairman of the board, the president, or such other persons, if any, as are specified in the bylaws. In addition, special meetings of members for any lawful purpose may be called by 5 percent or more of the members.

Corp. C. § 7511. Notice To Members; Waiver.

(a) Whenever members are required or permitted to take any action at a meeting, a written notice of the meeting shall be given not less than 10 nor more than 90 days before the date of the meeting to each member who, on the record date for notice of the meeting, is entitled to vote there at; provided, however, that if notice is given by mail, and the notice is not mailed by first-class, registered, or certified mail, that notice shall be given not less than 20 days before the meeting. Subject to subdivision (f), and subdivision (b) of Section 7512, the notice shall state the place, date and time of the meeting and (1) in the case of a special meeting, the general nature of the business to be transacted, and no other business may be transacted, or (2) in the case of the regular meeting, those matters which the board, at the time the notice is given, intends to present for action by the members, but, except as provided in subdivision (b) of Section 7512, any proper matter may be presented at the meeting for the action. The notice of any meeting at which directors are to be elected shall include the names of all those who are nominees at the time the notice is given to members.

(b) Notice of a members' meeting or any report shall be given either personally or by mail or other means of written communication, addressed to a member at the address of the member appearing on the books of the corporation or given by the member to the corporation for purpose of notice; or if no such address appears or is given, at the place where the principal office of the corporation is located or by publication at least once in a newspaper of general circulation in the county in which the principal office is located. An affidavit of giving of any notice or report in accordance with the provisions of this part, executed by the secretary, assistant secretary or any transfer agent, shall be *prima facie* evidence of the giving of the notice or report.

If any notice or report addressed to the member at the address of the member appearing on the books of the corporation is returned to the corporation by the United States Postal Service marked to indicate that the United States Postal Service is unable to deliver the notice or report to the member at the address, all future notices or reports shall be deemed to have been duly given without further mailing if the same shall be available for the member upon written demand of the member at the principal office of the corporation for a period of one year from the date of the giving of the notice or report to all other members.

(c) Upon request in writing to the chairman of the board, president, vice president, or secretary by any person (other than the board) entitled to call a special meeting of members, the officer forthwith shall cause notice to be given to the members entitled to vote that a meeting will be held at a time fixed by the board not less than 35 nor more than 90 days after the receipt of the request. If the notice is not given within 20 days after receipt of the request, the persons entitled to call the meeting may give the notice or the superior court of the proper county shall summarily order the giving of the notice, after notice to the corporation giving it an opportunity to be heard. The court may issue such orders as may be appropriate, including, without limitation, orders designating the time and place of the meeting, the record date for determination of members entitled to vote, and the form of notice.

(d) When a members' meeting is adjourned to another time or place, unless the bylaws otherwise require and except as provided in this subdivision, notice need not be given of the adjourned meeting if the time and place thereof are announced at the meeting at which the adjournment is taken. No meeting may be adjourned for more than 45 days. At the adjourned meeting the corporation may transact any business which might have been transacted at the original meeting. If after the adjournment a new record date is fixed for notice or voting, a notice of the adjourned meeting shall be given to each member who, on the record date for notice of the meeting, is entitled to vote at the meeting.

(e) The transactions of any meeting of members however called and noticed, and wherever held, are as valid as though had at a meeting duly held after regular call and notice, if a quorum is present either in person or by proxy, and if, either before or after the meeting, each of the persons entitled to vote, not present in person or by proxy, signs a written waiver of notice or a consent to the holding of the meeting or an approval of the minutes thereof. All such waivers, consents and approvals shall be filed with the corporate records or made a part of the minutes of the meeting. Attendance of a person at a meeting shall constitute a waiver of notice of and presence at the meeting, except when the person objects, at the beginning of the meeting, to the transaction of any business because the meeting is not lawfully called or convened and except that attendance at a meeting is not a waiver of any right to object to the consideration of matters required by this part to be included in the notice but not so included, if the objection is expressly made at the meeting. Neither the business to be transacted at nor the purpose of any regular or special meeting of members need be specified in any written waiver of notice, consent to the holding of the meeting or approval of the minutes thereof, unless otherwise provided in the articles or bylaws, except as provided in subdivision (f).

(f) Any approval of the members required under Sections 7222, 7224, 7233, 7812, 8610, or 8719, other than unanimous approval by those entitled to vote, shall be valid only if the general nature of the proposal so approved was stated in the notice of meeting or in any written waiver of notice.

(g) A court may find that notice not given in conformity with this section is still valid, if it was given in a fair and reasonable manner.

Corp. C. § 7512. Quorum.

(a) A majority of the voting power, represented in person or by proxy, shall constitute a quorum at a meeting of members, but, subject to subdivisions (b) and (c), a bylaw may set a different quorum. Any bylaw amendment to increase the quorum may be adopted only by approval of the members (Section 5034). If a quorum is present, the affirmative vote of the majority of the voting power represented at the meeting, entitled to vote, and voting on any matter shall be the act of the members unless the vote of a greater number or voting by classes is required by this part or the articles or bylaws.

(b) Where a bylaw authorizes a corporation to conduct a meeting with a quorum of less than one-third of the voting power, then the only matters that may be voted upon at any regular meeting actually attended, in person or by proxy, by less than one-third of the voting power are matters notice of the general nature of which was be given, pursuant to the first sentence of subdivision (a) of Section 7511.

(c) Subject to subdivision (b), the members present at a duly called or held meeting at which a quorum is present may continue to transact business until adjournment notwithstanding the withdrawal of enough members to leave less than a quorum, if any action taken (other than adjournment) is approved by at least a majority of the members required to constitute a quorum.

(d) In the absence of a quorum, any meeting of members may be adjourned from time to time by the vote of a majority of the votes represented either in person or by proxy, but no other business may be transacted except as provided in subdivision (c).

Corp. C. § 7513. Acts Without Meeting; Written Ballot.

(a) Subject to subdivision (e), and unless prohibited in the articles or bylaws, any action which may be taken at any regular or special meeting of members may be taken without a meeting if the corporation distributes a written ballot to every member entitled to vote on the matter. Such ballot shall set forth the proposed action, provide an opportunity to specify approval or disapproval of any proposal, and provide a reasonable time within which to return the ballot to the corporation.

(b) Approval by written ballot pursuant to this section shall be valid only when the number of votes cast by ballot within the time period specified equals or exceeds the quorum required to be present at a meeting authorizing the action, and the number of approvals equals or exceeds the number of votes that would be required to approve at a meeting at which the total number of votes cast was the same as the number of votes cast by ballot.

(c) Ballots shall be solicited in a manner consistent with the requirements of subdivision (b) of Section 7511 and Section 7514. All such solicitations shall indicate the numbery of responses needed to meet the quorum requirement and, with respect to ballots other than for the election of directors, shall state the percentage of approvals necessary to pass the measure submitted. The solicitation must specify the time by which the ballot must be received in order to be counted.

(d) Unless otherwise provided in the articles or bylaws, a written ballot may not be revoked.

(e) Directors may be elected by written ballot under this section, where authorized by the articles or bylaws, except that election by written ballot may not be authorized where the directors are elected by cumulative voting pursuant to Section 7615.

(f) When directors are to be elected by written ballot and the articles or bylaws prescribe a nomination procedure, the procedure may provide for a date for the close of nominations prior to the printing and distributing of the written ballots.

Corp. C. § 7514. Voting By Proxy Or Written Ballot.

(a) Any form of proxy or written ballot distributed to 10 or more members of a corporation with 100 or more members shall afford an opportunity on the proxy or form of written ballot to specify a choice between approval and disapproval of each matter or group of related matters intended, at the time the written ballot or proxy is distributed, to be acted upon at the meeting for which the proxy is solicited or by such written ballot, and shall provide, subject to reasonable specified conditions, that where the person solicited specifies a choice with respect to any such matter the vote shall be cast in accordance therewith.

(b) In any election of directors, any form of proxy or written ballot in which the directors to be voted upon are named therein as candidates and which is marked by a member "withhold" or otherwise marked in a manner indicating that the authority to vote for the election of directors is withheld shall not be voted either for or against the election of a director.

(c) Failure to comply with this section shall not invalidate any corporate action taken, but may be the basis for challenging any proxy at a meeting or written ballot and the superior court may compel compliance therewith at the suit of any member.

Corp. C. § 7515. Court Order For Meeting Or A Written Ballot.

(a) If for any reason it is impractical or unduly difficult for any corporation to call or conduct a meeting of its members, delegates or directors, or otherwise obtain their consent, in the manner prescribed by its articles or bylaws, or this part, then the superior court of the proper county, upon petition of a director, officer, delegate or member, may order that such a meeting be called or that a written ballot or other form of obtaining the vote of members, delegates or directors be authorized, in such a manner as the court finds fair and equitable under the circumstances.

(b) The court shall, in an order issued pursuant to this section, provide for a method of notice reasonably designed to give actual notice to all parties who would be entitled to notice of a meeting held pursuant to the articles, bylaws and this part, whether or not the method results in actual notice to every such person, or conforms to the notice requirements that would otherwise apply. In a proceeding under this section the court may determine who the members or directors are.

(c) The order issued pursuant to this section may dispense with any requirement relating to the holding of and voting at meetings or obtaining of votes, including any requirement as to quorums or as to the number or percentage of votes needed for approval, that would otherwise be imposed by the articles, bylaws, or this part.

(d) Wherever practical any order issued pursuant to this section shall limit the subject matter of the meetings or other forms of consent authorized to items, including amendments to the articles or bylaws, the resolution of which will or may enable the corporation to continue managing its affairs without further resort to this section; provided, however, that an order under this section may also authorize the obtaining of whatever votes and approvals are necessary for the dissolution, merger, sale of assets or reorganization of the corporation.

(e) Any meeting or other method of obtaining the vote of members, delegates or directors conducted pursuant to an order issued under this section, and which complies with all the provisions of such order, is for all purposes a valid meeting or vote, as the case may be, and shall have the same force and effect as if it complied with every requirement imposed by the articles, bylaws, and this part.

Corp. C. § 7516. Written Consent Of Members.

Any action required or permitted to be taken by the members may be taken without a meeting, if all members shall individually or collectively consent in writing to the action. The written consent or consents shall be filed with the minutes of the proceedings of the members. The action by written consent shall have the same force and effect as the unanimous vote of the members.

CHAPTER 15

ADDITIONAL PROVISIONS RELATING TO ELECTION OF DIRECTORS

(Corporations Code §§ 7520-7527)

Corp. C. § 7520. Election Of Directors By Members; Procedure.

As to directors elected by members, there shall be available to the members reasonable nomination and election procedures given the nature, size and operations of the corporation. The procedures shall include:

(a) A reasonable means of nominating persons for election as directors.

(b) A reasonable opportunity for a nominee to communicate to the members the nominee's qualifications and the reasons for the nominee's candidacy.

(c) A reasonable opportunity for all nominees to solicit votes.

(d) A reasonable opportunity for all members to choose among the nominees.

(e) Subject to the provisions of subdivisions (a), (b), and (d) of Section 7616, the superior court of the proper county shall enforce the provisions of this section.

Corp. C. § 7521. Nomination.

Except for directors who are elected as authorized by Section 7152 or 7153, and except as provided in Section 7522, any person who is qualified to be elected to the board of directors of a corporation with 500 or more members may be nominated:

(a) By any method authorized by the bylaws, or if no method is set forth in the bylaws by any method authorized by the board;

(b) By petition delivered to an officer of the corporation, signed within 11 months preceding the next time directors will be elected, by members representing the following number of votes:

Number of Votes Eligible to be Cast for Director Disregarding Any Provision For Cumulative Voting	Number of Votes
Under 5,000	2% of voting power
5,000 or more	1/20 of 1% of voting power, but not less than 100.

This subdivision does not apply to a corporation described in subdivision (c).

(c) In corporations with one million or more members engaged primarily in the business of retail merchandising of consumer goods, by petition delivered to an officer of the corporation, signed within 11 months preceding the next time directors will be elected, by such reasonable number of members as is set forth in the bylaws, or if no number is set forth in the bylaws, by such reasonable number of members as is determined by the directors.

(d) If there is a meeting to elect directors, by any member present at the meeting in person or by proxy if proxies are permitted.

Corp. C. § 7522. Close Of Nominations; When Election Not Required.

(a) The provisions of this section shall apply to any election of a director or directors by members of a corporation with 5,000 or more members except for an election authorized by Section 7152 or 7153.

(b) The corporation's articles or bylaws shall set a date for the close of nominations for the board. The date shall not be less than 50 nor more than 120 days before the day directors are to be elected. No nominations for the board can be made after the date set for the close of nominations.

(c) If more people are nominated for the board than can be elected, the election shall take place by means of a procedure which allows all nominees a reasonable opportunity to solicit votes and all members a reasonable opportunity to choose among the nominees.

(d) If after the close of nominations the number of people nominated for the board is not more than the number of directors to be elected, the corporation may without further action declare that those nominated and qualified to be elected have been elected.

Corp. C. § 7523. Publication Of Material Soliciting Votes; Nominees Rights.

Where a corporation with 500 or more members publishes any material soliciting a vote for any nominee for director in any publication owned or controlled by the corporation, it shall make available to all other nominees, in the same issue of the publication, an equal amount of space, with equal prominence, to be used by the nominee for a purpose reasonably related to the election.

Corp. C. § 7524. Request To Corporation To Mail Election Material.

Upon written request by any nominee for election to the board and the payment of the reasonable costs of mailing (including postage), a corporation shall within 10 business days after such request (provided payment has been made) mail to all members, or such portion of them as the nominee may reasonably specify, any material, which the nominee may furnish and which is reasonably related to the election, unless the corporation within five business days after the request allows the nominee, at the corporation's option, the rights set forth in either paragraph (1) or (2) of subdivision (a) of Section 8330.

Corp. C. § 7525. Refusal To Publish Or Mail Material; Liability For Contents.

(a) Except as provided in subdivision (c), no corporation may decline to publish or mail material, otherwise required to be published or mailed on behalf of any nominee under this article, on the basis of the content of such material.

(b) Neither the corporation, nor its agents, officers, directors, or employees, may be held criminally liable, liable for any negligence (active or passive) or otherwise liable for damages to any person on account of any material which is supplied by a nominee for director and which it mails or publishes pursuant to Section 7523 or 7524 but the nominee on whose behalf such material was published or mailed shall be liable and shall indemnify and hold the corporation, its agents, officers, directors, and employees and each of them harmless from all demands, costs, including reasonable legal fees and expenses, claims, damages and causes of action arising out of such material or any such mailing or publication.

(c) Nothing in this section shall prevent a corporation or any of its agents, officers, directors, or employees from seeking a court order relieving the corporation from its obligation under Sections 7523 and 7524 on the ground the material will expose the moving party to liability.

Corp. C. § 7526. Use Of Corporate Funds To Support Nominee.

Without authorization of the board, no corporation funds may be expended to support a nominee for director after there are more people nominated for director than can be elected.

Corp. C. § 7527. Time To Contest Election, Appointment, Or Removal Of Director; Defect In Notice.

An action challenging the validity of any election, appointment or removal of a director or directors must be commenced within nine months after the election, appointment or removal. If no such action is commenced, in the absence of fraud, any election, appointment or removal of a director is conclusively presumed valid nine months thereafter.

CHAPTER 16

VOTING OF MEMBERSHIPS
(Corporations Code §§ 7610-7616)

Corp. C. § 7610. One Vote Per Member; Exceptions.

Except as provided in a corporation's articles or bylaws or Section 7615, each member shall be entitled to one vote on each matter submitted to a vote of the members. Single memberships in which two or more persons have an indivisible interest shall be voted as provided in Section 7612.

Corp. C. § 7611. Record Date; Determining Member Eligible To Vote.

(a) The bylaws may provide or, in the absence of such provision, the board may fix, in advance, a date as the record date for the purpose of determining the members entitled to notice of any meeting of members. Such record date shall not be more than 90 nor less than 10 days before the date of the meeting. If no record date is fixed, members at the close of business on the business day preceding the day on which notice is given or, if notice is waived, at the close of business on the business day preceding the day on which the meeting is held are entitled to notice of a meeting of members. A determination of members entitled to notice of a meeting of members shall apply to any adjournment of the meeting unless the board fixes a new record date for the adjourned meeting.

(b) The bylaws may provide or, in the absence of such provision, the board may fix, in advance, a date as the record date for the purpose of determining the members entitled to vote at a meeting of members. Such record date shall not be more than 60 days before the date of the meeting. Such record date shall also apply in the case of an adjournment of the meeting unless the board fixes a new record date for the adjourned meeting. If no record date is fixed, members on the day of the meeting who are otherwise eligible to vote are entitled to vote at the meeting of members or, in the case of an adjourned meeting, members on the day of the adjourned meeting who are otherwise eligible to vote are entitled to vote at the adjourned meeting of members.

(c) The bylaws may provide or, in the absence of such provision, the board may fix, in advance, a date as the record date for the purpose of determining the members entitled to cast written ballots (Section 7513). Such record date shall not be more than 60 days before the day on which the first written ballot is mailed or solicited. If no record date is fixed, members on the day the first written ballot is mailed or solicited who are otherwise eligible to vote are entitled to cast written ballots.

(d) The bylaws may provide or, in the absence of such provision, the board may fix, in advance, a date as the record date for the purpose of determining the members entitled to exercise any rights in respect of any other lawful action. Such record date shall not be more than 60 days prior to such other action. If no record date is fixed, members at the close of business on the day on which the board adopts the resolution relating thereto, or the 60th day prior to the date of such other action, whichever is later, are entitled to exercise such rights.

Corp. C. § 7612. Memberships In Two Or More Names.

If a membership stands of record in the names of two or more persons, whether fiduciaries, members of a partnership, joint tenants, tenants in common, husband and wife as community property, tenants by the entirety, persons entitled to vote under a voting agreement or otherwise, or if two or more persons (including proxyholders) have the same fiduciary relationship respecting the same membership, unless the secretary of the corporation is given written notice to the contrary and is furnished with a copy of the instrument or order appointing them or creating the relationship wherein it is so provided, their acts with respect to voting shall have the following effect:

(a) If only one votes, such act binds all; or

(b) If more than one vote, the act of the majority so voting binds all.

Corp. C. § 7613. Proxies.

(a) Any member may authorize another person or persons to act by proxy with respect to such membership except that this right may be limited or withdrawn by the articles or bylaws, subject to subdivision (f). Any proxy purported to be executed in accordance with the provisions of this part shall be presumptively valid.

(b) No proxy shall be valid after the expiration of 11 months from the date thereof unless otherwise provided in the proxy, except that the maximum term of any proxy shall be three years from the date of execution. Every proxy continues in full force and effect until revoked by the person executing it prior to the vote pursuant thereto, except as otherwise provided in this section. Such revocation may be effected by a writing delivered to the corporation stating that the proxy is revoked or by a subsequent proxy executed by the person executing the prior proxy and presented to the meeting, or as to any meeting by attendance at such meeting and voting in person by the person executing the proxy. The dates contained on the forms of proxy presumptively determine the order of execution, regardless of the postmark dates on the envelopes in which they are mailed.

(c) A proxy is not revoked by the death or incapacity of the maker or the termination of a membership as a result thereof unless, before the vote is counted, written notice of such death or incapacity is received by the corporation.

(d) Unless otherwise provided in the articles or bylaws, the proxy of a member which states that it is irrevocable for the period specified therein (notwithstanding subdivisions (b) and (c)) when it is held by any of the following or a nominee of any of the following:

(1) A person who has purchased or who has agreed to purchase the membership;

(2) A creditor or creditors of the corporation or the member who extended or continued credit to the corporation or the member in consideration of the proxy if the proxy states that it was given in consideration of such extension or continuation of credit and the name of the person extending or continuing the credit; or

(3) A person who has contracted to perform services as an employee of the corporation, if the proxy is required by the contract of employment and if the proxy states that it was given in consideration of such contract of employment, the name of the employee and the period of employment contracted for.

Notwithstanding the period of irrevocability specified, the proxy becomes revocable when the agreement to purchase is terminated; the debt of the corporation or the member is paid; or the period of employment provided for in the contract of employment has terminated. In addition to the foregoing paragraphs (1) through (3), a proxy of a member may be made irrevocable (notwithstanding subdivision (c)) if it is given to secure the performance of a duty or to protect a title, either legal or equitable, until the happening of events which, by its terms, discharge the obligations secured by it.

(e) A proxy may be revoked, notwithstanding a provision making it irrevocable by a transferee of a membership without knowledge of the existence of the provision unless the existence of the proxy and its irrevocability appears on the certificate representing the membership.

(f) Subdivision (a) notwithstanding;

(1) No amendment of the articles or bylaws repealing, restricting, creating or expending proxy rights may be adopted without approval by the members (Section 5034); and

(2) No amendment of the articles or bylaws restricting or limiting the use of proxies may affect the validity of a previously issued irrevocable proxy during the term of its irrevocability, so long as it complied with applicable provisions, if any, of the articles or bylaws at the time of its issuance, and is otherwise valid under this section.

(g) Anything to the contrary notwithstanding, any revocable proxy covering matters requiring a vote of the members pursuant to Section 7222; Section 7224; Section 7233; paragraph (1) of subdivision (f) of this section; Section 7812; paragraph 2 of subdivision (a) of Section 7911; Section 8012; subdivision (a) of Section 8015; Section 8610; or subdivision (a) of Section 8719 is not valid as to such matters unless it sets forth the general nature of the matter to be voted on.

Corp. C. § 7614. Inspectors Of Election.

(a) In advance of any meeting of members, the board may appoint inspectors of election to act at the meeting and any adjournment thereof. If inspectors of election are not so appointed, or if any persons so appointed fail to appear or refuse to act, the chairman of any meeting of members may, and on the request of any member or a member's proxy shall, appoint inspectors of election (or persons to replace those who so fail or refuse) at the meeting. The number of inspectors shall be either one or three. If appointed at a meeting on the request of one or more members or proxies, the majority of members represented in person or by proxy shall determine whether one or three inspectors are to be appointed. In the case of any action by written ballot (Section 7513), the board may similarly appoint inspectors of election to act with powers and duties as set forth in this section.

(b) The inspectors of election shall determine the number of memberships outstanding and the voting power of each, the number represented at the meeting, the existence of a quorum, and the authenticity, validity and effect of proxies, receive votes, ballots or consents, hear and determine all challenges and questions in any way arising in connection with the right to vote, count and tabulate all votes or consents, determine when the polls shall close, determine the result and do such acts as may be proper to conduct the election or vote with fairness to all members.

(c) The inspectors of election shall perform their duties impartially, in good faith, to the best of their ability and as expeditiously as is practical. If there are three inspectors of election, the decision, act or certificate of a majority is effective in all respects as the decision, act or certificate of all. Any report or certificate made by the inspectors of election is *prima facie* evidence of the facts stated therein.

Corp. C. § 7615. Cumulative Voting; Determining Winner; When Ballots Are Required.

(a) If the articles or bylaws authorize cumulative voting, but not otherwise, every member entitled to vote at any election of directors may cumulate the member's votes and give one candidate a number of votes equal to the number of directors to be elected multiplied by the number of votes to which the member is entitled, or distribute the member's votes on the same principle among as many candidates as the member thinks fit. An article or bylaw provision authorizing cumulative voting may be repealed or amended only by approval of the members (Section 5034), except that the governing article or bylaw provision may require the vote of a greater proportion of the members, or of the members of any class, for its repeal.

(b) No member shall be entitled to cumulate votes for a candidate or candidates unless the candidate's name or candidates' names have been placed in nomination prior to the voting and the member has given notice at the meeting prior to the voting of the member's intention to cumulate votes. If any one member has given this notice, all members may cumulate their votes for candidates in nomination.

(c) In any election of directors by cumulative voting, the candidates receiving the highest number of votes are elected, subject to any lawful provision specifying election by classes.

(d) In any election of directors not governed by subdivision (c), unless otherwise provided in the articles or bylaws, the candidates receiving the highest number of votes are elected.

(e) Elections for directors need not be by ballot unless a member demands election by ballot at the meeting and before the voting begins or unless the bylaws so require.

Corp. C. § 7616. Action To Determine Validity Of Election Or Appointment Of Director; Notice To Attorney General.

(a) Upon the filing of an action therefor by any director or member or by any person who had the right to vote in the election at issue, the superior court of the proper county shall determine the validity of any election or appointment of any director of any corporation.

(b) In the case of a corporation holding assets in charitable trust, any person bringing an action under this section shall give notice of the action to the Attorney General, who may intervene.

(c) Upon the filing of the complaint, and before any further proceedings are had, the court shall enter an order fixing a date for the hearing, which shall be within five days unless for good cause shown a later date is fixed, and requiring notice of the date for the hearing and a copy of the complaint to be served upon the corporation and upon the person whose purported election or appointment is questioned and upon any person (other than the plaintiff) whom the plaintiff alleges to have been elected or appointed, in the manner in which a summons is required to be served, or, if the court so directs, by registered mail; and the court may make such further requirements as to notice as appear to be proper under the circumstances.

(d) The court, consistent with the provisions of this part and in conformity with the articles and bylaws to the extent feasible, may determine the person entitled to the office of director or may order a new election to be held or appointment to be made, may determine the validity, effectiveness and construction of voting agreements and voting trusts, the validity of the issuance of memberships and the right of persons to vote and may direct such other relief as may be just and proper.

CHAPTER 17

RECORDS, REPORTS AND RIGHTS OF INSPECTION

(Corporations Code §§ 8310-8338)

Corp. C. § 8310. Records Subject To Inspection To Be Written.

If any record subject to inspection pursuant to this chapter is not maintained in written form, a request for inspection is not complied with unless and until the corporation at its expense makes such records available in written form. For the purposes of this chapter "written" or "in writing" also includes cathode ray tube and similar electronic communications methods.

Corp. C. § 8311. Inspection By Agent Or Attorney; Right To Copy.

Any inspection under this chapter may be made in person or by agent or attorney and the right of inspection includes the right to copy and make extracts.

Corp. C. § 8313. No Limitation On Inspection Rights.

The rights of members provided in this chapter may not be limited by contract or the articles or bylaws.

Corp. C. § 8320. Records Required To Be Kept; Form Of Records.

(a) Each corporation shall keep:

(1) Adequate and correct books and records of account;

(2) Minutes of the proceedings of its members, board and committees of the board; and

(3) A record of its members giving their names and addresses and the class of membership held by each.

(b) Minutes shall be kept in written form. Other books and records shall be kept either in written form or in any other form capable of being converted into written form.

Corp. C. § 8330. Demand For Member's Names, Addresses, And Voting Rights; By Member.

(a) Subject to Sections 8331 and 8332, and unless the corporation provides a reasonable alternative pursuant to subdivision (c), a member may do either or both of the following as permitted by subdivision (b):

(1) Inspect and copy the record of all the members' names, addresses and voting rights, at reasonable times, upon five business days' prior written demand upon the corporation which demand shall state the purpose for which the inspection rights are requested; or

(2) Obtain from the secretary of the corporation, upon written demand and tender of a reasonable charge, a list of the names, addresses and voting rights of those members entitled to vote for the election of directors, as of the most recent record date for which it has been compiled or as of a date specified by the member subsequent to the date of demand. The demand shall state the purpose for which the list is requested. The membership list shall be made available on or before the later of ten business days after the demand is received or after the date specified therein as the date of which the list is to be compiled.

(b) The rights set forth in subdivision (a) may be exercised by:

(1) Any member, for a purpose reasonably related to such person's interest as a member. Where the corporation reasonably believes that the information will be used for another purpose, or where it provides a reasonable alternative pursuant to subdivision (c), it may deny the member access to the list. In any subsequent action brought by the member under Section 8336, the court shall enforce the rights set forth in subdivision (a) unless the corporation proves that the member will allow use of the information for purposes unrelated to the person's interest as a member or that the alternative method offered reasonably achieves the proper purpose set forth in the demand.

(2) The authorized number of members for a purpose reasonably related to the members' interest as members.

(c) The corporation may, within ten business days after receiving a demand under subdivision (a), deliver to the person or persons making the demand a written offer of an alternative method of achieving the purpose identified in said demand without providing access to or a copy of the membership list. An alternative method which reasonably and in a timely manner accomplishes the proper purpose set forth in a demand made under subdivision (a) shall be deemed a reasonable alternative, unless within a reasonable time after acceptance of the offer the corporation fails to do those things which it offered to do. Any rejection of the offer shall be in writing and shall indicate the reasons the alternative proposed by the corporation does not meet the proper purpose of the demand made pursuant to subdivision (a).

Corp. C. § 8331. Petition By Corporation To Set Aside Demand; Time; Procedure; Grounds.

(a) Where the corporation, in good faith, and with a substantial basis, believes that the membership list, demanded under Section 8330 by the authorized number (Section 5036), will be used for a purpose not reasonably related to the interests as members of the person or persons making the demand (hereinafter called the requesting parties) as members or provides a reasonable alternative pursuant to subdivision (c) of Section 8330, it may petition the superior court of the proper county for an order setting aside the demand.

(b) Except as provided in subdivision (c), a petition for an order to show cause why a protective order pursuant to subdivision (d) should not issue shall be filed within 10 business days after the demand by the authorized number under Section 8330 or receipt of a written rejection by the authorized number of an offer made pursuant to subdivision (c) of Section 8330, whichever is later. The petition shall be accompanied by an application for a hearing on the petition. Upon the filing of the petition, the court shall issue a protective order staying production of the list demanded until the hearing on the order to show cause. The court shall set the hearing on the order to show cause not more than 20 days from the date of the filing of the petition. The order to show cause shall be granted unless the court finds that there is no reasonable probability that the corporation will make the showing required under subdivision (f).

(c) A corporation may file a petition under this section more than 10 business days after the demand or rejection under Section 8330, but only upon a showing the delay was caused by excusable neglect. In no event, however, may any petition under this section be considered if filed more than 30 days after the requesting parties' demand or rejection, whichever is later.

(d) Upon the return day of the order to show cause, the court may issue a protective order staying production of the list demanded until final adjudication of the petition filed pursuant to this section. No protective order shall issue under this subdivision unless the court finds that the rights of the requesting parties can reasonably be preserved and that the corporation is likely to make the showing required by subdivision (f) or the court is likely to issue a protective order pursuant to subdivision (g).

(e) If the corporation fails to file a petition within the time allowed by subdivision (b) or (c), whichever is applicable, or fails to obtain a protective order under subdivision (d), then the corporation shall comply with the demand, and no further action may be brought by the corporation under this section.

(f) The court shall issue the final order setting aside the demand only if the corporation proves:

> (1) That there is a reasonable probability that the requesting parties will permit use of the membership list for a purpose unrelated to their interests as members; or
>
> (2) That the method offered by the corporation is a reasonable alternative in that it reasonably achieves the proper purpose set forth in the requesting parties' demand and that the corporation intends and is able to effectuate the reasonable alternative.

(g) In the final order, the court may, in its discretion, order an alternate mechanism for achieving the proper purposes of the requesting parties, or impose just and proper conditions upon the use of the membership list which reasonably assures compliance with Section 8330 and Section 8338.

(h) The court shall award reasonable costs and expenses including reasonable attorneys' fees, to requesting parties who successfully oppose any petition or application filed pursuant to this section.

(i) Where the corporation has neither, within the time allowed, complied with a demand by the authorized number (Section 5036) under Section 8330, nor obtained a protective order staying production of the list, or a final order setting aside the demand, which is then in effect, the requesting parties may petition the superior court of the proper county for a writ of mandamus pursuant to Section 1085 of the Code of Civil Procedure compelling the corporation to comply with the demand. At the hearing, the court shall hear the parties summarily, by affidavit or otherwise, and shall issue a peremptory writ of mandamus unless it appears that the demand was not made by an authorized number (Section 5036), that the demand has been complied with, that the corporation, pursuant to subdivision (c) of Section 8330, made an offer which was not rejected in writing within a reasonable time, or that a protective or final order properly issued under subdivision (d), (f) or (g) is then in effect. No inquiry may be made in such proceeding into the use for which the authorized number seek the list. The court shall award reasonable costs and expenses, including reasonable attorneys' fees to persons granted an order under this subdivision.

(j) Nothing in this section shall be construed to limit the right of the corporation to obtain damages for any misuse of a membership list obtained under Section 8330, or otherwise, or to obtain injunctive relief necessary to restrain misuse of a member list. A corporation shall be entitled to recover reasonable costs and expenses, including reasonable attorneys' fees, incurred in successfully bringing any such action.

Corp. C. § 8332. Power Of Court To Limit Rights Under Section 8330; Temporary Order Suspending Time Limit.

(a) Upon petition of the corporation or any member, the superior court of the proper county may limit or restrict the rights set forth in Section 8330 where, and only where, such limitation or restriction is necessary to protect the rights of any member under the Constitution of the United States or the Constitution of the State of California. An order issued pursuant to this subdivision shall provide, insofar as possible, for alternative mechanisms by which the persons seeking to exercise rights under Section 8330 may communicate with members for purposes reasonably related to their interests as members.

(b) Upon the filing of a petition under subdivision (a), the court may, if requested by the person making the petition, issue a temporary order suspending the running of any time limit specified in Section 8330 for compliance with that section. Such an order may be extended, after notice and hearing, until final adjudication of the petition, wherever it appears that the petitioner may prevail on the merits, and it is otherwise equitable to do so.

Corp. C. § 8333. Inspection Of Accounting Books, Records, Minutes; By Member.

The accounting books and records and minutes of proceedings of the members and the board and committees of the board shall be open to inspection upon the written demand on the corporation of any member at any reasonable time, for a purpose reasonably related to such person's interests as a member.

Corp. C. § 8337. Award Of Costs, Expenses, Attorneys' Fees.

In any action or proceeding under this article, and except as required by Section 8331, if the court finds the failure of the corporation to comply with a proper demand thereunder was without justification, the court may award the member reasonable costs and expenses, including reasonable attorneys' fees, in connection with such action or proceeding.

Corp. C. § 8338. Prohibited Uses Of Membership Lists; Damages For Misuse.

(a) A membership list is a corporate asset. Without consent of the board a membership list or any part thereof may not be used by any person for any purpose not reasonably related to a member's interest as a member. Without limiting the generality of the foregoing, without the consent of the board a membership list or any part thereof may not be:

> (1) Used to solicit money or property unless such money or property will be used solely to solicit the vote of the members in an election to be held by their corporation.

(2) Used for any purpose which the user does not reasonably and in good faith believe will benefit the corporation.

(3) Used for any commercial purpose or purpose in competition with the corporation.

(4) Sold to or purchased by any person.

(b) Any person who violates the provisions of subdivision (a) shall be liable for any damage such violation causes the corporation and shall account for and pay to the corporation any profit derived as a result of said violation. In addition, a court in its discretion may award exemplary damages for a fraudulent or malicious violation of subdivision (a).

(c) Nothing in this article shall be construed to limit the right of a corporation to obtain injunctive relief necessary to restrain misuse of a membership list or any part thereof.

(d) In any action or proceeding under this section, a court may award the corporation reasonable costs and expenses, including reasonable attorneys' fees, in connection with such action or proceeding.

(e) As used in this section, the term "membership list" means the record of the members' names and addresses.

CHAPTER 18

STANDING OF AN OWNERS' ASSOCIATION TO SUE & STATUTES OF LIMITATIONS

(Code of Civil Procedure §§ 383, 337-339.5)

CCP § 383. Owners Association For Common Interest Development; Standing To Sue.

(a) An association established to manage a common interest development shall have standing to institute, defend, settle, or intervene in litigation, arbitration, mediation, or administrative proceedings in its own name as the real party in interest and without joining with it the individual owners of the common interest development, in matters pertaining to the following:

(1) Enforcement of the governing documents.

(2) Damage to the common areas.

(3) Damage to the separate interests which the association is obligated to maintain or repair.

(4) Damage to the separate interests which arises out of, or is integrally related to, damage to the common areas or separate interests that the association is obligated to maintain or repair.

(b) In any action maintained by an association pursuant to paragraph (2), (3), or (4) of subdivision (a), the amount of damages recovered by the association shall be reduced by the amount of damages allocated to the association or its managing agents in direct proportion to their percentage of fault based upon principles of comparative fault. In such an action, the comparative fault of the association or its managing agents may be raised by way of defense, but shall not be the basis for any cross-action or separate action against the association or its managing agents for contribution or implied indemnity, where the only damage was sustained by the association or its members. It is the intent of this Legislature in enacting this subdivision to require that comparative fault be pled as an affirmative defense, rather than a separate cause of action, where the only damage was sustained by the association or its members.

(c) In any action involving damages described in paragraph (2), (3), or (4) of subdivision (a), the defendant or cross-defendant may allege and prove the comparative fault of the association or its managing agents as a setoff to his or her liability even it the association is not a party to the litigation or is no longer a party whether by reason of settlement, dismissal, or otherwise.

(d) Subdivisions (b) and (c) apply to actions commenced on or after January 1, 1993.

(e) Nothing in this section shall affect (1) any person's liability under Section 1431 of the Civil Code, or (2) the liability of the association or its managing agent for any act or omission which causes damages to another.

CCP § 337. Four Years; Written Contract; Exception; Book Account; Account Stated Based Upon Account In Writing; Balance Of Mutual, Open And Current Accounts In Writing; Rescission Of Written Contract.

Within four years:

1. An action upon any contract, obligation or liability founded upon an instrument in writing, except as provided in Section 336a of this code; provided, that the time within which any action for a money judgment for the balance due upon an obligation for the payment of which a deed of trust or mortgage with power of sale upon real property or any interest therein was given as security, following the exercise of the power of sale in such deed of trust or mortgage, may be brought shall not extend beyond

three months after the time of sale under such deed of trust or mortgage.

2. An action to recover (1) upon a book account whether consisting of one or more entries; (2) upon an account stated based upon an account in writing, but the acknowledgement of the account stated need not be in writing; (3) a balance due upon a mutual, open and current account, the items of which are in writing; provided, however, that where an account stated is based upon an account of one item, the time shall begin to run from the date of said item, and where an account stated is based upon an account of more than one item, the time shall begin to run from the date of the last item.

3. An action based upon the rescission of a contract in writing. The time begins to run from the date upon which the facts that entitle the aggrieved party to rescind occurred. Where the ground for rescission is fraud or mistake, the time does not begin to run until the discovery by the aggrieved party of the facts constituting the fraud or mistake. Where the ground for rescission is misrepresentation under Section 359 of the Insurance Code, the time does not begin to run until the representation becomes false.

CCP § 337.1. Four Years; Actions For Damages From Persons Performing Or Furnishing Design, Specifications, Surveying, Planning, Supervision Or Observation Of Construction Or Construction Of Improvement To Realty.

(a) Except as otherwise provided in this section, no action shall be brought to recover damages from any person performing or furnishing the design, specifications, surveying, planning, supervision or observation of construction or construction of an improvement to real property more than four years after the substantial completion of such improvement for any of the following:

(1) Any patent deficiency in the design, specifications, surveying, planning, supervision or observation of construction or construction

of an improvement to, or survey of, real property;

(2) Injury to property, real or personal, arising out of any such patent deficiency; or

(3) Injury to the person or for wrongful death arising out of any such patent deficiency.

(b) If by reason of such patent deficiency, an injury to property or the person or an injury causing wrongful death occurs during the fourth year after such substantial completion, an action in tort to recover damages for such an injury or wrongful death may be brought within one year after the date on which such injury occurred, irrespective of the date of death, but in no event may such an action be brought more than five years after the substantial completion of construction of such improvement.

(c) Nothing in this section shall be construed as extending the period prescribed by the laws of this state for the bringing of any action.

(d) The limitation prescribed by this section shall not be asserted by way of defense by any person in actual possession or the control, as owner, tenant or otherwise, of such an improvement at the time any deficiency in such an improvement constitutes the proximate cause of the injury or death for which it is proposed to bring an action.

(e) As used in this section, "patent deficiency" means a deficiency which is apparent by reasonable inspection.

(f) Subdivisions (a) and (b) shall not apply to any owner-occupied single-unit residence.

CCP § 337.15. Ten Years; Developer, Contractor, Architect, Etc. Of Real Property; Latent Deficiency In Design, Supervision, etc.; Injury To Property.

(a) No action may be brought to recover damages from any person, or the surety of a person, who develops real property or performs or furnishes the design, specifications, surveying, planning, supervision, testing, or observation of construction or construction of an improvement to real property more than 10 years after the substantial completion of the development or improvement for any of the following:

(1) Any latent deficiency in the design, specification, surveying, planning, supervision, or observation of construction or construction of an improvement to, or survey of, real property.

(2) Injury to property, real or personal, arising out of any such latent deficiency.

(b) As used in this section, "latent deficiency" means a deficiency which is not apparent by reasonable inspection.

(c) As used in this section, "action" includes an action for indemnity brought against a person arising out of that person's performance or furnishing of services or materials referred to in this section, except that a cross-complaint for indemnity may be filed pursuant to subdivision (b) of Section 428.10 in an action which has been brought within the time period set forth in subdivision (a) of this section.

(d) Nothing in this section shall be construed as extending the period prescribed by the laws of this state for bringing any action.

(e) The limitation prescribed by this section shall not be asserted by way of defense by any person in actual possession or the control, as owner, tenant or otherwise, of such an improvement, at the time any deficiency in the improvement constitutes the proximate cause for which it is proposed to bring an action.

(f) This section shall not apply to actions based on willful misconduct or fraudulent concealment.

(g) The 10-year period specified in subdivision (a) shall commence upon substantial completion of the improvement, but not later than the date of one of the following, whichever first occurs:

(1) The date of final inspection by the applicable public agency.

(2) The date of recordation of a valid notice of completion.
(3) The date of use or occupation of the improvement.
(4) One year after termination or cessation of work on the improvement.

The date of substantial completion shall relate specifically to the performance or furnishing design, specifications, surveying, planning, supervision, testing, observation of construction or construction services by each profession or trade rendering services to the improvement.

CCP § 338. Three Years; Statutory Liability; Exception; Trespass Or Injury To Realty; Taking, Detaining Or, injuring Goods Or Chattels; Fraud Or Mistake; Bond Of Public Official; Notary Public; Slander Of Title; False Advertising; Water Quality And Hazardous Wastes; Physical Damage To Private Property; Air Resources.

Within three years:

(a) An action upon a liability created by statute, other than a penalty or forfeiture.

(b) An action for trespass upon or injury to real property.

(c) An action for taking, detaining, or injuring any goods or chattels including actions for the specific recovery of personal property. The cause of action in the case of theft, as defined in Section 484 of the Penal Code, of any article of historical, interpretative, scientific, or artistic significance is not deemed to have accrued until the discovery of the whereabouts of the article by the aggrieved party, his or her agent, or the law enforcement agency which originally investigated the theft.

(d) An action for relief on the ground of fraud or mistake. The cause of action in that case is not to be deemed to have accrued until the discovery, by the aggrieved party, of the facts constituting the fraud or mistake.

(e) An action upon a bond of a public official except any cause of action based on fraud or embezzlement is not to be deemed to have accrued until the discovery, by the aggrieved party or his or her agent, of the facts constituting the cause of action upon the bond.

(f) An action against a notary public on his or her bond or in his or her official capacity except that any cause of action based on malfeasance or misfeasance is not deemed to have accrued until discovery, by the aggrieved party or his or her agent, of the facts, constituting the cause of action; provided that any action based on malfeasance or misfeasance shall be commenced within one year from discovery, by the aggrieved party or his or her agent, of the facts constituting the cause of action or within three years from the performance of the notarial act giving rise to the action, whichever is later; and provided further, that any action against a notary public on his or her bond or in his or her official capacity shall be commenced within six years.

(g) An action for slander of title to real property.

(h) An action commenced under Section 17536 of the Business and Professions Code. The cause of action in that case shall not be deemed to have accrued until the discovery by the aggrieved party, the Attorney General, the district attorney, the county counsel, the city prosecutor, or the city attorney of the facts constituting grounds for commencing such an action.

(i) An action commenced under the Porter-Cologne Water Quality Control Act (Division 7 (commencing with Section 13000) of the Water Code). The cause of action in that case shall not be deemed to have accrued until the discovery by the State Water Resources Control Board or a regional water quality control board of the facts constituting grounds for commencing actions under their jurisdiction.

(j) An action to recover for physical damage to private property under Section 19 of Article 1 of the California Constitution.

(k) An action commenced under division 26 (commencing with Section 39000) of the Health and Safety Code. These causes of action shall not be deemed to have accrued until the discovery by the State Air Resources Board or by a district, as defined in Section 39025 of the Health and Safety Code, of the facts constituting grounds for commencing the action under its jurisdiction.

CCP § 339. Two Years; Oral Contract; Certificate, Abstract Or Guaranty Of Title; Title Insurance Policy; Sheriff; Coroner; Constable; Rescission Of Oral Contract.

Within two years:

1. An action upon a contract, obligation or liability not founded upon an instrument of writing, except as provided in Section 2725 of the Commercial Code or subdivision 2 of Section 337 of this code; or an action founded upon a contract, obligation or liability, evidenced by a certificate, or abstract or guaranty of title of real property, or by a policy of title insurance; provided, that the cause of action upon a contract, obligation or liability evidenced by a certificate, or abstract or guaranty of title of real property or policy of title insurance shall not be deemed to have accrued until the discovery of the loss or damage suffered by the aggrieved party thereunder.

2. An action against a sheriff, coroner, or constable upon a liability incurred by the doing of an act in an official capacity and in virtue of office, or by the omission of an official duty including the nonpayment of money collected in the enforcement of a judgment.

3. An action based upon the rescission of a contract not in writing. The time begins to run from the date upon which the facts that entitle the aggrieved party to rescind occurred. Where the ground for rescission is fraud or mistake, the time does not begin to run until the discovery by the aggrieved party of the facts constituting the fraud or mistake.

CCP § 339.5. Lease Not In Writing; Period For Action After Breach.

Where a lease of real property is not in writing, no action shall be brought under Section 1951.2 of the Civil Code more than two years after the breach of the lease and abandonment of the property, or more than two years after the termination of the right of the lessee to possession of the property, whichever is the earlier time.

CHAPTER 19

EMPLOYEE INJURY PREVENTION
(Labor Code §§ 6401.7 & 6409.1)

Lab. C. § 6401.7. Injury Prevention Programs.

(a) Every employer shall establish, implement, and maintain an effective injury prevention program. The program shall be written, except as provided in subdivision (e), and shall include, but not be limited to, the following elements:

(1) Identification of the person or persons responsible for implementing the program.

(2) The employer's system for identifying and evaluating work place hazards, including scheduled periodic inspections to identify unsafe conditions and work practices.

(3) The employer's methods and procedures for correcting unsafe or unhealthy conditions and work practices in a timely manner.

(4) An occupational health and safety training program designed to instruct employees in general safe and healthy work practices and to provide specific instruction with respect to hazards specific to each employee's job assignment.

(5) The employer's system for communicating with employees on occupational health and safety matters, including provisions designed to encourage employees to inform the employer of hazards at the worksite without fear of reprisal.

(6) The employer's system for ensuring that employees comply with safe and healthy work practices, which may include disciplinary action.

(b) The employer shall correct unsafe and unhealthy conditions and work practices in a timely manner based on the severity of the hazard.

(c) The employer shall train all employees when the training program is first established, all new employees, and all employees given a new job assignment, and shall train employees whenever new substances, processes, procedures, or equipment are introduced to the workplace and represent a new hazard, and whenever the employer receives notification of a new or previously unrecognized hazard. Beginning January 1, 1994, an employer in the construction industry who is required to be licensed under Chapter 9 (commencing with Section 7000) of Division 3 of the Business and Professions Code may use employee training provided to the employer's employees under a construction industry occupational safety and health training program approved by the division to comply with the requirements of subdivision (a) relating to employee training, and shall only be required to provide training on hazards specific to an employee's job duties.

(d) The employer shall keep appropriate records of steps taken to implement and maintain the program. Beginning January 1, 1994, an employer in the construction industry who is required to be licensed under Chapter 9 (commencing with Section 7000) of Division 3 of the Business and Professions Code may use records relating to employee training provided to the employer in connection with an occupational safety and health training program approved by the division to comply with the requirements of this subdivision, and shall only be required to keep records of those steps taken to implement and maintain the program with respect to hazards specific to an employee's job duties.

(e) (1)The standards board shall adopt a standard setting forth the employer's duties under this Section, on or before January 1, 1991, consistent with the requirements specified in subdivisions (a), (b), (c), and (d). The standards board, in adopting the standard, shall include substantial compliance criteria for use in evaluating an employer's injury prevention program. The board may adopt less stringent criteria for employers with few employees and for employers in industries with insignificant occupational safety or health hazards.

(2) Notwithstanding subdivision (a), for employers with fewer than 20 employees who are in industries that are not on a designated list of high hazard industries and who have a workers' compensation experience modification rate of 1.1 or less, and for any employers with fewer than 20 employees who are in industries that are on a designated list of low hazard industries, the board shall adopt a standard setting for the employer's duties under this section consistent with the requirements specified in subdivisions (a), (b), and (c), except that the standard shall only require written documentation to the extent of documenting the person or persons responsible for implementing the program pursuant to paragraph (1) of subdivision (a), keeping a record of periodic inspections pursuant to paragraph (2) of subdivision (a), and keeping a record of employee training pursuant to paragraph (4) of subdivision (a). To any extent beyond the specifications of this subdivision, the standard shall not require the employer to keep the records specified in subdivision (d).

(3) The division shall establish a list of high hazard industries using the methods prescribed in Section 6314.1 for identifying and targeting employers in high hazard industries. For purposes of this subdivision, the "designated list of high hazard industries" shall be the list established pursuant to this paragraph.

For the purpose of implementing this subdivision, the Department of Industrial Relations shall periodically review, and as necessary revise, the list.

(4) For the purpose of implementing this subdivision, the Department of Industrial Relations shall also establish a list of low hazard industries, and shall periodically review, and as necessary revise, that list.

(f) The standard adopted pursuant to subdivision (e) shall specifically permit employer and employee occupational safety and health committees to be included in the employer's injury prevention program. The board shall establish criteria for use in evaluating employer and employee occupational safety and health committees. The criteria shall include minimum duties, including the following:

(1) Review of the employer's (A) periodic, scheduled worksite inspections, (B) investigation of causes of incidents resulting in injury, illness, or exposure to hazardous substances, and (c) investigation of any alleged hazardous condition brought to the attention of any committee member. When determined necessary by the committee, the committee may conduct its own inspections and investigations.

(2) Upon request from the division, verification of abatement action taken by the employer as specified in division citations.

If any employer's occupational safety and health committee meets the criteria established by the board, it shall be presumed to be in substantial compliance with paragraph (5) of subdivision (a).

(g) The division shall adopt regulations specifying the procedures for selecting employee representatives for employer-employee occupational health and safety committees when these procedures are not specified in an applicable collective bargaining agreement. No employee or employee organization shall be held liable for any act or omission in connection with a health and safety committee.

(h) The employer's injury prevention program, as required by this section, shall cover all of the employer's employees and all other workers who the employer controls or directs and directly supervises on the job to the extent these workers are exposed to worksite and job assignment specific hazards. Nothing in this subdivision shall affect the obligations of a contractor or other employer which controls or directs and directly supervises its own employees on the job.

(i) Where a contractor supplies its employee to a state agency employer on a temporary basis, the state agency employer may assess a fee upon the contractor to reimburse the state agency for the additional costs, if any, of including the contract employee within the state agency's injury prevention program.

(j) (1) The division shall prepare a Model Injury and Illness Prevention Program for Non-High-Hazard Employment, and shall make copies of the model program prepared pursuant to this subdivision available to employers, upon request, for posting in the workplace. An employer who adopts and implements the model program prepared by the division pursuant to this paragraph in good faith shall not be assessed a civil penalty for the first citation for a violation of this section issued after the employer's adoption and implementation of the model program.

(2) For purposes of this subdivision, the division shall establish a list of non-high-hazard industries in California, that may include the industries that, pursuant to Section 14316 of Title 8 of the California Code of Regulations, are not currently required to keep records of occupational injuries and illnesses under Article 2 (commencing with Section 14301) of Subchapter 1 of Chapter 7 of Division 1 of Title 8 of the California Code of Regulations. These industries, identified by their Standard Indus-

trial Classification Codes, as published by the United States Office of Management and Budget in the Manual of Standard Industrial Classification Codes, 1987 Edition, are apparel and accessory stores (Code 56), eating and drinking places (Code 58), miscellaneous retail (Code 59), finance, insurance, and real estate (Codes 60-67), personal services (Code 72), business services (Code 73), motion pictures (Code 78) except motion picture production and allied services (Code 781), legal services (Code 81), educational services (Code 82), social services (Code 83), museums, art galleries, and botanical and zoological gardens (code 84), membership organizations (Code 86), engineering, accounting, research, management, and related services (Code 87), private households (Code 88), and miscellaneous services (Code 89). To further identify industries that may be included on the list, the division shall also consider data from a rating organization as defined in Section 11750.1 of the Insurance Code, the Division of Labor Statistics and Research, including the logs of occupational injuries and illnesses maintained by employers on Form CAL/OSHA No. 200, or its equivalent, as required by Section 14301 of the Title 8 of the California Code of Regulations, and all other appropriate information. The list shall be established by June 30, 1994, and shall be reviewed, and as necessary revised, biennially.

(3) The division shall prepare a Model Injury and Illness Prevention Program for Employers in Industries with Intermittent Employment, and shall determine which industries have historically utilized seasonal or intermittent employees. An employer in an industry determined by the division to have historically util-

ized seasonal or intermittent employees shall be deemed to have complied with the requirements of subdivision (a) with respect to a written injury prevention program if the employer adopts the model program prepared by the division pursuant to this paragraph and complies with any instructions relating thereto.

(k) With respect to any county, city, city and county, or district, of any public of quasi-public corporation or public agency therein, including any pubic entity, other than a state agency, that is a member of, or created by, a joint powers agreement, the provisions of subdivision (d) shall not apply.

LC § 6409.1. Occupational Injury Or Illness Reports

(a) Every employer shall file a complete report of every occupational injury or occupational illness, as defined in subdivision (b) of Section 6409, to each employee which results in lost time beyond the date of the injury or illness, or which requires medical treatment beyond first aid, with the Department of Industrial Relations, through its Division of Labor Statistics and Research or, if an insured employer, with the insurer, on a form prescribed for that purpose by the Division of Labor Statistics and Research. A report shall be filed concerning each injury and illness which has, or is alleged to have, arisen out of and in the course of employment, within five days after the employer obtains knowledge of the injury or illness. Each report of occupational injury or occupational illness shall indicate the social security number of the injured employee. In the case of an insured employer, the insurer shall file with the division immediately upon receipt, a copy of the employer's report, which has been received from the insured employer. In the event an employer has filed a report of injury or illness pursuant to this subdivision and the employee subsequently dies as a result of the reported injury or illness, the employer shall file an amended report indicating the death with the Department of Industrial Relations, through its Division of Labor Statistics and Research or, if an insured employer, with the insurer, within five days after the employer is notified or learns of the death. A copy of any amended reports received by the insurer shall be filed with the division immediately upon receipt.

(b) In every case involving a serious injury or illness, or death, in addition to the report required by subdivision (a), a report shall be made immediately by the employer to the Division of Occupational Safety and Health by telephone or telegraph.

CHAPTER 20

TAX EXEMPTION
(United States Internal Revenue Code 528)
(California Revenue & Taxation Code §§ 23701, 23701t)

Internal Rev. C. (Federal) § 528. Certain Homeowner Associations.

(a) General rule.

A homeowners association (as defined in subsection (c)) shall be subject to taxation under this subtitle only to the extent provided in this section. A homeowners association shall be considered an organization exempt from income taxes for the purpose of any law which refers to organizations exempt from income taxes.

(b) Tax imposed.

A tax is hereby imposed for each taxable year on the owners association taxable income of every homeowners association. Such tax shall be equal to 30 percent of the homeowners association taxable income.

(c) Homeowners association defined. For purposes of this section

(1) Homeowners association.

The term "homeowners association" means: an organization which is a condominium management association or a residential real estate management association if

(A) such organization is organized and operated to provide for the acquisition, construction, management, maintenance, and care of association property,

(B) sixty percent or more of the gross income of such organization for the taxable year consists solely of amounts received as membership dues, fees, or assessments from

(i)owners of residential units in the case of a condominium management association, or

(ii)owners of residences or residential lots in the case of a residential real estate management association.

(C) ninety percent or more of the expenditures of the organization for the taxable year are expenditures for the acquisition, construction, management, maintenance, and care of association property,

(D) no part of the net earnings of such organization inures (other than by acquiring, constructing, or providing management, maintenance, and care of association property, and other than by a rebate of excess membership dues, fees, or assessments) to the benefit of any private shareholder or individual, and

(E) such organization elects (at such time and in such manner as the Secretary by regulations prescribes) to have this section apply for the taxable year.

(2) Condominium management association.

The term "condominium management association" means any organization meeting the requirement of subparagraph (A) of paragraph (1) with respect to a condominium project substantially all of the units of which are used by individuals for residences.

(3) Residential real estate management association.

The term "residential real estate management association" means any organization meeting the requirements of subparagraph (A) of paragraph (1) with respect to a subdivision, development, or similar area substantially all the lots or buildings of which may only be used by individuals for residences.

(4) Association property.

The term "association property" means:

(A) property held by the organization

(B) property commonly held by the members of the organization

(C) property within the organization privately held by the members of the organization, and

(D) property owned by a governmental unit and used for the benefit of residents of such unit.

(d) Homeowners association taxable income defined.

(1) Taxable income defined. For purposes of this section, the homeowners association taxable income of any organization for any taxable year is an amount equal to the excess (if any) of

(A) the gross amount for the taxable year (excluding any exempt function income), over

(B) the deductions allowed by this chapter which are directly connected with the production of the gross income (excluding exempt function income), computed with the modifications provided in paragraph (2).

(2) Modifications. For purposes of this subsection

(A) there shall be allowed a specific deduction of $100,

(B) no net operating loss deduction shall be allowed under Section 172, and

(C) no deduction shall be allowed under part VIII of subchapter B (relating to special deductions for corporations).

(3) Exempt function income. For purposes of this subsection, the term "exempt function income" means any amount received as membership dues, fees, or assessments from

(A) owners of condominium housing units in the case of a condominium management association, or

(B) owners of real property in the case of a residential real estate management association.

Rev. & Tax. C. (California) § 23701. Exemption of Specified Organizations.

Organizations which are organized and operated for nonprofit purposes within the provisions of a specific section of this article, or are defined in Section 23701h (relating to certain title-holding companies) or Section 23701x (relating to certain title-holding companies), are exempt from taxes imposed under this part, except as provided in this article or in Article 2 (commencing with Section 23731) of this chapter, if:

(a) An application for exemption is submitted in the form prescribed by the Franchise Tax Board; and

(b) A filing fee of twenty-five dollars ($25) is paid with each application for exemption filed with the Franchise Tax Board after December 31, 1969; and

(c) The Franchise Tax Board issues a determination exempting the organization from tax.

This section shall not prevent a determination from having a retroactive effect and does not prevent the issuance of a determination with respect to a domestic organization which was in existence prior to January 1, 1970, and exempt under prior law without the submission of a formal application or payment of a filing fee. For the purposes of this section, the term "domestic" means created or organized under the laws of this state.

The Franchise Tax Board may issue rulings and regulations as are necessary and reasonable to carry out the provisions of this article.

Rev. & Tax. C. (California) § 23701t. Homeowners' Association Conditions; Definitions.

(a) A homeowners' association organized and operated to provide for the acquisition, construction, management, maintenance, and care of residential association property if:

(1) Sixty percent or more of the gross income of such organization for the taxable year consists solely of amounts received as membership dues, fees and assessments from tenant-stockholders or owners of residential units, residences or lots;

(2) Ninety percent or more of the expenditures of the organization for the taxable year are expenditures for the acquisition, construction, management, maintenance, and care of association property;

(3) No part of the net earnings inures (other than by providing management, maintenance and care of association property or by a rebate of excess membership dues, fees or assessments) to the benefit of any private shareholder or individual; and

(4) Amounts received as membership dues, fees and assessments not expended for association purposes during the taxable year are transferred to and held in trust to provide for the management, maintenance, and care of association property and common areas.

(b) The term "association property" means

(1) Property held by the organization,

(2) Property held in common by the members of the organization, and

(3) Property within the organization privately held by the members of the organization.

(c) A homeowners association shall be subject to tax under this part with respect to its "homeowners association taxable income," and such income shall be subject to tax as provided by Chapter 3 (commencing with Section 23501) of this part.

(1) For purposes of this section, the term "homeowners association taxable income" of any organization for any taxable year means an amount equal to the excess over one hundred dollars ($100) (if any) of

(A) The gross income for the taxable year (excluding any exempt function income), over

(B) The deductions allowed by this part which are directly connected with the production of the gross income (excluding exempt function income).

(2) For purposes of this section, the term "exempt function income" means any amount received as membership fees, dues and assessments from tenant-shareholders or owners of residential units, residences or lots.

(d) The term "homeowners' association" includes a condominium management association, a residential real estate management association, and a cooperative housing corporation.

(e) "Cooperative housing corporation" includes, but is not limited to, a limited-equity housing cooperative, as defined in Section 33007.5 of the Health and Safety Code, organized either as a nonprofit benefit corporation pursuant to Part 2 (commencing with Section 5110) of Division 2 of Title 1 of the Corporations Code, or a nonprofit mutual benefit corporation pursuant to Part 3 (commencing with Section 7110) of Division 2 of Title 1 of the Corporations Code.

CHAPTER 21

BUILDING PLANS AND ASBESTOS DISCLOSURE

(Health & Safety Code §§ 19850-19851; 25915.2- 25915.5)

1. BUILDING RECORDS

Health & Saf. C. § 19850. Filing, Building Plans By City Or County.

The building department of every city or county shall maintain an official copy, which may be on microfilm or other type of photographic copy, of the plans of every building, during the life of the building, for which the department issued a building permit.

"Building Department" means the department, bureau, or officer charged with the enforcement of laws or ordinances regulating the erection, construction, or alteration of buildings.

Except for plans of a common interest development as defined in Section 1351 of the Civil Code, plans need not be filed for:

(a) Single or multiple dwellings not more than two stories and basement in height.

(b) Garages and other structures appurtenant to buildings described under subdivision (a).

(c) Farm or ranch buildings.

(d) Any one-story building where the span between bearing walls does not exceed 25 feet. The exemption in this subdivision does not, however, apply to a steel frame or concrete building.

Health & Saf. C. § 19851. Inspection Of Records; Duplication Of Plans.

(a) The official copy of the plans maintained by the building department of the city or county provided for under Section 19850 shall be open for inspection only on the premises of the building department as a public record. The copy may not be duplicated in whole or in part except (1) with the written permission, which permission shall not be unreasonably withheld as specified in subdivision (f), of the certified, licensed or registered professional or his or her successor, if any, who signed the original documents and the written permission of the original or current owner of the building, or, if the building is part of a common interest development, with the written permission of the board of directors or governing body of the association established to manage the common interest development, or (2) by order of a proper court.

(b) Any building department of a city or county, which is requested to duplicate the official copy of the plans maintained by the building department, shall request written permission to do so from the certified, licensed, or registered professional, or his or her successor, if any, who signed the original documents and from (1) the original or current owner of the building or (2), if the building is part of a common interest development, from the board of directors or other governing body of the association established to manage the common interest development.

(c) The building department shall also furnish the form of an affidavit to be completed and signed by the person requesting to duplicate the official copy of the plans, which contains provisions stating all of the following:

(1) That the copy of the plans shall only be used for the maintenance, operation, and use of the building.

(2) That drawings are instruments of professional service and are incomplete without the interpretation of the certified, licensed, or registered professional of record.

(3) That subdivision (a) of Section 5536.25 of the Business and Professions Code states that a licensed architect who signs plans, specifications, reports, or documents shall not be responsible for damage caused by subsequent changes to, or use of, those plans, specifications, reports, or documents where the subsequent changes or uses, including changes or uses made by state or local governmental agencies, are not authorized or approved by the licensed architect who originally signed the plans, specifications, reports, or documents, provided that the architectural service rendered by the architect who signed the plans, specifications, reports, or documents was not also a proximate cause of the damage.

(d) The request by the building department to a licensed, registered, or certified professional may be made by the building department sending a registered letter to the licensed, registered, or certified professional requesting his or her permission to duplicate the official copy of the plans and sending with the registered letter, a copy of the affidavit furnished by the building department which has been completed and signed by the person requesting to duplicate the official copy of the plans. The registered letters shall be sent by the building department to the most recent address of the licensed, registered, or certified professional available from the California State Board of Architectural Examiners.

(e) The governing body of the city or county may establish a fee to be paid by any person who requests the building department of the city or county to duplicate the official copy of any plans pursuant to this section, in an amount which it determines is reasonably necessary to cover the costs of the building department pursuant to this section.

(f) The certified, licensed, or registered professional's refusal to permit the duplication of the plans is unreasonable if, upon request from the building department, the professional does either of the following:

(1) Fails to respond to the local building department within 30 days of receipt by the professional of the request. However, if the building department determines that professional is unavailable to respond within 30 days of receipt of the request due to serious illness, travel, or other extenuating circumstances, the time period shall be extended by the building department to allow the professional adequate time to respond, as determined to be appropriate to the individual circumstance, but not to exceed 60 days.

(2) Refuses to give his or her permission for the duplication of the plans after receiving the signed affidavit and registered letter specified in subdivisions (c) and (d).

2. ASBESTOS DISCLOSURE

Health & Saf. C. § 25915.2 Written Notice To Employees, Other Owners And Employees Of Contractors; Exceptions.

(a) Notice provided pursuant to this chapter shall be provided in writing to each individual employee, and shall be mailed to other owners designated to receive the notice pursuant to subdivision (a) of Section 25915.5, within 15 days of the first receipt by the owner of information identifying the presence or location of asbestos-containing construction materials in the building. This notice shall be provided annually thereafter. In addition, if new information regarding those items specified in paragraphs (1) to (5), inclusive, of subdivision (a) of Section 25915 has been obtained within 90 days after the notice required by this subdivision is provided or any subsequent 90-day period, then a supplemental notice shall be provided within 15 days of the close of that 90-day period.

(b) Notice provided pursuant to this chapter shall be provided to new employees within 15 days of commencement of work in the building.

(c) Notice provided pursuant to this chapter shall be mailed to any new owner designated to receive the notice pursuant to subdivision (a) of Section 25915.5 within 15 days of the effective date of the agreement under which a person becomes a new owner.

(d) Subdivisions (a) and (c) shall not be construed to require owners of a building or part of a building within a residential common interest development to mail written notification to other owners of a building or part of a building within the residential common interest development, if all the following conditions are met:

> (1) The association conspicuously posts, in each building or part of a building, known to contain asbestos-containing materials, a large sign in a prominent location that fully informs persons entering each building or part of a building within the common interest development that the association knows the building contains asbestos-containing materials.
>
> The sign shall also inform persons of the location where further information, as required by this chapter, is available about the asbestos-containing materials known to be located in the building.
>
> (2) The owners or association disclose, as soon as practicable before the transfer of title of a separate interest in the common interest development, to a transferee the existence of asbestos-containing material in a building or part of a building within the common interest development.

Failure to comply with this section shall not invalidate the transfer of title of real property. This paragraph shall only apply to transfers of title of separate interests in the common interest development of which the owners have knowledge. As used in this section, "association" and "common interest development" are defined in Section 1351 of the Civil Code.

(e) If a person contracting with an owner receives notice pursuant to this chapter, that contractor shall provide a copy of the notice to his or her employees or contractors working within the building.

(f) If the asbestos-containing construction material in the building is limited to an area or areas within the building that meet all the following criteria:

(1) Are unique and physically defined.

(2) Contain asbestos-containing construction materials in structural, mechanical, or building materials which are not replicated throughout the building.

(3) Are not connected to other areas through a common ventilation system; then, an owner required to give notice to his or her employees pursuant to subdivision (a) of Section 25915 or Section 25915.1 may provide that notice only to the employees working within or entering that area or those areas of the building meeting the conditions above.

(g) If the asbestos-containing construction material in the building is limited to an area or areas within the building that meet all the following criteria:

(1) Are accessed only by building maintenance employees or contractors and are not accessed by tenants or employees in the building, other than on an incidental basis.

(2) Contain asbestos-containing construction materials in structural, mechanical, or building materials which are not replicated in areas of the building which are accessed by tenants and employees.

(3) The owner knows that no asbestos fibers are being released or have the reasonable possibility to be released from the material; then, as to that asbestos-containing construction material, an owner required to give notice to his

or her employees pursuant to subdivision (a) of Section 25915 or Section 25915.1 may provide that notice only to its building maintenance employees and contractors who have access to that area or those areas of the building meeting the conditions above.

(h) In those areas of a building where the asbestos-containing construction material is composed only of asbestos fibers which are completely encapsulated, if the owner knows that no asbestos fibers are being released or have the reasonable possibility to be released from that material in its present condition and has no knowledge that other asbestos-containing material is present, then an owner required to give notice pursuant to subdivision (a) of Section 25915 shall provide the information required in paragraph (2) of subdivision (a) of Section 25915 and may substitute the following notice for the requirements of paragraphs (1), (3), (4), and (5) of subdivision (a) of Section 25915:

(1) The existence of, conclusions from, and a description or list of the contents of, that portion of any survey conducted to determine the existence and location of asbestos-containing construction materials within the building that refers to the asbestos materials described in this subdivision, and information describing when and where the results of the survey are available pursuant to Section 25917.

(2) Information to convey that moving, drilling, boring, or otherwise distributing the asbestos-containing construction material identified may present a health risk and, consequently, should not be attempted by an unqualified employee. The notice shall identify the appropriate person the employee is required to contact if the condition of the asbestos-containing construction material deteriorates.

Health & Saf. C. § 25915.5. Notice To Persons Having Privy Of Contract With Owner; Effect Of Notice Or Lack Of Notice; Method Of Delivery; Liability Of Owner; Owners Within A Residential Common Interest Development Or Association.

(a) An owner required to give notice to employees pursuant to this chapter, in addition to notifying his or her employees, shall mail, in accordance with this subdivision, a copy of that notice to all other persons who are owners of the building or part of the building, with whom the owner has privity of contract. Receipt of a notice pursuant to this section by an owner, lessee or operator shall constitute knowledge that the building contains asbestos-containing construction materials for purposes of this chapter. Notice to an owner shall be delivered by first-class mail addressed to the person and at the address designated for the receipt of notices under the lease, rental agreement, or contract with the owner.

(b) The delivery of notice under this section or negligent failure to provide that notice shall not constitute a breach of any covenant under the lease or rental agreement, and nothing in this chapter enlarges or diminishes any rights or duties respecting constructive eviction.

(c) No owner who, in good faith, complies with the provisions of this section shall be liable to any other owner for any damages alleged to have resulted from his or her compliance with the provisions of this section.

(d) This section shall not be construed to apply to owners of a building or part of a building within a residential common interest development or association, if the owners comply with the provisions of subdivision (d) of Section 25915.2. For purposes of this section, "association" and "common interest development" are defined in Section 1351 of the Civil Code.

CHAPTER 22

REMOVAL OF PARKED AN ABANDONED VEHICLES

(Vehicle Code §§ 27658-22658.2)

Veh. C. § 22658. Removal From Private Property.

(a) Except as provided in Section 22658.2, the owner or person in lawful possession of any private property, subsequent to notifying, by telephone or, if impractical, by the most expeditious means available, *the local traffic law enforcement agency* may cause the removal of a vehicle parked on the property to the nearest public garage under any of the following circumstances:

(1) There is displayed, in plain view at all entrances to the property, a sign not less than 17 by 22 inches in size, with lettering not less than one inch in height, prohibiting public parking and indicating that vehicles will be removed at the owner's expense, and containing the telephone number of the local traffic law enforcement agency. The sign may also indicate that a citation may also be issued for the violation, or

(2) The vehicle has been issued a notice of parking violation, and 96 hours have elapsed since the issuance of that notice.

(3) The vehicle is on private property and lacks an engine, transmission, wheels, tires, doors, windshield, or any other major part or equipment necessary to operate safely on the highways, the owner or person in lawful possession of the private property has notified

the *local traffic law enforcement agency*, and 24 hours have elapsed since that notification.

(4) The lot or parcel upon which the vehicle is parked is improved with a single-family dwelling.

(b) The person causing removal of the vehicle, if the person knows or is able to ascertain from the registration records of the Department of Motor Vehicles the name and address of the registered and legal owner of the vehicle, shall immediately give, or cause to be given, notice in writing to the registered and legal owner of the fact of the removal, the grounds for the removal, and indicate the place to which the vehicle has been removed. If the vehicle is stored in a public garage, a copy of the notice shall be given to the proprietor of the garage. The notice provided for in this section shall include the amount of mileage on the vehicle at the time of removal. If the person does not know and is not able to ascertain the name of the owner or for any other reason is unable to give the notice to the owner as provided in this section, the person causing removal of the vehicle shall comply with the requirements of subdivision (c) of Section 22853 relating to notice in the same manner as applicable to an officer removing a vehicle from private property.

(c) This section does not limit or affect any right or remedy which the owner or person in lawful possession of private property may have by virtue of other provisions of law authorizing the removal of a vehicle parked upon private property.

(d) The owner of a vehicle removed from private property pursuant to subdivision (a) may recover for any damage to the vehicle resulting from any intentional or negligent act of any person causing the removal of, or removing, the vehicle.

(e) Any owner or person in lawful possession of any private property, or an "association" pursuant to Section 22658.2, causing the removal of a vehicle parked on that property is liable for double the storage or towing charges whenever there has been a failure to comply with Paragraph (1), (2), or (3) of subdivision (a) or to state the grounds for the removal of the vehicle if requested by the legal or registered owner of the vehicle as required by subdivision (f).

(f) Any owner or person in lawful possession of any private property, or an "association" pursuant to Section 22658.2, causing the removal of a vehicle parked on that property shall state the grounds for the removal of the vehicle if requested by the legal or registered owner of that vehicle. Any towing company that removes a vehicle from private property with the authorization of the property owner or the property owner's agent shall not be held responsible in any situation relating to the validity of the removal. Any towing company that removes the vehicle under this section shall be responsible for (1) any damage to the vehicle in the transit and subsequent storage of the vehicle and (2) the removal of a vehicle other than the vehicle specified by the owner or other person in lawful possession of the private property.

(g) Possession of any vehicle under this section shall be deemed to arise when a vehicle is removed from private property and is in transit.

(h) A towing company may impose a charge of not more than one-half of the regular towing charge for the towing of a vehicle at the request of the owner of private property or that owner's agent pursuant to this section if the owner of the vehicle or the owner's agent returns to the vehicle before it is removed from the private property. The regular towing charge may only be imposed after the vehicle has been removed from the property and is in transit.

(i) A charge for towing or storage, or both, of a vehicle under this section is excessive if the charge is greater than that which would have been charged for towing or storage, or both, made at the request of a law enforcement agency under an agreement between the law enforcement agency and a towing company in the city or county in which is located the private property from which the vehicle was, or was attempted to be, removed.

If a request to release a vehicle is made within 24 hours from the time the vehicle is brought into the storage facility, regardless of the calendar date, the storage charge shall be for only one day. Not more than one day's storage charge may be required for any vehicle released the same day that it is stored.

(j) Any person who charges a vehicle owner a towing, service, or storage charge at an excessive rate, as described in subdivision (i), is liable to the vehicle owner for four times the amount charged.

(k) Persons operating or in charge of any storage facility where vehicles are stored pursuant to this section shall accept a valid bank credit card or cash for payment of towing and storage by a registered owner or the owner's agent claiming the vehicle. A person operating or in charge of any storage facility who refuses to accept a valid bank credit card is liable to the registered owner of the vehicle for four times the amount of the towing and storage charges, but not to exceed five hundred dollars ($500). In addition, persons operating or in charge of the storage facility shall have sufficient moneys on the premises to accommodate, and make change in, a reasonable monetary transaction.

Credit charges for towing and storage services shall comply with Section 1748.1 of the Civil Code. Law enforcement agencies may include the costs of providing for payment by credit when making agreements with towing companies as described in subdivision (i).

(l) (1) A towing company shall not remove or commence the removal of a vehicle from private property without first obtaining written authorization from the property owner or lessee, or an employee or agent thereof, who shall be present at the time of removal. General authorization to remove or commence the removal of a vehicle at the towing company's discretion shall not be delegated to a towing company or its affiliates except in the case of a vehicle unlawfully parked within 15 feet of a fire hydrant or in a fire lane, or in a manner which interferes with any entrance to, or exit from, the private property.

(2) If a towing company removes a vehicle without written authorization and that vehicle is unlawfully parked within 15 feet of a fire hydrant or in a fire lane, or in a manner which interferes with any entrance to, or exit from, the private property, the towing company shall take, prior to the removal of that vehicle, a photograph of the vehicle which clearly indicates that parking violation. The towing company shall keep one copy of the photograph taken pursuant to this paragraph, and shall present that photograph to the owner or an agent of the owner, when that person claims the vehicle.

(3) Any towing company, or any affiliate of a towing company, which removes, or commences removal of, a vehicle from private property without first obtaining written authorization from the property owner or lessee, or an employee or agent thereof, who is present at the time of removal, or commencement of the removal, except as permitted by paragraph (1), is liable to the owner of the vehicle for four times the amount of the towing and storage charges, in addition to any applicable criminal penalty, for a violation of paragraph (1).

Veh. C. § 22658.1. Damaging Of Fence While Removing Vehicle; Location And Notification Of Property Owner By Towing Company.

(a) Any towing company that, in removing a vehicle, cuts, removes, otherwise damages, or leaves open a fence without the prior approval of the property owner of the person in charge of the property shall then and there do either of the following:

(1) Locate and notify the owner or person in charge of the property of the damage or open condition of the fence, the name and address of the towing company, and the license, registration, or identification number of the vehicle being removed.

(2) Leave in a conspicuous place on the property the name and address of the towing company, and the license, registration, or identification number of the vehicle being removed, and shall without unnecessary delay, notify the police department of the city in which the property is located, or if the property is located in unincorporated territory, either the sheriff or the local headquarters of the Department of the California Highway Patrol, of that information and the location of the damaged or opened fence.

(b) Any person failing to comply with all the requirements of this section is guilty of an infraction.

Veh. C. § 22658.2. Removal Of Vehicles From Common Interest Development.

(a) Except as provided in subdivision (b), an "association", as defined in subdivision (a) of Section 1351 of the Civil Code, of a common interest development, as defined in subdivision (c) of Section 1351 of the Civil Code, may cause the removal of a vehicle parked on that property to the nearest public garage if all of the following requirements are satisfied:

(1) A sign not less than 17 by 22 inches in size with lettering not less than one inch in height appears at each
entrance to the common interest development and contains both of the following:

(A)A statement that public parking is prohibited and all vehicles not authorized to park on the common interest development will be removed at the owner's expense.

(B)The telephone number of the local traffic law enforcement agency.

The sign may also indicate that a citation may be issued for the violation.

(2) If the identity of the registered owner of the vehicle is known or readily ascertainable, the president of the association or his or her designee shall, within a reasonable time, notify the owner of the removal by first-class mail. If the identity of the owner of the vehicle is not known or ascertainable, the president of the association or his or her designee shall comply with subdivision (c) of Section 22853.

(3) The president of the association or his or her designee, gives or causes to be given, notice of the removal to the local traffic law enforcement agency immediately after the vehicle has been removed. The notice shall include a description of the vehicle, the license plate number, and the address from where the vehicle was removed.

(b) The association may cause the removal without notice of any vehicle parked in a marked fire lane, within 15 feet of a fire hydrant, in a parking space designated for handicapped without proper authority, or in a manner which interferes with any entrance to, or exit from, the common interest development or any separate interest contained therein.

(c) Notwithstanding Section 1708 of the Civil Code, the association shall not be liable for any damages incurred by the vehicle owner because of the removal of a vehicle in compliance with this section or for any damage to the vehicle caused by the removal. However, the owner of a vehicle removed pursuant to this section may recover for any damage to the vehicle which results from any intentional or negligent act of the association or any person causing the removal of, or removing, the vehicle.

(d) Notwithstanding any other provision of law, subdivisions (f) to (k), inclusive, of Section 22658 apply to the removal of vehicles pursuant to this section.

CHAPTER 23

BASIC PARLIAMENTARY PROCEDURE

1. GENERAL

Parliamentary procedure originated in the English Parliament as a way of debating public affairs even when matters became heated. The rules were introduced to meetings in America with the first settlers from England and, as we know them today, were established in 1876 by Henry M. Robert when he published his first manual on parliamentary law entitled Robert's Rules of Order. The original procedural system has evolved into a sophisticated set of rules that have become the standard method of conducting business at organizational meetings.

The purpose of this segment of the book is to set forth the basic rules of parliamentary procedure so that they can be easily understood and adapted to fit the needs of your organization. It is important to remember that parliamentary procedure, while allowing for democratic rule, should be flexible enough to protect the rights of all members - including the opposition. A sense of fair play can be established by providing everyone with an opportunity to be heard. Like any system, parliamentary procedure works when it is used properly by those in charge and treats with respect the rights of all members.

This is a basic summary of a complex set of rules that will serve as a guide for most routine matters. However, when technical issues arise it may be necessary to consult a primary text on parliamentary procedure.

2. ORDER OF BUSINESS

Organizations using parliamentary procedure usually follow a fixed order of business. The following is a typical example:

1. CALL TO ORDER: The chairperson says, "The meeting will please come to order."
2. ROLL CALL: Members say "present" as their names are called.
3. READING AND APPROVAL OF MINUTES: The secretary reads the record of the last meeting and calls for approval, modification or addition by motion.
4. OFFICERS' REPORTS: Often limited to a report without discussion from officers (e.g., treasurer), but others may report at this time.
5. COMMITTEE REPORTS: First come reports from "standing" committees or permanent committees, then come reports from "ad hoc" or special committees, usually in the order of importance.
6. SPECIAL BUSINESS: Important business previously designated for consideration at the meeting.
7. UNFINISHED BUSINESS: Business left over from previous meetings.
8. NEW BUSINESS: Introduction and discussion of new topics.
9. ANNOUNCEMENTS: Informing the meeting of other subjects and events germane to the business of the organization.
10. ADJOURNMENT: The meeting ends by vote or general consensus recorded in the minutes; or under special circumstances by the chair's decision <u>if</u> time of adjournment was prearranged by vote.

3. TYPES OF MOTIONS

There are four types of motions:

1) Main motions
2) Subsidiary motions
3) Privileged motions
4) Incidental motions

Each type has a specific purpose and a relative priority. The order of precedence is: privileged motions, subsidiary motions and then main motions. Incidental motions have no order of precedence; they must be decided as soon as they arise. A table of the various types of motions and the parliamentary procedure for each is set forth in Section VI.

1. MAIN MOTIONS introduce subjects to the assembly for its consideration. They cannot be made when another motion is before the assembly. Only one main motion may be considered at a time, but it must yield to privileged, subsidiary and incidental motions. For example, a main motion might be introduced as follows: "I move that we purchase . . ."

2. SUBSIDIARY MOTIONS change or affect how the main motion is handled and they are voted on before the main motion. Subsidiary motions include a motion to amend, a motion to refer to committee, a motion to postpone, a motion to limit or extend debate, a motion to close debate and a motion to table. A subsidiary motion may be introduced by saying, "I move the question be amended by striking out . . ."

3. PRIVILEGED MOTIONS are those that are most urgent. They usually deal with a special or important matter not directly related to the pending business. Some examples are: a motion to recess, a motion to adjourn at a pre-determined time, a question to complain about heat,

noise or other conditions, a question to protest breach of rules or conduct, a question to avoid improper matter, etc.

4. INCIDENTAL MOTIONS raise questions of procedure that relate to other pending motions and must be considered before a vote on the related motion. For example, an incidental motion may involve a motion to appeal the chair's decision to the assembly, a motion to suspend the rules, a point of order, a parliamentary inquiry, a request to withdraw a motion, a request for division of the motion into parts, verification of a vote, a motion for reconsideration of hasty action, etc.

4. CONSIDERATION OF MOTIONS

Generally, a motion is in order if it relates to the business at hand and is presented at the right time. It must not be obstructive, frivolous or against the by-laws. Usually, a second is required. A second indicates that another member would like to consider the motion. A second is not required for certain types of motions, but if a second is required, the motion will die without a second. The procedure of a second prevents spending time on a question that interests only one person.

Most motions once made can be amended by striking out, inserting, or both at once. Amendments, however, must relate to the subject presented by the main motion. Both the main motion and all amendments are debatable. Parliamentary procedure guards the right to free and full debate on most motions. Some privileged and incidental motions are not debatable.

Some motions are so important that the speaker may be interrupted to make them. The original speaker regains the floor after the interruption has been attended to.

Most motions require a majority vote. But motions concerning the rights of the assembly or its members need a 2/3 vote to be adopted. Once passed, most motions can be re-debated and re-voted to give the members a chance to change their minds. The move to reconsider, however, must come from the winning side.

5. PRESENTING A MOTION

A motion is a proposal that the assembly take a stand or take action on some issue. A member can present a motion by making a proposal with the introduction, "I move . . ." A member may second a motion expressing support for the decision to discuss another member's motion. Following a second, if a second is required, a member may debate the pending motion or related business by giving an opinion or raising a question about the business at hand. Finally a member may call for a vote on the disposition of the motion.

The procedure for presenting a motion is relatively simple. First, the member should wait until the last speaker is finished and obtain the floor by addressing the chair. The member should say, "Mr. or (Ms.) Chairperson (or President)" and give his or her name. The chair will recognize the member by repeating the member's name. Next, the member should state the motion in clear and concise terms. The motion should be stated affirmatively, not negatively. For example, a motion should be phrased, "I move that we . . ." instead of, "I move that we do not . . ." All motions should avoid personalities, innuendo and irrelevancies.

Once the motion has been made, the member should wait for a second. Another member will second the motion by saying, "I second the motion." Or, if a second is not immediately forthcoming, the chair will call for a second. If there is no second and one is required for the motion, the motion will not be considered.

Following a second, the chair will say, "It is moved and seconded that we . . ." and debate will commence. The motion is now "assembly property" that can't be changed without the consent of the members by a vote.

A pending motion may be expanded. The initial moving member, however, is allowed to speak first. The mover should direct all comments to the chair. Keep to time limits for speaking as stated in the by-laws or as pre-determined by the members or the chair. The other members may speak after the mover is finished, and the mover may speak again after all other members have finished speaking. A mover may speak only twice unless a motion is passed by a 2/3 vote to suspend the rules authorizing the mover to more than two turns.

At the conclusion of debate, the chair will ask, "Are you ready for the question?" If there is no more discussion, a vote is taken. Alternatively, a motion for a previous question may be adopted.

Parliamentary Procedure Tables

6. PARLIAMENTARY PROCEDURE TABLES

PARLIAMENTARY PROCEDURE . . . at a glance

TO DO THIS:	YOU SAY THIS:
ADJOURN MEETING	"I move that we adjourn."
CALL AN INTERMISSION	"I move that we recess for..."
COMPLAIN ABOUT	"I rise to a question of privilege."
SUSPEND FURTHER CONSIDERATION OF AN ISSUE	"I move to table the motion."
END DEBATE AND AMENDMENTS	"I move the previous question."
POSTPONE DISCUSSION FOR A CERTAIN TIME	"I move to postpone the discussion until..."
GIVE CLOSER STUDY TO SOMETHING	"I move to refer the matter to committee."
AMEND A MOTION	"I move to amend the motion by. ."
INTRODUCE BUSINESS	"I move that..."

Here are some motions you might make, how to make them, and what to expect of the rules. The motions below are listed in order of precedence.

MAY YOU INTERRUPT THE SPEAKER?	DO YOU NEED A SECOND?	IS IT DEBAT-ABLE?	CAN IT BE AMENDED?	WHAT VOTE IS NEEDED?	CAN IT BE RECON-SIDERED?
NO	YES	NO	NO	MAJORITY	NO
NO	YES	NO	YES	MAJORITY	NO
YES	NO	NO	NO	NO VOTE	NO
NO	YES	NO	NO	MAJORITY	NO
NO	YES	NO	NO	2/3	NO[1]
NO	YES	YES	YES	MAJORITY	YES
NO	YES	YES	YES	MAJORITY	YES[2]
NO	YES	YES[3]	YES	MAJORITY	YES
NO	YES	YES	YES	MAJORITY	YES

[1] Unless vote on the question is not yet taken.

[2] Unless the committee has already taken up the subject.

[3] Only if the motion to be amended is debatable.

There is no order of precedence with the following motions....

TO DO THIS:	YOU SAY THIS:
PROTEST BREACH OF RULES OR CONDUCT	"I raise to a point of order."
VOTE ON A RULING OF THE CHAIR	"I appeal the chair's decision"
SUSPEND RULES TEMPORARILY	"I move to suspend the rules so that ."
AVOID CONSIDERING AN IMPROPER MATTER	"I object to consideration of this motion."
VERIFY A VOICE VOTE BY HAVING MEMBERS STAND	"I call for a division, or, DIVISION."
REQUEST INFORMATION	"Point of information."
TAKE UP A MATTER PREVIOUSLY TABLED	"I move to take from the table..."
RECONSIDER A HASTY ACTION	"I move to reconsider the vote on..."

MAY YOU INTERRUPT THE SPEAKER?	DO YOU NEED A SECOND?	IS IT DEBAT-ABLE?	CAN IT BE AMENDED?	WHAT VOTE IS NEEDED?	CAN IT BE RECON-SIDERED?
YES	NO	NO	NO	NO VOTE[4]	NO
YES	YES	YES	NO	MAJORITY[5]	YES
NO	YES	NO	NO	2/3	NO
YES	NO	NO	NO	2/3[6]	—[7]
YES	NO	NO	NO	NO VOTE	NO
YES	NO	NO	NO	NO VOTE	NO
NO	YES	NO	NO	MAJORITY	NO
YES	YES	—[8]	NO	MAJORITY	NO

[4]Except in doubtful cases.

[5]A majority vote in the negative is needed to reverse the ruling of the chair

[6]A 2/3 vote in the negative is needed to prevent consideration of the main motion.

[7]Only if the main question or motion was not, in fact, considered.

[8]Only if the motion to be reconsidered is debatable.

7. VOTING ON A MOTION

The method of voting on a motion depends on the situation and the by-laws. Generally, there are five methods of voting on a motion: 1) by a voice vote, 2) by a show of hands, 3) by a roll call, 4) by a ballot and 5) by general consent.

A voice vote is taken by the chair asking those in favor to say "Aye" and those opposed to say "No." This method may be used for a majority vote only. It may not be used for a 2/3 vote. A member may move for an exact count at his or her option on any type of vote.

A vote by a show of hands is taken by members raising their hands as sight verification of or as an alternative to a voice vote. It does not require a count. However, any member may move for an exact count.

A vote by roll call is taken by the chair calling out the name of each member who then answers "Yes" or "No" as his or her name is called. The secretary will record the roll call vote as taken when a record of each person's vote is needed.

A vote taken by ballot requires the members to write their vote on a slip of paper. This method of voting is used when secrecy is desired.

A vote by general consent is used when a motion isn't likely to be opposed. It is introduced by the chair saying, "If there is no objection . . ." Members show agreement by their silence. If a member says, "I object," the matter must be put to a roll call or ballot vote.

A motion (or question) is pending so long as it has been stated by the chair but not yet voted on. The last motion stated by the chair is the first pending. The main motion is always the last voted on.

A vote can be delayed for either a predetermined period or indefinitely. Postponement involves two types of motions: a motion to table or a motion to postpone indefinitely. A motion to table is often used in an attempt to "kill" a motion. There is always the option to "take from the table" later by a motion for reconsideration by the assembly. A tabled motion will remain tabled until reconsidered. A motion to postpone indefinitely allows members to dispose of a motion without making a decision for or against the matter presented. It is useful in the case of a badly chosen main motion for which either a "Yes" or "No" vote would have undesirable consequences. Again, a motion postponed indefinitely may be reconsidered when a motion for reconsideration is passed.

8. 20 TIPS FOR A SUCCESSFUL MEETING

1. RESPECT TRADITION. Follow established parliamentary procedure.
2. Have a WRITTEN AGENDA and stick to it.
3. Allot a DESIGNATED AMOUNT OF TIME for each controversial matter and schedule after routine business.
4. RESTATE EACH MOTION so that it may be accurately recorded and fully understood. Repeat again if necessary.
5. CONTROL DISCUSSION and debate through the chair. Require recognition before allowing a member to speak.
6. LIMIT DISCUSSION to matters pertinent to the pending motion. Don't let anyone make a major issue of a minor one.
7. PERMIT FULL DEBATE even if it requires delaying a vote until the next meeting.
8. ALLOW ALL SIDES TO SUBMIT privileged, subsidiary and incidental motions.
9. RAISE A POINT OF ORDER whenever there is an error, mistake, omission or misunderstanding.

10. DO NOT USE parliamentary technicalities for tactical advantage alone.
11. CALL FOR A FINAL VOTE on all motions and in the proper order of their respective precedence.
12. DISPOSE OF ALL NON-CONTROVERSIAL MATTERS by a general consensus vote.
13. REQUIRE A VOTE BY BALLOT on all important contested matters.
14. ALLOW THE CHAIR to resolve procedural questions unless an appeal is taken to the assembly questioning the chair's action.
15. RECORD ALL MOTIONS WHETHER THEY ARE defeated or succeed. Record non-controversial motions adopted by general consensus.
16. DO NOT RECORD individual opinion, personal criticism, comments made in debate, motives behind motions or motions that have been withdrawn.
17. PERMIT THE ENTIRE ASSEMBLY to decide when debate should end.
18. DO NOT SPEND VALUABLE MEETING TIME worrying about who is right or wrong. Nothing is as important as it seems at first.
19. BE WILLING TO LOSE A BATTLE OR TWO in order to win the war.
20. GET ACQUAINTED with a good lawyer, CPA and parliamentarian.

CHAPTER 24

FORMS

Form No. 1	Board Resolution
Form No. 2	Notice of Annual Membership Meeting
Form No. 3	Notice of Special Membership Meeting
Form No. 4	Notice of Regular Board Meeting
Form No. 5	Notice of Special Board Meeting
Form No. 6	Approval of Board Action Without Meeting
Form No. 7	Approval of Board Meeting Without Notice
Form No. 8	Proxy Form
Form No. 9	Proxy Revocation Form
Form No. 10	Ballot
Form No. 11	Request for Alternative Dispute Resolution
Form No. 12	Response to Request For Alternative Dispute Resolution
Form No. 13	Notice of Violation of Governing Documents
Form No. 14	Release of Notice of Violation of Governing Documents
Form No. 15	Notice of Delinquent Assessment
Form No. 16	Release of Notice of Delinquent Assessment

FORM NO. 1

MODEL HOMEOWNERS' ASSOCIATION

RESOLUTION OF THE BOARD OF DIRECTORS

RECITALS

Whereas, (state date, time of meeting) .

Whereas, (state facts upon which resolution is based) .

Whereas, (state additional facts, as necessary) .

RESOLUTION

It is hereby resolved by the Board of Directors for the Model Homeowners' Association that (state substance of resolution) ______________________________
____
____.

Executed this ____ day of (month) , 1995.

By: ______________________________
President
Model Homeowners' Association

FORM NO. 2

MODEL HOMEOWNERS' ASSOCIATION

NOTICE
TO HOMEOWNERS

ANNUAL MEMBERSHIP MEETING

Date: ______________________________

Time: ______________________________

Location: ______________________________

Notice is hereby given that the annual meeting of Model Homeowners' Association will be held on (date), at (time). The issues to be discussed will include (describe issues to be discussed or reference an attached meeting agenda). There will be a vote of the membership on the following issues: (list items on the ballot). Members who will be unable to attend the meeting should execute the enclosed proxy and return it to the (name and address of individual in charge of collecting proxies) by (date).

The meeting will be held at the (name of facility), located at (address of facility). Directions to the (name of facility) are available from (name and phone number of person who can give directions - or enclose a map showing directions to the facility from the Development).

The Board of Directors
Model Homeowners' Association

FORM NO. 3

MODEL HOMEOWNERS' ASSOCIATION

NOTICE
TO HOMEOWNERS

SPECIAL MEMBERSHIP MEETING

Date: ______________________________
Time: ______________________________
Location: ______________________________

Notice is hereby given that on (date), at (time), there will be a special meeting of the members of the Model Homeowners' Association to discuss (describe issues to be discussed). There will be a vote of the membership on the following issues: (list items on the ballot). Members who will be unable to attend the meeting should execute the enclosed proxy and return it to the (name and address of individual in charge of collecting proxies) by (date).

The meeting will be held at the (name of facility), located at (address of facility). Directions to the (name of facility) are available from (name and phone number of person who can give directions - or enclose a map showing directions to the facility from the Development).

The Board of Directors
Model Homeowners' Association

FORM NO. 4

MODEL HOMEOWNERS' ASSOCIATION

NOTICE TO HOMEOWNERS

REGULAR BOARD OF DIRECTORS MEETING

Date: ______________________________

Time: ______________________________

Location: ______________________________

Notice is hereby given that the regular (monthly/quarterly) meeting of the Board of Directors for the Model Homeowners' Association will be held on (date), at (time). The issues to be discussed will include (describe issues to be discussed or reference an attached meeting agenda).

The meeting will be held at the (name of facility), located at (address of facility). Directions to the (name of facility) are available from (name and phone number of person who can give directions - or enclose a map showing directions to the facility from the Development).

The Board of Directors
Model Homeowners' Association

FORM NO. 5

MODEL HOMEOWNERS' ASSOCIATION

NOTICE
TO HOMEOWNERS

SPECIAL BOARD OF DIRECTORS MEETING

Date: ______________________________

Time: ______________________________

Location: ______________________________

Notice is hereby given that a special meeting of the Board of Directors for the Model Homeowners' Association will be held on (date), at (time). The issues to be discussed will include (describe issues to be discussed or reference an attached meeting agenda).

The meeting will be held at the (name of facility), located at (address of facility). Directions to the (name of facility) are available from (name and phone number of person who can give directions - or enclose a map showing directions to the facility from the Development).

The Board of Directors
Model Homeowners' Association

FORM NO. 6

MODEL HOMEOWNERS' ASSOCIATION

CONSENT TO BOARD OF DIRECTORS ACTION WITHOUT HOLDING A MEETING

We, the undersigned, being all the directors of (Model Homeowner Association), a California non-profit corporation, hereby consent to the following action by the Board of Directors in the absence of a meeting:

(description of action to be taken)________________
____
____
____
____.

Dated: __________ ____________________
(Signature of Director)

____
(Signature of Director)

____
(Signature of Director)

____
(Signature of Director)

____
(Signature of Director)

[Please note, this document must be filed with the minutes of the Board of Directors meetings.]

FORM NO. 7

MODEL HOMEOWNERS' ASSOCIATION

WAIVER OF NOTICE AND CONSENT TO HOLDING OF BOARD OF DIRECTORS MEETING

We, the undersigned directors of the (Model Homeowner Association), a California non-profit corporation, waive notice of the (specify regular or special) meeting of the Board of Directors of the (name of association) on (date), at (location), California, and consent to this meeting being held at the time and place stated above and to the transaction of any and all business by the directors at this meeting including, but not limited to, (state agenda items to be acted on such as election of offices or adoption of contracts).

Dated: ___________ ___________________________
(Signature of Director)

____
(Signature of Director)

____
(Signature of Director)

____
(Signature of Director)

____
(Signature of Director)

[Please note, this document should be filed with the records of the Board of Directors.]

FORM NO. 8

MODEL HOMEOWNERS' ASSOCIATION

PROXY FOR ANNUAL MEETING

I/we, ______________________, hereby designate (__________) to act on my/our behalf at the (__________) meeting to be held on (date) at (location of meeting), California. I/we authorize (______________________) to exercise my/our vote on all matters which come regularly before the (annual membership) at the (date) meeting as follows:

(Brief description of item to be voted on)
____
____.

___ I/we approve. ___ I/we disapprove.

(Brief description of the next item to be voted on)
____
____.

___ I/we approve. ___ I/we disapprove.

Date: ______ Signature:______________________
(unit owner)

Date: ______ Signature:______________________
(co-owner)

Your proxy can be revoked by you at any time prior to the (date) meeting by executing the enclosed proxy revocation form and returning it to (name of person or entity in charge of collecting proxies), by executing a later dated proxy or by personally voting at the meeting.

Form No. 7 (Cont.)
PROXY FOR ANNUAL MEETING

[Please note, if your association has fewer than 100 members or if you solicit proxies from less than 10 members of the association then you only need to describe the matters to be voted on if they include any of the following: 1) Removing a director without cause; 2) electing director(s); 3) Amending the Articles of Incorporation; 4) Approving transaction in which a director has a financial interest; 5) Approving a change in the proxy rights; 6) Selling or disposing of all or substantially all of the corporate assets; 7) Merging with another corporation; 8) Dissolving or winding up the corporation; 9) Approving a distribution of assets upon liquidation which is inconsistent with the liquidation rights of any class of stock/membership; and 10) Any matter which requires written approval for a valid proxy under the applicable provisions of your association's CC&Rs or bylaws.]

FORM NO. 9

MODEL HOMEOWNERS' ASSOCIATION

PROXY REVOCATION

I/we, ____________________________, hereby revoke our proxy executed on ___________. (Name of Board President or person authorized by proxy) is not authorized to exercise my/our vote at the (Board/Membership) meeting on (date) at (location), California.

I/we understand that if I/we do not execute a new proxy or personally vote at the meeting my/our vote will not be counted on any matter.

Date: ________ Signature: ____________________________
(Owner)

Date: ________ Signature: ____________________________
(Co-owner)

FORM NO. 10

MODEL HOMEOWNERS' ASSOCIATION

SOLICITATION MATERIALS

The owner(s) of each unit are entitled to cast one vote per unit owned. Please read the following ballot measure(s) carefully and indicate whether you wish to vote for or against each ballot measure listed. Your vote will be cast in accordance with your choice as set forth on this ballot form.

The association must receive executed ballots from at least (number of votes needed for a quorum) homeowners for this vote to be valid. In addition each measure must be approved by (percentage of homeowners needed to pass measure) of the homeowners in order to be enacted. Ballots should be returned to the Association's (office/property management company) by (date) *.

BALLOT

(Set forth a description of the proposed action to be voted on.) ______________________________
____
____
____
______________________________.

I/We, hereby, cast my/our vote for or against the above action as follows:

____ For
____ Against

***You must allow a reasonable time for return of the ballots.**

Form No. 10 (Cont.)
BALLOT

(Set forth a description of the proposed action to be voted on.)____________________________________
____
____
____
____
____.

I/We, hereby, cast my/our vote for or against the above action as follows:

____ For

____ Against

[Please note that a written ballot form may not be used to elect directors and officers unless specifically authorized by the articles or by-laws of your association]

FORM NO. 11

MODEL HOMEOWNERS' ASSOCIATION

REQUEST FOR ALTERNATIVE DISPUTE RESOLUTION

Requesting Party: ______________________________

Street Address: ______________________________

City, State, Zip: ______________________________

Responding Party: ______________________________

Responding Party: ______________________________

Nature of Dispute:______________________________.

Under Civil Code 1354, a person or entity seeking declaratory or injunctive relief or monetary relief of $5,000 or less relating to the enforcement of the governing documents of a common interest development shall seek to have the dispute resolved through a method of resolution alternative to the commencement of a civil court action.

PURSUANT TO CIVIL CODE § 1354, A COPY OF THE STATUTE IS BEING SERVED ALONG WITH THIS REQUEST FOR ALTERNATIVE DISPUTE RESOLUTION.

You are hereby requested to agree to submit the above describe dispute to the form of Alternative Dispute Resolution (ADR), indicated below:

___ Mediation ___ Non-Binding Arbitration ___ Binding Arbitration

This Request for Alternative Dispute Resolution is being made in accordance with the provisions of California Civil Code § 1354.

FORM NO. 12

MODEL HOMEOWNERS' ASSOCIATION

RESPONSE TO REQUEST FOR ALTERNATIVE DISPUTE RESOLUTION

I agree to submit this dispute to alternative dispute resolution.

Responding Party: ________________________________

Responding Party: ________________________________

Nature of Dispute: ________________________________

____

Signature: ________________________________

Date: ________________________________

[The person(s) or entity(ies) named as responding party(ies) above are required to respond to a request for alternative dispute resolution within 30 days of receipt, or it will be deemed rejected. Responses should be sent to the requesting party at the address indicated on the request.

If you choose to accept a form of Alternative Dispute Resolution, alternative dispute resolution shall be completed within 90 days of receipt of your acceptance, unless all parties to the dispute agree otherwise in writing.]

Form No. 12 (Cont.)
RESPONSE TO REQUEST

MEDIATION

Mediation is a dispute settlement process which allows you to fully participate in negotiation a satisfactory resolution of a claim. In this process, you and the initiating party submit the dispute to a third party neutral (the mediator) who works with both sides to reach a settlement of the dispute.

It is not binding. The mediator does not have the authority to impose a settlement on the parties. The mediator serves to facilitate negotiations.

Experience has shown that when parties mediate, they reach a settlement 80% to 95% of the time.

ARBITRATION

Arbitration is the submission of a dispute to one or more mutually selected, impartial persons for either a non-binding or a final, binding decision. Arbitration is a complete substitute for a trial by a judge or jury. In arbitration, the hearing procedure is less formal than in the court. Discovery is limited and the rules of evidence are relaxed. These and other features of arbitration provide for flexibility, the availability of expert neutral arbitrators and considerable savings of time and expense for the parties in reaching a final determination of their dispute. Arbitrations are governed by state or federal law in the United States.

FORM NO. 13

MODEL HOMEOWNERS' ASSOCIATION

NOTICE OF VIOLATION OF THE GOVERNING DOCUMENTS*

RECORDING REQUESTED BY,
AND WHEN RECORDED RETURN TO:
(Name and address of Association)

____

In accordance with Article (No.) of the Declaration of Covenants, Conditions and Restrictions ("CC&Rs") for the (name of association) recorded on (date) as Instrument No. (insert number--the instrument number will be indicated on the recording stamp at the top of the CC&Rs), of the Official Records of (name) County, California, the (name of association) hereby records a notice of a violation of Article (no.) of the (name of association) CC&Rs against the real property described in paragraph 1 below.

1. The property against which this notice is imposed is commonly known as (insert street address of unit) and more particularly described as (insert the legal description of the property i.e. the lot and tract numbers or reference an attached exhibit which contains this description such as a grant deed).

2. The record owner of the property described in paragraph 1 is (name of property owner).

3. The nature of the violation is (describe).

Date:_______ Signature:______________________
President
Model Homeowners' Association

*Please note a Notice of Violation can only be recorded if authorized by your Association's CC&Rs.

FORM NO. 14

MODEL HOMEOWNERS' ASSOCIATION

RELEASE OF NOTICE OF VIOLATION OF THE GOVERNING DOCUMENTS

RECORDING REQUESTED BY,
AND WHEN RECORDED RETURN TO:

(Name and address of Association)
____
____

In accordance with Article (No.) of the Declaration of Covenants, Conditions and Restrictions ("CC&Rs") for the (name of association) recorded on (date) as Instrument No. (insert number--the instrument number will be indicated on the recording stamp at the top of the Notice), of the Official Records of (name) County, California, the undersigned hereby certifies that the Notice of a Violation dated (date) and recorded on (date) as Instrument No. (number) of the Official Records of (name) County, California, against the real property described as (insert legal description or refer to attached exhibit) owned by (name of property owner at time of recording of Notice), the then record owner, is released effective on the date of recordation of this notice in the office of the (name) County Recorder.

Date:_______ Signature:______________________
President
Model Homeowners' Association

FORM NO. 15

MODEL HOMEOWNERS' ASSOCIATION

NOTICE OF DELINQUENT ASSESSMENT* (LIEN)

This NOTICE OF DELINQUENT ASSESSMENT is being given pursuant to California Civil Code § 1367 and the provisions of the Declaration of Covenants, Conditions and Restrictions (CC&Rs) of the Homeowners Association as follows:

Association claimant: (Name of Association) __________
Declaration of CC&Rs recorded on: __________
Instrument No.: __________
County: __________

The description of the common interest development property against which this notice is being recorded is as follows:
Common address: __________
Lot ______ Tract ______ Unit ______ per Map recorded in Book ___ Page ___ as shown on the Condominium Plan recorded __________ as Document No. __________ APN# __________
The reputed owner is: __________
Owner's mailing address: __________

DELINQUENCY

Assessments due for: (Dates) $______
Late fees, attorney's fees, costs & interest $______
Total amount of delinquency: $______

Date: __________ Signed: (Authorized signatory)

* Forms 15 and 16 are adapted from forms provided by Association Lien Services, 11900 West Olympic Blvd., Suite 700, Los Angeles, CA 90064. Tel. (800) 372-2207, Fax (310) 207-2115.

FORM NO. 16

MODEL HOMEOWNERS' ASSOCIATION

RELEASE OF NOTICE OF DELINQUENT ASSESSMENT*

NOTIFICATION IS HEREBY GIVEN:

That the lien claimed by (Name of Association) against ____________________ upon the following described real property in (City), (County) County, State of California:

Lot ____ Tract _____ Unit __ in the County of ____, State of California as per map recorded in Book ___ Page ___, inclusive of Maps in the Offices of the County Recorder of _____, County, California is hereby released, the claim thereunder having been fully paid and satisfied, and that certain Notice of Assessment of Lien recorded as Instrument No. _____ on _____, Official Records of _____ County, California, is hereby satisfied and discharged.

Date: ___________

Signed: (Authorized Signatory)

* Forms 15 and 16 are adapted from forms provided by Association Lien Services, 11900 West Olympic Blvd., Suite 700, Los Angeles, CA 90064. Tel. (800) 372-2207, Fax (310) 207-2115.

Form No. 16 (Cont.)
RELEASE OF NOTICE
OF DELINQUENT ASSESSMENT*

STATE OF CALIFORNIA)
) ss
COUNTY OF (Name of County))

On (date), before me, (Name), personally appeared (Name), personally known to me (or proved to me on the basis of satisfactory evidence) to be the person whose name is subscribed to the within instrument and acknowledged that she executed the same in her authorized capacity, and that by her signature on the instrument, the person, or the entity upon behalf of which the person acted, executed the instrument.

WITNESS my hand and official seal.

(seal) (Signature)

CHAPTER 25

SERVICE ORGANIZATIONS, GOVERNMENT AGENCIES & INFORMATION SERVICES

1. TRADE ORGANIZATIONS

Executive Counsel of Home Owners
ECHO
P.O. Box 23177
San Jose, California 95153
TEL: (408) 297-3246
FAX: (408) 297-3517

California Association of Community Managers
CACM
18662 MacArthur Blvd., Suite 340
Irvine, California 92715
TEL: (714) 263-CACM
FAX: (714) 263-3789

Club Lake Association of Northern California
CLANC
c/o Bill Stewart
11509 Northwoods Blvd.
Truckee, California 96161
TEL: (916) 587-9494
FAX: (916) 587-9419

Council of Condominium Homeowner Associations
COCHA
P.O. Box 4484
Walnut Creek, California 94596
TEL: (510) 937-0177
FAX: (510) 930-6653

CAI-California Legislative Action Committee
CLAC
2848 Arden Way, Suite 200
Sacramento, California 95825
TEL: (916) 974-1141
FAX: (916) 974-8380

California Parks & Recreation Society
CPRS
P.O. Box 161118
Sacramento, California 95816
TEL: (916) 446-2777
FAX: Not available to public

Sacramento Area Condominium Association
SACA
PO Box 160246
Sacramento, CA 95816
TEL: (916) 923-2203

Community Association Institute
CAI
1630 Duke Street
Alexandria, Virginia 22314
TEL: (703) 548-8600
FAX: (703) 684-1581

CAI Local Chapters

Bay Area Chapter
1989A Santa Rita Rd., Suite 260
Pleasanton, Ca. 94566
TEL: (510) 803-0860
FAX: (510) 803-0861

Coachella Valley Chapter
41-865 Boardwalk, St 121
Palm Desert, Ca. 92211
TEL: (619) 779-5627
FAX: (619) 341-8843

Northern Counties Chapter
2848 Arden Way, St. 200
Sacramento, Ca. 95825
TEL: (916) 974-8390
FAX: (916) 974-8380

Greater Inland Empire Chapter
P.O. Box 8478
Moreno Valley, Ca. 92552
TEL: (909) 653-5893
FAX: (909) 653-2283

Central California Chapter
P.O. Box 70262
Stockton, Ca. 95267
TEL: (209) 477-7314
FAX: (209) 474-2406

Greater Los Angeles Chapter
P.O. Box 84303
Los Angeles, Ca. 90073
TEL: (310) 393-7041
FAX: (310) 576-0485

Channel Islands Chapter
P.O. Box 3575
Ventura, Ca. 93006
TEL: (805) 658-1438
FAX: (805) 658-7011

Southern Counties Chapter
23421 South Pointe Dr., Suite 145
Laguna Hills, Ca. 92653
TEL: (714) 380-7360
FAX: (714) 380-4312

2. GOVERNMENT AGENCIES

Department of Insurance
Los Angeles Office
300 South Spring Street
Los Angeles, California 90013
TEL: (800) 927-4357
FAX: Not available to public

San Francisco Office
425 Market Street, 6th Floor
San Francisco, California 94105
TEL: (800) 927-4357
FAX: Not available to public

Sacramento Office
320 Capital Mall
Sacramento, California 95814
TEL: (916) 322-3555
FAX: Not available to public

San Diego Office
1350 Front Street, Suite 6060
San Diego, California 92101
TEL: (619) 525-4157
FAX: Not available to public

Department of Consumer Affairs
400 "R" Street, Suite 3060
Sacramento, California 95814
TEL: (916) 445-4465
FAX: (916) 445-8769

Department of Corporations
1115 11th Street
Sacramento, California 95814
TEL: (916) 445-7205
FAX: Not available to public

Department of Real Estate
Sacramento Office
2201 Broadway
Sacramento, California 95818
TEL: (916) 227-0931
FAX: Not available to public

San Francisco Office
185 Berry Street
San Francisco, California 94107
TEL: (415) 904-5925
FAX: Not available to public

Los Angeles Office
107 South Broadway, Suite 8107
Los Angeles, California 90012
TEL: (213) 897-3399
FAX: Not available to public

San Diego Office
1350 Front Street, Suite 3064
San Diego, California 92101
TEL: (619) 525-4192
FAX: Not available to public

Secretary of State
1230 "J" Street
Sacramento, California 95814
TEL: (916) 445-2900
FAX: Not available to public

Contractors State Licensing Board
9835 Goethe Road
Sacramento, California 95827
TEL: (916) 255-3900
FAX: (916) 364-0130

3. INFORMATION SERVICES

Access 2
3240 Stone Valley Road West, Suite 103
Alamo, California 94507
TEL: 1-800-400-1484
FAX: (510) 820-5592
(Communication/information on-line service exclusively for the community association industry.)

The CID Registry of California
P.O. Box 1308
Roseville, California 95661
TEL: 1-800-350-8333 (Toll Free)
(Locating service for an association contact person anywhere in California. Directories, labels and disks available.)

The Condominium Bluebook®
B & B Publications
4 Embarcadero Center, Suite 3440
San Francisco, California 94111
TEL: (415) 433-1233
FAX: (415) 433-2985
(Reference Book with the latest statutes, rules, regulations and other information pertaining to community associations.)

HOA-Info
1611 Telegraph Avenue, Suite 1450
Oakland, California 94612
TEL: (510) 465-2073
FAX: (510) 465-7035
(Database information on community associations cross-reference in a number of different categories.)

The Real Estate Register
10044 Bianchi Way
P.O. Box 1207
Cupertino, California 95015
TEL: 1-800-208-8880
TEL: (408) 996-9679
FAX: (408) 996-2246
(Mailing lists of homeowner and various businesses in the real estate fields.)

CHAPTER 26

CHECKLISTS

Checklist No. 1	Transition From Developer Control
Checklist No. 2	Standard Agenda Board of Directors Meeting
Checklist No. 3	Association Duties
Checklist No. 4	Quarterly Financial Review
Checklist No. 5	Annual Financial Review
Checklist No. 6	Rule Enforcement
Checklist No. 7	Construction Contract Review

CHECKLIST. NO. 1

TRANSITION FROM DEVELOPER CONTROL

A. DOCUMENTS TO OBTAIN

- ☐ Original recorded CC&Rs and any amendments.
- ☐ Original corporate minute book containing articles of incorporation, bylaws, and rules and regulations.
- ☐ Corporate seal, letterhead, books and records.
- ☐ Original recorded condominium plan or tract map.
- ☐ Original minutes of all board of director meetings.
- ☐ Original minutes of all member meetings.
- ☐ Membership roster from inception to date.
- ☐ All bank records, including: a) Checkbooks, passbooks and other access documents; b) Bank statements and reconciliations; c) Cancelled checks and check registers; and d) Bank account and borrowing resolutions.
- ☐ As-built plans and specifications.
- ☐ Inventory of moveable property.
- ☐ Tax records including: a) Returns (Federal and State); b) Board certifications to CPA; c) IRS and FTB correspondence; and d) Audit materials.

- ❑ Insurance policies including: a) General liability policies; b) Directors and officers liability; and c) Fidelity bonds.
- ❑ Maintenance contracts and records.
- ❑ Management contracts and records.
- ❑ *Pro forma* operating budgets from inception to date.
- ❑ Reserve studies and updates from inception to date.
- ❑ Bonds - subdivision maintenance bond, etc.
- ❑ Warranties and written contracts with product suppliers.
- ❑ Records of accounts payable and accounts receivable from inception to date.
- ❑ Statement of known defective conditions.

B. FINANCIAL AUDIT

- ❑ Review financial statements.
- ❑ Review *pro forma* operating budget.
- ❑ Review bank statements and cancelled checks.
- ❑ Review segregation of operation revenue from reserves.
- ❑ Review prior reserve studies.
- ❑ Review balances on deposit in reserve accounts.

- ❑ Conduct an audit if discrepancies appear.

C. CONSTRUCTION AUDIT

- ❑ Review all major systems on spot check basis including the roof system, siding system, foundation system, electrical system, plumbing system, seismic restraint system, and the landscape and drainage system.
- ❑ Retain expert consultants as necessary.
- ❑ Define any problems and method of repair.
- ❑ Determine cost of repair.
- ❑ Make demand on developer for compensation.

D. ORGANIZATION OF ASSOCIATION

- ❑ Review governing documents for compliance with requirements for officers and directors.
- ❑ Review committee structure for effective use.
- ❑ Review management contracts for compliance with current needs.
- ❑ Review service providers for adequacy.
- ❑ Review professional consultant contracts for adequacy and conflicts of interest.
- ❑ Establish reporting procedures for management and committees.

- ☐ Delegate tasks to Board members and committee members.
- ☐ Develop long range plan for overall management of project.

CHECKLIST NO. 2

STANDARD AGENDA
BOARD OF DIRECTORS MEETING

- [ ] Call to order by President.
- [ ] Determine whether a quorum is present.
- [ ] If quorum not present, adjourn and reschedule either by verbal or written notice as specified in CC&Rs or bylaws.
- [ ] If quorum present, proceed with meeting.
- [ ] Adopt minutes of last meeting by: a) Read minutes of the last meeting or vote to waive; b) Call for corrections; and c) Vote on adoption.
- [ ] Homeowner forum.
- [ ] Consent calendar (if appropriate).
- [ ] Present reports including: a) Treasurer; b) Architectural Committee; c) Landscape Committee; d) Newsletter Committee; e) Maintenance Committee; and f) Property manager.
- [ ] Unfinished Business.
- [ ] New Business.
- [ ] Executive session (if necessary).
- [ ] Adjournment.

CHECKLIST NO. 3

ASSOCIATION DUTIES

- ☐ Provide effective physical maintenance of common area and facilities for which it is responsible.
- ☐ Establish sound financial policy and procedures, including compliance with annual reporting requirements and government filings (e.g. tax, corporate, etc.)
- ☐ Review and adjust, as necessary, budget figures and assessment rates.
- ☐ Establish and implement a delinquent assessment policy.
- ☐ Establish, publicize and enforce rules and regulations, including penalties for violation.
- ☐ Select a financial consultant and arrange for prompt preparation of necessary reports.
- ☐ Employ a competent attorney.
- ☐ Employ a management agent or employee and prescribe the scope of the manager's duties.
- ☐ Establish and enforce architectural and other standards.
- ☐ Appoint committees. Coordinate and supervise their activities to ensure effective action.

- ❑ Develop and supervise an education and training program for board members.
- ❑ Establish and periodically review the insurance program to ensure adequate coverage.
- ❑ Ensure proper procedures (e.g. parliamentary, notice, etc.) are followed at all board and member meetings.
- ❑ Periodically review bonding of personnel handling funds.
- ❑ Communicate with members on matters that affect their property.
- ❑ Address owner concerns before they become a real problem.
- ❑ Avoid conflicts-of-interest and self-interest decisions.
- ❑ Decide matters based upon the best interests of the association as a whole.
- ❑ Understand the governing documents thoroughly.
- ❑ Hold regular board meeting and ensure proper records are kept.

CHECKLIST NO. 4

QUARTERLY FINANCIAL REVIEW

- ☐ Review Civil Code § 1365.5.
- ☐ Check to determine whether the governing documents impose more stringent standards than set forth below.
- ☐ Review a current reconciliation of the association's operating accounts.
- ☐ Review a current reconciliation of the association's reserve accounts.
- ☐ Review the current year's actual reserve revenues and expenses compared to the current year's budget.
- ☐ Review the latest account statements prepared by the financial institutions where the association has it operating and reserve accounts.
- ☐ Review an income and expense statement for the association's operating and reserve accounts.
- ☐ Investigate any apparent discrepancies.

CHECKLIST NO. 5

ANNUAL FINANCIAL REVIEW

- ☐ Review Civil Code § 1365.5.

- ☐ Review CC&R financial requirements.

- ☐ Review the most recent reserve study for compliance with Civil Code § 1365.5(d). Include the following in your review: a) Review the major components with a remaining useful life of 30 years or less for which the association is responsible; b) Review the probable remaining useful life of those major compenants as of the date of the study; c) Review the estimated cost of repair, replacement, restoration and maintenance during and at the end of their remaining useful lives; d) Review the total annual contribution necessary to defray the cost of repair, replacement, restoration and maintenance of those components as required; e) Review the total reserve funds on deposit as of the date of the study year; and f) Review the percent of reserves funded when the amount the current amount of accumulated cash reserves is divided by the current estimate of the amount of cash reserves necessary to maintain, repair or replace the major components.

- ☐ Review year to date expenses in all categories, including accounting, administrative, insurance, legal, maintenance, management, utilities, outside services, etc.

- ☐ Determine whether the association anticipates any substantial increases in operating expenses upcoming year.

- ☐ Determine whether there will be any capital improvements or new projects that will introduce new categories of expense into the budget and in what amount.

- ☐ Review delinquent accounts and whether enforcement action is necessary.

- ☐ Review the current delinquent assessment collection policy of the association for adequacy.

- ☐ Review the draft budget for the upcoming year.

- ☐ Review income from all sources, such as reimbursable expenses, penalties, interest, etc. (Note: interest income on reserve accounts is normally excluded from operating revenue for budget purposes.)

- ☐ Determine whether the current monthly assessment per unit is adequate, and, if not, adjust accordingly.

- ☐ Review prior years income and expense figures to determine whether there are any unusual disparities and, if so, investigate.

- ☐ Determine whether the time deadlines for financial reporting have been met in the past and ensure that they can be complied with in the future.

- ☐ Determine whether the overall financial program is serving the best interests of the association and, if not, how it should be restructured.

CHECKLIST NO. 6

RULE ENFORCEMENT

- ☐ Determine whether there has there been a violation or infraction of the governing documents (i.e. CC&Rs, bylaws, rules).
- ☐ Determine whether there is sufficient evidence (i.e. witnesses and/or documents) to sustain a rule enforcement proceeding.
- ☐ Determine whether the violator is someone subject to the restrictions in the governing documents. If not consider indirect enforcement action against the responsible owner.
- ☐ Determine whether there is authority in the governing documents to make and enforce the rule. This should have been done at the time of enactment.
- ☐ Determine whether the rule is reasonably related to the purposes it is intended to achieve. This should have been done at the time of enactment.
- ☐ Determine whether the violator has received adequate notice of the rule and related penalties in advance of the violation.
- ☐ Determine whether there are any defenses to enforcement, such as lack of notice, waiver, selective enforcement, illegality, etc.
- ☐ Give adequate notice of a hearing pursuant to an established enforcement program.

- ☐ Conduct a hearing in accordance with established procedure. Swear in all witnesses. Give limited weight to hearsay, particularly uncorroborated or inherently untrustworthy third party statements.

- ☐ Give the violator a full and fair opportunity to be heard and present evidence on his/her behalf.

- ☐ Render a prompt decision based upon the evidence. The decision should be a simple, concise statement of the ultimate decision.

- ☐ Commence and carry out enforcement without delay.

CHECKLIST NO. 7

CONSTRUCTION CONTRACT REVIEW

- ☐ Review identity and credentials of design professional (i.e. architect/ engineer), construction manager, general contractor, specialty subcontractors, and contact person with each.
- ☐ Review the final stamped (by the architect/ engineer) and approved (by the local building department) set of drawings and specifications. If a set cannot be located, obtain a complete set immediately.
- ☐ Review all change orders and other contract modifications.
- ☐ Determine whether the contract has been performed to date in accordance with the written documents.
- ☐ Determine whether the work is proceeding on schedule and, if not, why not.
- ☐ Determine whether holdback or retention has been deducted from periodic payments to contractor(s).
- ☐ Determine whether construction manager or other owner's representative has obtained lien releases for work covered by the periodic payments.
- ☐ Review adequacy and effectiveness of reporting channels.

INDEX

A

C

D

E

F

G

H

I

J

K

L

M

P